1004525638

William Miller, PhD, MLS
Rita M. Pellen, MLS
Editors

Internet Reference Support for Distance Learners

Internet Reference Support for Distance Learners has been co-published simultaneously as *Internet Reference Services Quarterly*, Volume 9, Numbers 3/4 2004.

Pre-publication
REVIEWS,
COMMENTARIES,
EVALUATIONS . . .

"**A**NY LIBRARIAN INVOLVED WITH THE DELIVERY OF INSTRUCTION OR REFERENCE SERVICE USING THE INTERNET WILL FIND THIS BOOK INVALUABLE. . . . Addresses a variety of important topics. . . . Of particular interest is the emphasis on establishing collaborative associations with other libraries to provide this electronic service."

Patrick Mahoney, MLS, MBA, BSBA
Off-Campus Librarian
Central Michigan University

Internet Reference Support for Distance Learners

Internet Reference Support for Distance Learners has been co-published simultaneously as *Internet Reference Services Quarterly*, Volume 9, Numbers 3/4 2004.

Monographic Separates from *Internet Reference Services Quarterly*™

For additional information on these and other Haworth Press titles, including descriptions, tables of contents, reviews, and prices, use the QuickSearch catalog at http://www.HaworthPress.com.

Internet Reference Support for Distance Learners, edited by William Miller, PhD, MLS, and Rita M. Pellen, MLS (Vol. 9, No. 3/4, 2004). *A guide to providing effective library reference services through online support to distance learners.*

Improving Internet Reference Services to Distance Learners, edited by William Miller, PhD, MLS, and Rita M. Pellen, MLS (Vol. 9, No. 1/2, 2004). *A look at the cooperative activities between librarians and those working outside the library to provide quality services to distance users.*

Virtual Reference Services: Issues and Trends, edited by Stacey Kimmel, MLS, and Jennifer Heise, MLS (Vol. 8, No. 1/2, 2003). *Offers practical advice and suggestions for product selection, policy setting, technical support, collaborative efforts, staffing, training, marketing, budgeting, evaluation, and administration.*

Database-Driven Web Sites, edited by Kristin Antelman, MS (Vol. 7, No. 1/2, 2002). *Profiles numerous successful uses of database-driven content to deliver common library services on the Internet.*

Bioterrorism and Political Violence: Web Resources, edited by M. Sandra Wood, MLS, MBA (Vol. 6, No. 3/4, 2002). *Describes how to find reliable information on bioterrorism via the Internet.*

The Challenge of Internet Literacy: The Instruction-Web Convergence, edited by Lyn Elizabeth M. Martin, BA, MLS (Vol. 2, No. 2/3, 1997). *"A source of valuable advice. . . . Recommended for institutions that collect library science materials on a comprehensive level." (Library & Information Science Annual 1999)*

Internet Reference Support for Distance Learners

William Miller
Rita M. Pellen
Editors

Internet Reference Support for Distance Learners has been co-published simultaneously as *Internet Reference Services Quarterly*, Volume 9, Numbers 3/4 2004.

The Haworth Information Press®
An Imprint of The Haworth Press, Inc.

New York • London • Victoria (AU)
www.HaworthPress.com

Published by

The Haworth Information Press®, 10 Alice Street, Binghamton, NY 13904-1580 USA

The Haworth Information Press® is an imprint of The Haworth Press, Inc., 10 Alice Street, Binghamton, NY 13904-1580 USA.

Internet Reference Support for Distance Learners has been co-published simultaneously as *Internet Reference Services Quarterly*, Volume 9, Numbers 3/4 2004.

The development, preparation, and publication of this work has been undertaken with great care. However, the publisher, employees, editors, and agents of The Haworth Press and all imprints of The Haworth Press, Inc., including The Haworth Medical Press® and Pharmaceutical Products Press®, are not responsible for any errors contained herein or for consequences that may ensue from use of materials or information contained in this work. Opinions expressed by the author(s) are not necessarily those of The Haworth Press, Inc. With regard to case studies, identities and circumstances of individuals discussed herein have been changed to protect confidentiality. Any resemblance to actual persons, living or dead, is entirely coincidental.

Cover design by Jennifer M. Gaska

Library of Congress Cataloging-in-Publication Data

Internet reference support for distance learners / William Miller, Rita M. Pellen, editors.
    p. cm.
    "Internet reference support for distance learners has been co-published simultaneously as Internet reference services quarterly, volume 9, numbers 3/4 2004."
    Includes bibliographical references and index.
    ISBN-13: 978-0-7890-2937-9 (hc. : alk. paper)
    ISBN-10: 0-7890-2937-5 (hc. : alk. paper)
    ISBN-13: 978-0-7890-2938-6 (pbk. : alk. paper)
    ISBN-10: 0-7890-2938-3 (pbk. : alk. paper)
    1. Internet in library reference services–United States. 2. Electronic reference services (Libraries)–United States. 3. Libraries and distance education–United States. I. Miller, William, 1947- II. Pellen, Rita M. III. Internet reference services quarterly.
Z711.47 .I58 2005
025.5'2–dc22
                                            2005003922

Indexing, Abstracting & Website/Internet Coverage

This section provides you with a list of major indexing & abstracting services and other tools for bibliographic access. That is to say, each service began covering this periodical during the year noted in the right column. Most Websites which are listed below have indicated that they will either post, disseminate, compile, archive, cite or alert their own Website users with research-based content from this work. (This list is as current as the copyright date of this publication.)

Abstracting, Website/Indexing Coverage . . . . Year When Coverage Began

- *Annual Bibliography of English Language & Literature "Abstracts Section" (in print, CD-ROM, and online)* 1996

- *Applied Social Sciences Index & Abstracts (ASSIA) (Online: ASSI via DataStar) (CDRom: ASSIA Plus) <http://www.csa.com>* 1996

- *CINAHL (Cumulative Index to Nursing & Allied Health Literature), in print, EBSCO, and SilverPlatter, DataStar, and PaperChase. (Support materials include Subject Heading List, Database Search Guide, and instructional video) <http://www.cinahl.com>* 1996

- *Computer and Information Systems Abstracts <http://www.csa.com>* 2004

- *Computer Science Index (CSI) (formerly Computer Literature Index) (EBSCO) <http://www.epnet.com>* 1997

- *Computing Reviews <http://www.reviews.com>* 1996

- *Current Cites [Digital Libraries] [Electronic Publishing] [Multimedia & Hypermedia] [Networks & Networking] [General] <http://sunsite.berkeley.edu/CurrentCites/>* 2004

- *EBSCOhost Electronic Journals Service (EJS) <http://ejournals.ebsco.com>* 2001

- *ERIC: Processing & Reference Facility* 1998

(continued)

- *European Association for Health Information & Libraries: selected abstracts in newsletter "Publications" section* 1996

- *FRANCIS. INIST/CNRS <http://www.inist.fr>* 1998

- *Google <http://www.google.com>* 2004

- *Google Scholar <http://scholar.google.com>* 2004

- *Haworth Document Delivery Center <http://www.HaworthPress.com/journals/dds.asp>* 1996

- *IBZ International Bibliography of Periodical Literature <http://www.saur.de>* 1998

- *Index to Periodical Articles Related to Law <http://www.law.utexas.edu>* 1996

- *Information Science & Technology Abstracts: indexes journal articles from more than 450 publications as well as books, research reports, and conference proceedings; EBSCO Publishing <http://www.epnet.com>* 1996

- *Informed Librarian, The <http://www.informedlibrarian.com>* 1996

- *INSPEC is the leading English-language bibliographic information service providing access to the world's scientific & technical literature in physics, electrical engineering, electronics, communications, control engineering, computers & computing, and information technology <http://www.iee.org.uk/publish/>* 1996

- *Internationale Bibliographie der geistes- und sozialwissenschaftlichen Zeitschriftenliteratur ... See IBZ <http://www.saur.de>* 1998

- *Internet & Personal Computing Abstracts (IPCA) (formerly Microcomputer Abstracts) provides access to concise and comprehensive information on the latest PC products & developments, covering over 120 of the most important publications: EBSCO Publishing <http://www.epnet.com/public/internet&personal.asp>* 1996

- *Journal of Academic Librarianship: Guide to Professional Literature, The* 1996

- *Konyvtari Figyelo (Library Review)* 1996

- *Library & Information Science Abstracts (LISA) <http://www.csa.com>* 1996

- *Library and Information Science Annual (LISCA) <http://www.lu.com>* 1999

- *Library Literature & Information Science <http://www.hwwilson.com>* 1998

- *Mathematical Didactics (MATHDI) <http://www.emis.de/MATH/DI.html>* 2000

- *PASCAL, c/o Institut de l'Information Scientifique et Technique. Cross-disciplinary electronic database covering the fields of science, technology & medicine. Also available on CD-ROM, and can generate customized retrospective searches <http://www.inist.fr>* 1998

(continued)

- *Referativnyi Zhurnal (Abstracts Journal of the All-Russian Institute of Scientific and Technical Information–in Russian) <http://www.viniti.ru>* 1996

- *SwetsWise <http://www.swets.com>* 2001

- *zetoc <http://zetoc.mimas.ac.uk/>* 2004

Special Bibliographic Notes related to special journal issues (separates) and indexing/abstracting:

- indexing/abstracting services in this list will also cover material in any "separate" that is co-published simultaneously with Haworth's special thematic journal issue or DocuSerial. Indexing/abstracting usually covers material at the article/chapter level.
- monographic co-editions are intended for either non-subscribers or libraries which intend to purchase a second copy for their circulating collections.
- monographic co-editions are reported to all jobbers/wholesalers/approval plans. The source journal is listed as the "series" to assist the prevention of duplicate purchasing in the same manner utilized for books-in-series.
- to facilitate user/access services all indexing/abstracting services are encouraged to utilize the co-indexing entry note indicated at the bottom of the first page of each article/chapter/contribution.
- this is intended to assist a library user of any reference tool (whether print, electronic, online, or CD-ROM) to locate the monographic version if the library has purchased this version but not a subscription to the source journal.
- individual articles/chapters in any Haworth publication are also available through the Haworth Document Delivery Service (HDDS).

Internet Reference Support
for Distance Learners

CONTENTS

Introduction: Providing Distance Learners
   with Reference Services Online   1
   William Miller

A Historical Overview of Internet Reference Services
   for Distance Learners   5
   Anne Marie Casey

Internet Reference Services for Distance Education: Guidelines
   Comparison and Implementation   19
   Marie F. Jones

Academic Library Web Sites for Distance Learners in Greater
   Western Library Alliance Member Institutions   33
   Mary Cassner
   Kate E. Adams

Keep IT Simple: Internet Reference Support for Distance
   Learners   43
   Marthea Turnage
   Wade Carter
   Randy McDonald

Ask a UT System Librarian: A Multi-Campus Chat Initiative
   Supporting Students at a Distance   55
   Kimberly Chapman
   Darcy Del Bosque

HawkHelp: From Chat to a Student Services Portal   81
   Nancy J. Burich
   Frances A. Devlin

One School's Experience with Virtual Reference 99
    Carol J. Tipton
    Vanessa J. Earp

Does Anyone Need Help Out There? Lessons from Designing
    Online Help 115
    Judith M. Arnold
    Floyd Csir
    Jennifer Sias
    Jingping Zhang

If You Build It, They Will Come, but Then What:
    A Look at Issues Related to Using Online Course Software
    to Provide Specialized Reference Services 135
    Linda L. Lillard
    Mollie Dinwiddie

Open Source Software to Support Distance Learning Library
    Services 147
    H. Frank Cervone

Integrating Library Reference Services in an Online Information
    Literacy Course: The Internet Navigator as a Model 159
    Amy Brunvand

Copyright and the Delivery of Library Services to Distance
    Learners 179
    Irmin Allner

From Cameras to Camtasia: Streaming Media
    Without the Stress 193
    Christopher Cox

Index 201

ABOUT THE EDITORS

William Miller, PhD, MLS, is Director of Libraries at Florida Atlantic University in Boca Raton. He formerly served as Head of Reference at Michigan State University in East Lansing, and as Associate Dean of Libraries at Bowling Green State University in Ohio. Dr. Miller is past President of the Association of College and Research Libraries, has served as Chair of the *Choice* magazine editorial board, and is a contributing editor of *Library Issues*. He was named Instruction Librarian of the Year in 2004 by the Association of College and Research Libraries Instruction Section.

Rita M. Pellen, MLS, is Associate Director of Libraries at Florida Atlantic University in Boca Raton. She was formerly Assistant Director of Public Services and Head of the Reference Department at Florida Atlantic. In 1993, Ms. Pellen received the Gabor Exemplary Employee Award in recognition for outstanding service to FAU, and in 1997, the "Literati Club Award for Excellence" for the outstanding paper presented in *The Bottom Line*. She has served on committees in LAMA, ACRL, and ALCTS, as well as the Southeast Florida Library Information Network, SEFLIN, a multi-type library cooperative in South Florida. Honor society memberships include Beta Phi Mu and Phi Kappa Phi.

Introduction:
Providing Distance Learners
with Reference Services Online

The articles in this volume show the range of attention that librarians are currently giving to the creation of reference and instructional services to distance learners. They reveal that librarians do not make a sharp distinction between reference and instruction in the distance learning context, and that there is no clear demarcation between "true" distance learners and more traditional students who might use the services designed with distance learners in mind. Nevertheless, librarians are being driven, in part by accreditation requirements and in part by their desire to serve users well, to provide distance learners with services that approximate those already provided on campus to the traditional user.

Anne Marie Casey, in "A Historical Overview of Internet Reference Services for Distance Learners," provides a comprehensive view of how reference services to such users have been delivered, before and after the creation of the Internet. Prior to the advent of online services, it was cumbersome and costly to provide reference to distance learners. Now it is easier, but still not easy. She surveys current methods of delivery including e-mail and chat reference, and points out that "separate library services for distance learners . . . are perhaps models of a bygone era."

Marie Jones provides a valuable service in "Internet Reference Services for Distance Education: Guidelines Comparison and Implementa-

[Haworth co-indexing entry note]: "Introduction: Providing Distance Learners with Reference Services Online." Miller, William. Co-published simultaneously in *Internet Reference Services Quarterly* (The Haworth Information Press, an imprint of The Haworth Press, Inc.) Vol. 9, No. 3/4, 2004, pp. 1-3; and: *Internet Reference Support for Distance Learners* (ed: William Miller, and Rita M. Pellen) The Haworth Information Press, an imprint of The Haworth Press, Inc., 2004, pp. 1-3. Single or multiple copies of this article are available for a fee from The Haworth Document Delivery Service [1-800-HAWORTH, 9:00 a.m. - 5:00 p.m. (EST). E-mail address: docdelivery@haworthpress.com].

Available online at http://www.haworthpress.com/web/IRSQ
Digital Object Identifier: 10.1300/J136v09n03_01

tion," by synthesizing various guidelines and standards that support provision of distance reference services. These include the ACRL Distance Learning Section's *Guidelines for Distance Learning Library Services*, highly influential on the authors included here and widely cited throughout this volume, which calls for services to distance learners which are equivalent to those offered on campus.

Mary Cassner and Kate Adams survey the variety of distance learning reference support services in a group of 30 research libraries, focusing on the libraries' specialized Web sites for distance learners. They conclude that the Web site and, in particular, the distance education home page are the crucial resources supporting distance reference services. In "Keep IT Simple: Internet Reference Support for Distance Learners," Marthea Turnage, Wade Carter, and Randy McDonald focus on the Web page also, and specifically on Web pages created to support particular courses, in collaboration with faculty. They advocate making the use of technology as simple as possible, and they worry that library Web pages are still too complex, and library technology too difficult for students to use easily and comfortably.

Three articles here focus on chat reference. In "Ask a UT System Librarian: A Multi-Campus Chat Initiative Supporting Students at a Distance," Kimberly Chapman and Darcy Del Bosque describe a University of Texas system-wide chat initiative in which librarians at every institution were available to all students within the system. They discover what those offering chat help often report: that distance learning students, in practice, do not make much use of this service, and that traditional on-campus students are as likely to use it as true distance learners. In "HawkHelp: From Chat to a Student Services Portal," Nancy Burich and Frances Devlin describe setting up a university chat service plus additional features such as providing a link to their statewide chat service. They provide extensive discussion of the software selection process, staff training, and assessment. They also discuss providing support for student services beyond the traditional provision of library resources, such as advising, enrollment, and payment of fees. Finally, in "One School's Experience with Virtual Reference," Carol Tipton and Vanessa Earp discuss the experience of ten libraries in the Texas A&M System in setting up a collaborative chat reference service.

Several articles in this volume focus on the design of software to support various features of online assistance. In "Does Anyone Need Help Out There? Lessons from Designing Online Help," Judith Arnold, Floyd Csir, Jennifer Sias, and Jingping Zhang discuss the creation of an online assistance site which incorporates online versions of "traditional print handouts, FAQs, online subject guides, course-specific guides, learning modules, and instructional videos in one central location where users can get assistance . . . at their point of need." In "If You Build It, They Will Come, but Then What: A Look at Issues Related to Using Online Course Software to Provide Specialized Reference Services," Linda Lillard and Mollie Dinwiddie discuss creation of online support for students in Blackboard courses. They discuss working with specific professors intensively to create materials in support of specific courses, and linking their resources from within the online course. In "Open Source Software to Support Distance Learning Library Services," H. Frank Cervone knowledgeably surveys a variety of open-source software that can help librarians provide enhanced services at a lower cost than commercial software, but he also describes the technical requirements and constraints of using such software.

Amy Brunvand, in "Integrating Library Reference Services in an Online Information Literacy Course: The Internet Navigator as a Model," discusses the creation of an online information literacy course created by a team of librarians in Utah, as "a model for teaching independent research skills to remote students." The course uses a self-paced, tutorial approach.

Two articles in this collection look at specialized aspects of service to distance learners. Irmin Allner, in "Copyright and the Delivery of Library Services to Distance Learners," thoroughly explores the implications of the Digital Millennium Copyright Act and other acts in terms of their implications for distance learning, and indicates how librarians can avoid copyright infringement while serving the needs of distance learners. Finally, in "From Cameras to Camtasia: Streaming Media Without the Stress," Christopher Cox discusses the use of Camtasia Studio, a screen capture program which "offers a simple, low-cost alternative to live video" for the creation of audio and video in online presentations.

It is remarkable to realize that, a decade ago, we were sending librarians on long trips to interact with distance learners, setting up far-flung physical satellite locations to serve them, and doing reference by telephone and snail mail. This volume shows the evolution into an online environment for such services, along with a movement to mainstream them because the difference between distance learners and others, which is already blurred, will ultimately disappear.

William Miller
Director of Libraries
Florida Atlantic University

A Historical Overview
of Internet Reference Services
for Distance Learners

Anne Marie Casey

SUMMARY. The advent of library services and collections on the Internet revolutionized reference services to students enrolled in distance learning programs. Prior to the Internet, reference librarians who supported distance learning programs had few methods, and many of them costly, to provide the equivalent library services advocated by the ACRL Guidelines. Through the Internet, these librarians were able to approximate the services and resources that had always been available to students who came into the library. This article describes the development of reference services on the Internet in a variety of libraries that support distance learners. *[Article copies available for a fee from The Haworth Document Delivery Service: 1-800-HAWORTH. E-mail address: <docdelivery@haworthpress.com> Website: <http://www.HaworthPress.com> © 2004 by The Haworth Press, Inc. All rights reserved.]*

KEYWORDS. Chat reference, e-mail reference, digital reference, virtual reference, distance learning, distance education, off-campus library services

Anne Marie Casey (Casey1am@cmich.edu) is affiliated with Central Michigan University, Park 407C, Mount Pleasant, MI 48859.

[Haworth co-indexing entry note]: "A Historical Overview of Internet Reference Services for Distance Learners." Casey, Anne Marie. Co-published simultaneously in *Internet Reference Services Quarterly* (The Haworth Information Press, an imprint of The Haworth Press, Inc.) Vol. 9, No. 3/4, 2004, pp. 5-17; and: *Internet Reference Support for Distance Learners* (ed: William Miller, and Rita M. Pellen) The Haworth Information Press, an imprint of The Haworth Press, Inc., 2004, pp. 5-17. Single or multiple copies of this article are available for a fee from The Haworth Document Delivery Service [1-800-HAWORTH, 9:00 a.m. - 5:00 p.m. (EST). E-mail address: docdelivery@haworthpress.com].

Available online at http://www.haworthpress.com/web/IRSQ
Digital Object Identifier: 10.1300/J136v09n03_02

With the proliferation of colleges, universities, and even companies that offer courses and degrees in higher education through the World Wide Web today, it would seem that the concept of teaching students who are away from the home campus arose with the omnipresence of the Internet in our culture. Actually, distance learning in the United States dates back to shortly after the Civil War when correspondence courses originated. However, there is little in the library literature on library services for distance learners prior to 1970. In the 1970s, the establishment of open learning universities in many countries and in the 1980s the growth of distance education programs in traditional colleges and universities both precipitated a substantial growth in the literature about library services in support of distance education (Slade and Kascus 1998, 262).

In the 1970s and 1980s, there were several ways in which distance learning library services provided reference assistance. One way was to negotiate contracts or set up memoranda of understanding with local libraries near where their distance students lived. Toll-free telephone and fax lines were another common approach. Students were encouraged to call the 800 number to talk to a dedicated distance learning reference librarian or be connected directly to the reference desk. Some distance learning programs set up branch campus libraries at established centers where several courses were taught. In addition, since library services to distance learning students were not always funded appropriately, a common practice was to simply refer students to local libraries in their home areas and hope for the best.

While some distance learning programs established separate library services to support their off-campus students, most did not. In the third edition of the *Off-Campus Library Services Directory*, 29 of the 161 respondents reported being a separate service dedicated to the needs of the distance students only (Casey and Cachero 1998, 91). The majority of library services supporting distance education maintained a reference department that was asked to balance the needs of traditional-aged, on-campus students who most normally came to the reference desk in person with distance students who were generally working adults in a compressed course who called or faxed in requests for reference assistance. Naturally students in distance learning programs turned to local libraries quite frequently for reference assistance and faculty teaching in distance programs tended to alter course expectations, planning more group projects and offering additional readings in course packs because they perceived that their distance students did not have the access to library services that on-campus students did.

Central Michigan University (CMU) developed Off-Campus Library Services (OCLS) in 1976 to support exclusively the needs of students in its burgeoning five-year-old distance learning division. From the beginning, OCLS had reference librarians based in the main campus library in Mt. Pleasant, as well as in major regional offices throughout the U.S. The locations of field-based librarians changed over the years as CMU student populations rose and fell throughout the U.S. In 2004, field librarians were based in suburban Detroit, suburban Washington, D.C., Kansas City, and Atlanta.

Although there is a small amount of face-to-face reference service in the field offices, the majority of reference work done historically at OCLS was by toll-free telephone. The most common type of reference assistance, which has remained constant throughout the history of OCLS, has been help in finding references to books and articles for research papers. At OCLS, as at many library services that supported distance learning students prior to easy access to the Internet, CMU students were helped with defining a topic and developing a list of controlled vocabulary if they indicated that they preferred to conduct their own research in a local library, or were mailed lists of references to their topics compiled by an OCLS librarian, if that were their preference.

Easy access to the Internet revolutionized libraries but arguably was more welcomed by distance learning librarians than by anyone else. Now their students would truly have equivalent access to many of the same resources that on-campus students did, as stipulated by the *ACRL Guidelines for Distance Learning Library Services* (ACRL 2003). Emphasis was placed on making online databases available to off-campus students. In 1995, the main criterion that the CMU Libraries used to choose an online database vendor was that access would be as easy for the off-campus students as for those on campus.

In the mid-1990s, as the concept of the digital library swept higher education, the emphasis seemed to be far more on access to digitized information then on access to information professionals. Our first priority at the beginning of the digital library era was to extend the collections of the library out to our off-campus students.

> Defining the digital library is an interesting, but somewhat daunting, task. There is no shortage of proposed definitions. One would think there would be some commonly accepted and fairly straightforward standard definition, but there does not appear to be. Rather, there are many. And one common thread among all these definitions is a heavy emphasis on resources and an apparent lack

of emphasis on librarians and the services they provide. (Sloan 1998, 118)

One would almost get the impression that the service tradition of the physical library will be unnecessary and redundant in the digital library environment. (Sloan 1998, 117)

Digital reference advocates say that patrons don't want to deal with flesh-and-blood librarians. The reality is more complicated than that. The reference people we know are open, discreet, knowledgeable, and committed guides to knowledge in all forms; and it's often the digital equipment our patrons seem to despise. Nevertheless, librarians have to take a run at some form of digital reference, not because it is comparable to face-to-face service, but because we have to keep our oar in the stream and a more inclusive model for reference makes sense. If librarians are players, delivering better quality service and better answers to their local patrons than Web-searching "experts" sitting at their terminals . . . , then maybe libraries can cement their place in the postmodern world. (Cameron and McCarty 2001, 9)

For the average person, there seems to be a growing belief that having access to digital resources on a 24/7 basis is enough. Reference librarians are still thought of as sitting behind a desk in a physical library and since information online is easy to find and easy to use, there is little need for them to move out from behind the desk into the digital world. Reference librarians, however, understand that for most lay people, conducting effective research in a digital library is at least as difficult as conducting research in a print-based library and they have been offering Internet reference assistance for years.

The professional literature contains an abundance of articles on various forms of digital reference that often include discussions about the important role it plays in today's libraries and the need for engaging in new technologies. Some of the discussion centers on the difficulties inherent in trying to conduct a reference interview in an electronic environment rather than face-to-face (Abels 1994; Abels 1996; Schilling-Eccles and Harzbecker 1998). Some discussion centers on the types of questions to answer, and how limits should be set up (Fishman 1998, 4). Internet-based reference is an enormous change from the way that academic reference librarians have been operating for most of the history of the profession. For most reference librarians, the ideal way to help a patron is face-to-face, where all of the different aspects that go into successful communication are in evidence. Moving to a different method of communicating with patrons has caused a great deal of trial and discussion in the traditional academic library. However, in the world of distance learning librarianship, the ability to communicate with patrons who were at a distance, in other formats than phone and mail, quickly revolutionized the reference services in the late 1980s and early 1990s as the Internet became available to the average person.

When the concepts of digital or virtual or Internet reference are discussed, most people tend to think of the most common: e-mail reference, video conferencing reference, and chat reference. There are also some other forms of digital reference that surface in the literature and in discussions. One is Internet reference that is offered through the World Wide Web. In the third edition of the *Off-Campus Library Services Directory* (160-162), 147 of 161 respondents reported using the World Wide Web as a method for providing reference services to off-campus students. Since this coincides exactly with the number who report providing e-mail reference in the same directory, it is reasonable to conclude that the WWW based reference referred to online reference request forms or "Ask-a-Librarian" services. Because the method of communication with those using Web forms is generally e-mail, the discussion of this type of reference service will be rolled into the discussion of e-mail reference to follow.

In addition, in some distance learning library services, access to online databases was considered a form of reference early on. Given that much of the reference assistance to distance learning students before the World Wide Web consisted of mailing custom-tailored bibliographies to students, the idea of making available online databases that students could search themselves was viewed as a type of reference assistance. When CMU began to offer dial-in and telnet access to four databases that were linked to the OPAC in the mid-1990s, the OCLS librarians did consider that we were extending reference service to our students beyond the hours that we were available. The librarians at Monash University College Gippsland in Australia also considered that a dial-in service to some of the CD-ROM databases in their library in 1991 would extend their reference service beyond the hours they were available and would greatly speed up the response time for students who normally had to wait to receive search results by mail (Van Dyk 1992).

E-mail reference is probably the oldest continuous method of conducting reference on the Internet and is fairly universal today. In 1998, 147 of 161 respondents to the third edition of the *Off-Campus Library*

Services Directory (158-160) reported using e-mail as a method for providing reference services to off-campus students. This was a significant increase over those who reported using e-mail for any service in the second edition of the same directory, where 27 of the 176 respondents reported supplying materials by e-mail (Jacob 1993, 178) and 59 reported receiving requests for service or materials this way (Jacob 1993, 189).

One of the earliest examples in the literature of a library extending digital reference service to distance learning students is found at Indiana University (IU). In February 1987, a library service was launched through the Academic Information Environment, maintained by the IU computing center, which included reference services. Full-time faculty and graduate students were given accounts to access the system (Copler 1989; Bristow and Buechley 1995).

The University of Alaska Fairbanks, which served students at five extended campuses and seven rural education centers throughout the state, started a library service for its distance students in 1989. By 1991, they were offering library service through e-mail (Smith and West, 1991).

In the late 1990s, some states began developing library services to support distance learners statewide. One was the Kentucky Virtual Library (KYVL), which was developed in 1999 to support the Kentucky Virtual University, whose mandate was to promote distance learning in Kentucky. Reference service was available to distance learners by telephone and by e-mail every day. "A large part of the service is handled completely electronically, e-mail to e-mail . . . " (Moore, Knight, and Kinnersley 2001, 33). Reference librarians at KYVL developed a series of answers to frequently asked questions that they have in templates to send out electronically whenever needed.

In 1997, the state of Florida established the Florida Distance Learning Reference and Referral Center (RRC) at the Tampa Campus of the University of South Florida. Until state funding ceased in 2001 and the RRC was forced to disband, the librarians supported distance learners taking courses at any public institution of higher education in the state of Florida. E-mail reference was part of the repertoire from the beginning as well as technical knowledge of the Web sites of the public college and university libraries in Florida (Ault and Viggiano 2000).

OCLS began to use e-mail for reference in 1993. The majority of CMU distance learning classes have historically been taught in compressed format in classroom locations, often in remote areas, in the U.S., Canada, and Mexico. One of the hallmarks of OCLS has been the guarantee that every graduate student and most undergraduate students would meet a reference librarian at least once during the course of a program when the regional librarian would come to class to teach library instruction methods during the required research class. Many of the classes were taught on military installations where students had e-mail access earlier than the general population. Feedback received from students during library instruction classes was that they would like to receive database searches and other reference responses by e-mail. Having recently concluded a study to determine the feasibility of sending database searches by fax and deciding that most students did not yet have access to fax machines powerful enough to easily receive the amount of data we normally sent, we concluded that e-mail might be a better way to send search results quickly.

As a result of the student feedback, OCLS created a departmental e-mail account in 1993 that was publicized to off-campus students and faculty. Those students who had e-mail access readily accepted the option to receive search results through e-mail rather than mail. In addition to speeding up the time it took for students to receive research results, there was an additional benefit. OCLS librarians began to notice that in the cases of more difficult searches, they were able to refine their search parameters by e-mailing students several search strategies and some sample search results in order to get a clearer idea of what a student truly needed but had not been able to communicate effectively during the reference interview over the telephone. In some ways, e-mail reference was able to mimic in-person reference better than telephone reference was. By having the ability to send some possibilities for a student to choose from, the librarian was working through the search process with a student in a way similar to helping a student navigate a search through a database in the reference department.

In 1996, OCLS created a Web site with links to services and databases for the distance learning students. Included on the Web site was an "Ask an OCLS Librarian" button. It was originally named this way because the OCLS Web site was an adjunct to the university library Web site and we were making every effort to distinguish the OCLS service from the University library "Ask a Librarian" service. Initially, when students filled out a Web form, they designated the CMU center where they were registered to take classes. Each of the centers was coded to fall into one of three regional offices. (Prior to 2000, two OCLS librarians each were located in the university library on campus and in field offices in suburban Detroit and suburban Washington, D.C.) An e-mail request derived from the form was sent to the e-mail addresses of both librarians in the regional office that provided reference services to students taking classes at the given CMU center. Whichever of the two librarians was scheduled to be "on the reference phone" also answered the e-mail questions that came in during that same shift.

Although e-mail reference and Web forms don't always provide the best way to conduct a reference interview with a student, the OCLS librarians were generally satisfied that the format of the Web form prompted students to ask their questions very succinctly. Students were informed that once the form was submitted they could expect to receive an answer by e-mail or a call from a librarian to clarify the question within 24 hours during the work week. The librarians found that they could answer most questions without having to call students. For their part, the students appeared to be very satisfied that they were able to ask for reference assistance at a time convenient for them and know that they would generally receive an answer quickly without having to take time out of their work days to speak to a librarian.

In 2000, OCLS reorganized and moved a librarian position from the Detroit and Washington offices to new offices in Atlanta and Kansas City. In addition, we centralized reference. Rather than calling librarians in the regional offices for reference assistance as they had historically, students were instructed to call the central 800 number in the OCLS office in the CMU library. Calls were then forwarded to the office of the librarian on reference duty. At the same time, an e-mail reference account was created that could be accessed by all of the librarians. That e-mail address was given out to students as one form of accessing reference assistance. In addition, the Web form was reprogrammed to send all e-mail requests to the new reference e-mail address. In turn, librarians began sending all answers to reference requests out through the reference e-mail address. This had two major benefits: librarians could access searches sent by other librarians if they were following up on a question and e-mail reference requests no longer sat unattended in a particular librarian's personal e-mail account while he or she was out of the office.

In the mid- to late-1990s, some libraries began experimenting with reference assistance using video conferencing equipment. This was not a very successful means of providing assistance to distance learning students because the majority of students were accessing the Internet from home or work computers with slow dial-in capabilities. However, there are some accounts of libraries that used video conferencing technology with students at branches or centers. Emory University Libraries experimented with reference and instruction using video conferencing in

1995. The Centre for Business Information, which supported the Executive and Evening MBA classes at an off-campus site, set up equipment at that site. Librarians were available for ready reference, in-depth consultation, and training on databases. Users did not adapt to the system as readily as expected, partly because marketing was not strong and partly because there was a perceived lack of support from the administration (Pagell 1996).

In 1999, the Dean of Libraries at CMU offered to buy video conferencing equipment for both OCLS and the university library reference services department. After much discussion, OCLS decided against trying a method that required specific equipment of our students. Another thing that shaped our decision was the experience of the OCLS Web master who had been using video conferencing technology to take part in meetings on campus from her office in Detroit. She found the quality of the experience to be so distracting that she went back to conferencing into the meetings by telephone. We thought that if the most technologically advanced of the OCLS librarians had difficulty with video conferencing, we would have many challenges trying to provide reference by that method.

Chat first began to appear in the distance learning library world in the mid-1990s although it became a more common method of providing reference assistance from 2000 on. One of the first accounts in the literature of a chat reference service to support distance learners appears in 1995. The librarians at Embry-Riddle Aeronautical University added a new Internet reference service to their established e-mail reference service. They began to "sit in" on CompuServe forums set up for the university's correspondence students. This allowed the reference librarians to answer reference questions that came up during the chat sessions and to build relationships with the students who continued to ask for reference assistance by phone or e-mail after the forums (Young 1995).

During the 1997-98 academic year, librarians at Austin Community College (ACC) built two fully functioning computer classrooms, one in Austin and the other in rural Fredericksburg, Texas, where ACC students were enrolled in a vocational Nursing program. The VTEL equipment allowed for conferencing through compressed audio and video over network and telephone lines. Among the services available was text chat with a reference librarian in Austin. The librarians also had scanners attached to their workstations so were able to scan appropriate print items that answered the students' reference questions and sent them through to a printer in the computer lab in Fredericksburg (Tinnin, Buckstead, and Richardson 1998).

By 2000, chat software was being designed to meet the needs of library reference and instruction services. Some of the products on the market, such as LSSI and 24/7 software, offered both the ability to chat and to co-browse. Librarians could maintain a conversation with a student by chatting while simultaneously sending Web pages to the student or taking control of the student's Web browser and guiding him or her through the research process. This format allowed for a reference interview almost as good as one a librarian could conduct in person and was extremely well-received by distance learning library services.

Many case studies of distance learning library services using chat for reference started to appear in the literature in 2000. The Florida RRC was offering reference assistance using chat software in 2000 (Ault & Viggiano, 2000). North Carolina State University conducted a chat reference pilot, in which off-site students were included, in 2000 and implemented a full service in January 2001 (Anderson, Boyer, & Ciccone 2000). Maricopa Community College extended chat reference services in a pilot study to its distance learning students in 2001 (Witten 2002). A chat reference trial was conducted with off-campus students in the School of Nursing at LaTrobe University in Australia in 2002 (Porter 2003). Steven F. Austin Sate University in Texas set up a chat trial in 2003 for its distance education students (McDonald and Turnage 2003). Southeastern Louisiana University (SLU), which has been a member of a chat consortium since 2002, conducted an innovative chat reference pilot in 2003. SLU librarians set up dedicated reference chat sessions with Nursing students in their distance education program. The dedicated sessions were with groups formed by the professor to work on projects together. The reference librarians provided reference assistance to the students as they were conducting research on their group projects (Guillot and Starr 2004).

At CMU, the OCLS librarians began discussing offering a chat reference service in late 2000. In 2001, in conjunction with the university library reference services department, OCLS purchased LSSI chat software. In the spring of 2002, OCLS librarians began to add chat reference sessions to the reference schedule on a limited basis. It was common to have no reference requests come in during a shift on chat reference. Because OCLS and the university library reference services department had shared the cost of the subscription to LSSI, we divided the week between the two services. The reference services department was getting a somewhat higher response from the on-campus students to the service but not one that was strong enough to continue to justify the drain on time of the librarians who had added chat reference shifts to all of their other duties. With the divided schedule, it was impossible to set up a consistent service that students could find every day at the same time.

In 2003, the OCLS and reference librarians met in a conference call to discuss ways to innovate the service in order to encourage higher use. For the first time since the establishment of OCLS in 1976, the reference librarians in both units decided to consider all CMU students one large group for the purposes of chat reference. Since all students using chat reference were remote, the differences in assisting them would be far less obvious than with traditional reference assistance to students on either side of the line. A regular schedule was set up for chat reference assistance and librarians from both reference services and OCLS were scheduled for chat reference sessions that were advertised to all CMU library users.

During the 2003-2004 academic year, chat reference was available for 24 hours per week. Of the approximately 400 sessions that were logged as true reference sessions rather than practices during the year, less than 1/3 were from distance learning students. At the end of the academic year, the library decided to suspend chat reference until a stronger financial climate at CMU would allow for more staff to dedicate to the service or until the library is able to participate in a chat consortium.

Although chat has many characteristics that make it preferable to other avenues of reference assistance to distance learning students, it is not without its challenges. If a student comes into the chat session on a slow modem, the session can be impossibly slow or crash. If the librarian spends too much time looking for an answer to a student's question, the students have been known to leave because they are not sure if they have been abandoned or disconnected. Finally, chat reference is almost universally an add-on service. Reference librarians do not generally give up telephone reference or e-mail reference to start offering chat reference. Normally they add another service into an already busy schedule and risk making mistakes and burning out.

As anyone knows, who has seen reference tools change rapidly from the card catalog and print indexes to the sophisticated Web search engines of today, a better technology to provide reference assistance on the Internet is always "just around the corner." Steve Coffman, who has been a leader in the field of virtual reference, discussed in a 2001 article two technologies that are currently available but perhaps not as widespread or as sophisticated as we might need for universal acceptance right now. One is VoIP or Voice over Internet Protocol. "VoIP . . . will allow the librarian and patron to hold a voice conversation on the same line they are using for the Web connection–meaning they will be able to browse the Web and talk back and forth at the same time, just as if they were on the phone" (Coffman 2001, 23). The other is the knowledge base. A good example of this, which is available now, is QuestionPoint, developed by OCLC and the Library of Congress. "QuestionPoint uses best-match routing from the Global Reference Network to find the institution best able to answer a question and builds and maintains a global Knowledge Base of previously asked and answered reference questions" (OCLC, 2004).

Separate library services for distance learners, such as CMU's Off-Campus Library Services, are perhaps models of a bygone era. With the proliferation of the World Wide Web and the continued addition of Web-based reference services, there is less and less to distinguish the working adult, in a compressed class or online class, who needs reference assistance at 2:00 a.m. from the student in the dorm, five-minutes walk from the library, who prefers to work on his own PC and also needs reference assistance at 2:00 a.m. It will be interesting to experience the ways in which reference librarians will continue to add the human interface to the virtual library and extend our service to our remote users wherever they are.

REFERENCES

Abels, E. G. 1996. The e-mail reference interview. *RQ* 35 (3): 345-358.

_____, and Liebscher, P. 1994. A new challenge for intermediary-client communication: The electronic network. *The Reference Librarian* 41/42: 185-196.

Anderson, E., J. Boyer, and K. Ciccone. 2000. Remote reference services at the North Carolina State University Libraries. In *The virtual reference desk: 2nd annual digital reference conference proceedings.* Syracuse, NY: Virtual Reference Desk Project. http://www.vrd.org/conferences/VRD2000/proceedings/boyer-anderson-ciccone12-14.shtml (accessed May 31, 2004).

Association of College and Research Libraries. 2003. *ACRL guidelines for distance learning library services.* Chicago: ACRL. http://www.ala.org/ala/acrl/acrlstandards/guidelinesdistancelearning.htm (accessed June 6, 2004).

Ault, M., and R. Viggiano. 2000. Going the distance: Traditional reference services for non-traditional users. *Florida Libraries* 43 (3): 6-7.

Bristow, A., and M. Buechley. 1995. Academic reference service over e-mail: An update. *C&RL News* 56 (7): 459-462.

Cameron, A. J., and L. McCarty. 2001. Distance education and digital reference: The yellow brick road? *Alki* 17 (1): 6-9.

Casey, A. M., and M. Cachero. 1998. *Off-Campus library services directory.* 3rd ed. Mount Pleasant: Central Michigan University.

Coffman, S. 2001. Distance education and virtual reference: Where are we headed? *Computers in Libraries* 21 (4): 20-25.

Copler, J. A. 1989. Reaching remote users–Library services through a systemwide computing network. In *The off-campus library services conference proceedings*, ed. B. M. Lessin, 78-84. Mount Pleasant: Central Michigan University.

Fishman, D. L. 1998. Managing the virtual reference desk: How to plan an effective reference e-mail system. *Medical Reference Services Quarterly* 17 (1): 1-10.

Guillot, L., and B. Stahr. 2004. A tale of two campuses: Providing virtual reference to distance nursing students. In *The eleventh off-campus library services conference proceedings*, ed. P. B. Mahoney, 105-114. Mount Pleasant: Central Michigan University.

Jacob, C. J. 1993. *Off-Campus library services directory*. 2nd ed. Mount Pleasant: Central Michigan University.

McDonald, R., and M. Turnage. 2003. Making the connection: Library services for distance education and off-campus students. *Texas Library Journal* 79 (2): 50-53.

Moore, E., E. Knight, and R. Kinnersley. 2001. WKU Libraries' Kentucky Virtual University support services. *Kentucky Libraries* 65 (4): 31-35.

OCLC. QuestionPoint: How it helps libraries: The global network. http://www.oclc.org/questionpoint/libraries/network/default.htm (accessed June 6, 2004).

Pagell, R. A. 1996. The virtual reference librarian: Using desktop videoconferencing for distance reference. *The Electronic Library* 14 (1): 21-26.

Porter, S. 2003. Chat: From the desk of a subject librarian. *Reference Services Review* 31 (1): 57-67.

Schilling-Eccles, K., and J. J. Harzbecker. 1998. The use of electronic mail at the reference desk: Impact of a computer-mediated communication technology on librarian-client interactions. *Medical Reference Services Quarterly* 17 (4): 17-27.

Slade, S., and M. Kascus. 1998. An international comparison of library services for distance learning. In *The eighth off-campus library services conference proceedings*, comp. P. S. Thomas and M. Jones, 259-297. Mount Pleasant: Central Michigan University.

Sloan, B. 1998. Service perspectives for the digital library remote reference services. *Library Trends* 47 (1): 117-143.

Smith, R. M., S. F. Race, and M. Ault. 2000. Virtual desk: Real reference. In *The ninth off-campus library services conference proceedings*, comp. P. S. Thomas, 245-252. Mount Pleasant: Central Michigan University.

Smith, S. L., and S. M. West. 1991. CD-ROM reference access and delivery. In *The fifth off-campus library services conference proceedings*, comp. C. J. Jacob, 273-280. Mount Pleasant: Central Michigan University.

Tinnin, N., J. Buckstead, and K. Richardson. 1998. Remote reference by microcomputer: Setup and installation. In *The eighth off-campus library services conference proceedings*, comp. P. S. Thomas and M. Jones, 299-312. Mount Pleasant: Central Michigan University.

Van Dyk, M. T. 1992. ROMOTE: An off-campus dial-up service for CD-ROM databases. *Lasie* 22 (6): 148-155.

Witten, S. 2002. Being RAD: Reference at a distance in a multi-campus institution. In *The tenth off-campus library services conference proceedings*, ed. P. B. Mahoney, 423-438. Mount Pleasant: Central Michigan University.

Young, J. B. 1995. Providing reference service to graduate independent study students worldwide. In *The seventh off-campus library services conference proceedings*, comp. C. J. Jacob, 399-402. Mount Pleasant: Central Michigan University.

Internet Reference Services for Distance Education: Guidelines Comparison and Implementation

Marie F. Jones

SUMMARY. Published guidelines for distance learning library services provide a framework for distance education librarians to use in planning services for off-campus students. Other literature in the arena of distance education librarianship provides concrete examples of how reference services have been offered in real settings. This paper attempts to synthesize these two types of literature in order to offer models of reference service for distance learners. *[Article copies available for a fee from The Haworth Document Delivery Service: 1-800-HAWORTH. E-mail address: <docdelivery@haworthpress.com> Website: <http://www.HaworthPress.com> © 2004 by The Haworth Press, Inc. All rights reserved.]*

KEYWORDS. Guidelines, standards, distance learners, distance learning, library services, reference services

Marie F. Jones (JONESMF@mail.etsu.edu) is Extended Campus Services Librarian, East Tennessee State University, Sherrod Library, Box 70665, Johnson City, TN 37614.

[Haworth co-indexing entry note]: "Internet Reference Services for Distance Education: Guidelines Comparison and Implementation." Jones, Marie F. Co-published simultaneously in *Internet Reference Services Quarterly* (The Haworth Information Press, an imprint of The Haworth Press, Inc.) Vol. 9, No. 3/4, 2004, pp. 19-32; and: *Internet Reference Support for Distance Learners* (ed: William Miller, and Rita M. Pellen) The Haworth Information Press, an imprint of The Haworth Press, Inc., 2004, pp. 19-32. Single or multiple copies of this article are available for a fee from The Haworth Document Delivery Service [1-800-HAWORTH, 9:00 a.m. - 5:00 p.m. (EST). E-mail address: docdelivery@haworthpress.com].

Reference services in academic libraries traditionally include professional assistance with general reference questions, information-gathering, development of research strategies, resource selection, and mediated database searching. However, when reference services begin to occur over a distance rather than in a face-to-face transaction, a shift must take place in how reference services are offered. This shift can, in part, be guided by a framework of published guidelines and standards. Published guidelines for distance learning library services provide a framework for distance education librarians to use in planning all types of services for off-campus students and faculty, and for administering programs of distance education services. Other literature in the arena of distance education librarianship provides concrete examples of how, practically, reference and instruction services have shifted to fit the needs of both the off-campus and the campus communities. This paper attempts to provide a synthesis of the guidelines and standards, supported by specific implementation examples, to provide a framework for distance education librarianship.

REVIEW OF THE LITERATURE

Guidelines and Standards

In the U.S., the Association of College and Research Libraries (ACRL) and its component organizations provide codified standards and guidelines on a variety of topics related to academic librarianship. These guidelines cross a wide range of topics in librarianship, from those for specific academic library types (e.g., college, branch, community college) to issues of professionalism (e.g., MLS requirements, collective bargaining, faculty status) (*Standards & guidelines by topic*, n.d.). The Distance Learning Section (DLS) of ACRL created and revised the *Guidelines for Distance Learning Library Services* (*ACRL Guidelines*, 2003). The DLS Guidelines describe the underlying principle for the document as follows:

> Library resources and services in institutions of higher education must meet the needs of all their faculty, students, and academic support staff, wherever these individuals are located, whether on a main campus, off campus, in distance learning or extended campus programs, or in the absence of a campus at all; in courses taken for credit or noncredit; in continuing education programs; in courses

attended in person or by means of electronic transmission; or any other means of distance learning. The "Guidelines" delineate the elements necessary to achieving this underlying and uncompromising principle.

The Medical Library Association (MLA) has set forth its own position paper for "Essential Library Support for Distance Education" (Ludwig, 2002). Like the ACRL guidelines, this position paper emphasizes the need for equivalent services for off-campus students. While it discusses some specific means for provision of services, it does not provide a thorough framework for librarians; rather, it provides a document to be used for lobbying for Federal funding.

The *Guidelines for Library Support of Distance and Distributed Learning in Canada* ([Canadian Guidelines], 2000) parallel much of the ACRL DLS guidelines. They are organized with the same structure; however, specifics vary. For example, the U.S. guidelines insist on formal agreements with local libraries while the Canadian guidelines allow for informal agreements, or even no agreements at all, if they don't seem necessary. The *Guidelines for Library Services to Distance Learners* from the Indian Library Association (n.d., *Guidelines for library services*) reflect the organizational structure of Indian education and the infrastructure in that country, but are organized similarly to the Canadian and U.S. Guidelines. Nonetheless, the underlying mission of distance education library services is the same as it is elsewhere, to provide "equitable library services to distance learners" (p. 2).

Library Literature

The library literature offers a plethora of articles discussing practical ways to serve the distance education community. Since providing reference services via the Internet is one of the major venues for reaching the distance education community, resources that concentrate on digital reference are important to this discussion. One useful resource in reference is Bernie Sloan's *Digital Reference Services Bibliography* (Sloan, 2003), a comprehensive and continuously updated bibliography. Another is the journal *Internet Reference Services Quarterly*, a scholarly journal devoted to reference services on the Internet.

One other very useful examination of the literature of service to distance education students is Gandhi's "Academic Librarians and Distance Education" (Gandhi, 2003). Gandhi presents three "opportunities and challenges for academic librarians: (1) globalization of information, (2) increase in student expectations, and (3) the reference interview" (p. 142).

First, Gandhi discusses how librarians, historically, were expected to have an in-depth knowledge only of their own library collections and limited knowledge of other collections. But "with the advent of virtual libraries and electronic resources, and an expanded repertoire of reference tools, even basic reference tasks have become more time-consuming. . . . Librarians must be well versed in all formats and know which format will serve as the best information source for a particular question. They must also be able to guide students to specific libraries that have the information students are seeking" (p. 142).

Gandhi goes on to point out that user expectations have grown to include even an expectation of 24/7 reference service. While librarians have always worked evenings and weekends, Helfer (2001) is one voice among many libraries for whom "the thought of having to answer a patron inquiry at 3 a.m. does not exactly excite me–or at least, not positively" (p. 69). The idea of 24-hour reference is one which has been discussed widely in library literature (e.g., Dougherty, 2002; "Library opens 24-hour," 2001; Dunn & Morgan, 2003; Jerant & Firestein, 2003).

A less dramatic strategy for dealing with increased expectations and the need to serve off-campus patrons comes from those libraries that offer digital reference services such as e-mail reference (e.g., Sullivan, 2003; Kratzert, Richey, & Wassmann, 2001) and live chat reference services (e.g., Katz, 2003; Stormont, 2002; Heise & Kimmel, 2003; Connor, 2002). Much literature is also devoted to creating quality library Web pages for distance education (e.g., Adams & Cassner, 2002; Bao, 2001; Buckstead, 2001; Linden, 2000; Stacy-Bates, 2000).

Gandhi's third point about distance education and reference services relates to the reference interview. He notes that librarians "can provide some reference assistance to distance learners through user guides, Webliographies, and electronic pathfinders," and that the actual reference interview is more challenging when it is conducted over a geographic distance by "Internet chat, paging and instant messaging, e-mail, audio-and videoconferencing, fax, Web forms, regular mail, and the telephone (some libraries have toll-free numbers)" (p. 143). Gandhi discusses the difficulty of question negotiation minus the nonverbal cues of the face-to-face interview and points out "the librarian and the student may need to trade a number of e-mail or chat messages to clarify the student's information needs, making the reference question negotiation process lengthier and more time-intensive" (p. 143). Pease and

Power (1994) observe, "It is easier to demonstrate the use of a reference resource than to explain it in writing or over the phone" (p. 49). Even co-browsing sessions where the librarian can demonstrate the use of an online resource take more time, as typing is still slower than speaking. Audio and video-conferencing technologies may address these concerns, but bandwidth and available hardware/software on the user end still limit the practical application of this type of technology.

The library literature also discusses the importance of establishing a library presence in course management systems (courseware such as Blackboard or WebCT). Shank and Dewald (2003) have named two types of involvement, Macro-Level Library Courseware Involvement (MaLLCI) and Micro-Level Library Courseware Involvement (MiLLCI). The former method involves working with courseware developers and programmers to integrate a generic library presence into the software; the latter method involves individual librarians working with faculty to participate in developing customized instruction and resource components within the courseware. Many of the articles written about courseware focus on using it for library instruction (Shank & Dewald, 2003), but Cote (2001) suggests that reference services are enhanced when academic librarians actively participate in bulletin board and e-mail discussions so that they become more visible in the online environment so that students and faculty can feel comfortable enough to ask questions.

DISCUSSION

Generally, the guidelines from various organizations cover the same topics. For the purposes of this discussion, the organization and wording of the *ACRL Guidelines for Distance Learning Library Services* (2003) will be used as the framework on which other guidelines and standards are placed, and then specific examples for implementation are provided. The reader should be aware that only those aspects which may have a direct or indirect impact on reference services are included here; the guidelines cover many areas of library service beyond reference.

Equivalent Services

"Members of the distance learning community are entitled to library services and resources equivalent to those provided for students and faculty in traditional campus settings" (*ACRL Guidelines*, 2003, Philosophy section, para. 1). Jones (2003) writes that equivalency "doesn't necessarily mean *exactly the same*, but it does mean that distance learning students should have access, somehow, to library/learning resources and services, designed to support the specific programs offered. These services/resources should meet the same standard of academic quality as the same courses offered in traditional settings" (p. 1). Jones continues by defining how this might be accomplished. One can do so either by providing the service directly, in a technology-mediated manner, or by way of formal agreements with other institutions or organizations. If reference service to distance learners is provided through the same service point as that to on-campus students, it is important that distance education students don't "get short shrift from librarians who may be too quick to tell callers that 'you'll have to come into the library for that'" (Goodson, 2001, p. 71).

Personalization

Both the Canadian and U.S. Guidelines point out that students and faculty in distance education programs, because they do not have direct access to services and materials, may require more personalized services than might be expected on campus. The MLA position paper (Ludwig, 2002) approaches it from a slightly different perspective, stating that these library services are "more labor intensive than on-campus services" (para. 5). Personalization of services comes naturally in a distance education library setting where service is valued foremost. Because each individual distance education student comes to the librarian with a different set of circumstances–this one has no fax number, that one cannot be called during working hours, another cannot access a computer right now (and is taking face-to-face classes at a very distant site)–the distance education librarian personalizes service to help individuals find what they need regardless of circumstances. There is no "one size fits all" reference service that can provide all answers to all questions. Some can be answered by e-mail, some by phone. Sometimes, you can e-mail a link to a reference article, sometimes you can fax it, and sometimes you send by mail. Certainly, a standard procedure can be put in place, but long-time distance education librarians have found that those procedures don't always fit everyone's circumstance. In order to offer equitable service, distance education librarians need to have a whole range of tools in their reference toolbox.

Pro-Active Librarianship

When serving a distance education population, we cannot passively sit at the reference desk and expect students to come to us. Planning becomes more important, and we must become more aggressive about letting people know what we can do for them. (See sections on marketing and promotion for more examples.) "Special funding arrangements, proactive planning, and promotion are necessary to deliver equivalent library services and to achieve equivalent results in teaching and learning" (*ACRL Guidelines*, 2003, Philosophy section, para. 3). Since the fact that help even exists is not immediately obvious to a student who takes courses hundreds of miles away from the physical reference desk, our emphasis needs to be on advocating the services we offer and educating our clientele not only in areas of information literacy but also in the simple knowledge of what resources and services are available.

Innovation

Providing equivalent services may require "innovative approaches to the design and evaluation of special procedures or systems to meet these needs" (*ACRL Guidelines*, 2003, Philosophy section, para. 9). For example, libraries supporting distance education programs were among the first to implement innovations such as chat reference services. Innovation ties in neatly with the idea of personalization, discussed earlier. If your campus has a variety of off-campus locations and a variety of distance education media (face-to-face, interactive television, online, telecourses), serving that variety takes innovative and diverse thinking.

Partnerships with Other Libraries

The MLA position paper (Ludwig, 2002) emphasizes "partnering institutions" and says "Librarians, with their strong tradition of inter-institutional cooperation and outreach services, are in a unique position to advise, lead, and contribute to these efforts." The ACRL Guidelines (2003) say that the librarian-administrator should "initiate dialogue leading to cooperative agreements and possible resource sharing and/or compensation for unaffiliated libraries" (Management section, para. 9). The Canadian Library Association Guidelines allow for a more informal arrangement in regard to patrons' use of other libraries. The Indian Guidelines (*Guidelines for library services*, n.d.) consider partnerships and resource sharing so important that they put them in the Philosophy section of their document as one of the bases for distance education in that country.

Regardless, patrons *will* use the libraries closest to them, and patrons will also ask reference questions at those libraries. Formal or informal communication with regional libraries lets their librarians know how to direct reference questions from your students back to the appropriate department in your institution, as necessary.

Libraries have worked together for years in consortia for resource-sharing, consortial borrowing, interlibrary loan, and other activities. Most recently, some libraries have created partnerships for Internet reference services in the form of shared 24/7 chat reference services. Groups that have set up chat consortia include Q&A NJ and the Boston Library Consortium. Quite a number of academic libraries use 24/7 Reference software and participate in group reference through that company (see <http://www.247ref.org/communities.htm> for a list of participating libraries).

Mission Statement

The DLS guidelines state that distance education librarians should "promote the incorporation of the distance learning mission statement, goals, and objectives into those of the library and of the originating institution as a whole" (*ACRL Guidelines*, 2003, Management section, para. 4). Therefore, libraries should examine their existing mission statements for reference services, and make sure that they include the needs of distance learners as well as those of on-campus students. Institutionally, incorporating library issues into other distance education statements requires negotiation and communication with other departments and administrators, and will be influenced by institutional politics. It therefore becomes necessary for distance education librarians to muster support not only within the library, but elsewhere in the institution. These political considerations are one of the many reasons that experienced distance education librarians recommend actively networking across campus (Jones, 2002).

Evaluation

As with face-to-face reference services, reference for distance education must be evaluated in order for it to be continuously revised and improved. The guidelines point out that the librarian-administrator of distance education should "assess the existing library support for distance learning, its availability, appropriateness, and effectiveness, using qualitative, quantitative, and outcomes measurement devices, as well as the written profile of needs" (*ACRL Guidelines*, 2003, Management section, para. 6). In libraries where Internet reference services are provided for both distant and local learners at the same service point, it may be harder to separate out the distance education transactions. Nonetheless, the guidelines offer the following specific measures that might be used for reference evaluation:

- Asking focus groups of students, faculty, staff and alumni to comment on their experiences using distance learning library services over a period of time;
- Employing assessment and evaluation by librarians from other institutions and/or other appropriate consultants, including those in communities where the institution has concentrations of distance learners;
- Conducting reviews of specific library and information service areas and/or operations which support distance learning services [e.g., reference];
- Considering distance learning library services in the assessment strategies related to institutional accreditation;
- Comparing the library . . . with its peers (*ACRL Guidelines*, 2003, Management section, para. 6).

Promotion and Marketing

The librarian who administers distance education is encouraged to be proactive, spending much of her/his energies to "promote library support services to the distance learning community" (*ACRL Guidelines*, 2003, Management section, para. 9). The Indian guidelines (*Guidelines for library services*, n.d.) put it this way: "It is for the Library and Information Science professionals to create awareness and demand for library and information services in the distance learning mode" (p. 3). They also require that the "programme guide" list facilities, resources, and services and that library schedules be widely published (p. 7). The Canadian Guidelines (2000) provide a detailed list of examples of publicity that distance education librarians should use. Included among the list are items which serve either reference or instruction purposes: "library instruction sessions for distant learners conducted either in person, through print or audio-visual materials, on the World Wide Web, or by computer-audio- or teleconferencing methods" (Publicity section, para. 7). Here, the word "sessions" may be misleading; print handouts or tutorials are seldom referred to as a "session" but nonetheless serve the purpose intended by this statement.

Finances

Essentially, the DLS Guidelines (2003) call for a separate library budget for distance education, and for adequate funding that increases as needs and demands increase (Funding section). Funding for Internet-based reference service involves additional technology and telecommunication costs; it may also involve development costs for new materials, including tutorials, Web pages, and expert systems. The Introduction to the Canadian Guidelines (2000) points out that the "tremendous growth in the size and importance of distance education/distributed learning" are accompanied simultaneously with "sky-rocketing costs of library resources, especially journal subscriptions and electronic databases" at a time when "libraries have had to cut back collections budgets and staff" (para. 1).

If funding fails to cover the basics for local users, it is going to be impossible to make that same funding stretch to meet the needs of distant users, as well. The MLA position paper (Ludwig, 2002) also emphasizes the need for funding; MLA's solution is to lobby for federal grants and other federal programs funding to help cover costs of distance education for health science libraries. In some institutions, additional funding may be available for reference resources for distance education students by tapping into funds of distance education administrative units on campus. In this case, networking and negotiating with these departments is an important activity for the distance education librarian, in order to create funding partnerships outside the library.

Personnel

Issues of personnel for Internet reference will depend on the configuration of an individual library's reference department, its distance library services (DLS) department, and the overall staffing patterns of the library. While all of the guidelines indicate that one person should take responsibility for coordinating DLS, it is not likely that the same person can also serve all of the reference needs of the distance education community, unless that community is very small or the DLS department is well-staffed enough to essentially be a self-contained public services and document delivery unit. The Canadian Guidelines (2000) are more specific about reference personnel and their function in reference service: "The Library should ensure that distant learners and their instructors have access, as required, to the collective specialized reference staff of the originating institution" (Personnel section, para. 3). If reference services for distance education are supplied through the central reference desk, then it is important that those who staff that service point are trained to serve distance education learners and faculty, and to know all of the services available to distant populations.

Facilities and Resources

Although not directly related to reference, the issues of appropriate facilities and resources are vital to distance education departments and major sections of the Guidelines are devoted to these topics. It is important to note that in order for quality reference work to happen in an online environment, quality resources must be available in online formats. While document delivery can provide quality print materials to distance learners, timeliness of delivery becomes a factor. In the current library environment, it is vital to have online reference tools available for distance education students.

Reference Services

The DLS Guidelines list essential services for DLS, including reference assistance and consultative services, but do not go into any detail about how those services might be delivered. The Canadian Guidelines (2000) provide the most comprehensive and specific discussion of reference services, saying that students and instructors should have a means to "consult with a librarian from the originating institution, either in person or by telephone, fax, e-mail or some other means of electronic mediated communication" (Services section, para. 2). They should also be able to have access to "specialized reference staff" to "receive instruction . . . in the use of libraries, library resources, or in automated library systems," and to "request general reference assistance" (Services section, para. 4). Other literature in the field (see literature review, mentioned earlier) helps to flesh out what, exactly, a library can offer in the way of reference and consultative services for distance education. Among the options are:

- Toll-free telephone reference;
- On-site reference services, in which a librarian goes to an off-campus site to provide reference service to students by appointment;

- E-mail reference;
- Chat reference, possibly including co-browsing capabilities where the librarian and patron can view search screens simultaneously;
- Informational Web pages, including links to resources, FAQs, and tutorials;
- Course-specific Web pages designed for distance education courses;
- Reference services within courseware for online courses.

CONCLUSION

Reference services designed to meet the needs of distance education students require making changes to our way of thinking about the reference transaction, and to constantly be rethinking and changing as distance education technology and library technology evolve. As these changes occur, guidelines and standards continue to provide a framework for service, while the particulars of implementation change over time. Yet even while negotiating the shifting sands of new technologies, we must keep service to the individual in mind. Says Goodson (2001), "Providing reference services to distance learners is no picnic. . . . Each question is specific and often unique to the individual asking, thus requiring that the responder from the library possess comprehensive knowledge of institutional procedures, policies, and available resources" (p. 73). Flexibility and knowledge may therefore be the most vital attributes we, as reference librarians, need to bring to our work with distance learners.

REFERENCES

ACRL guidelines for distance learning library services. (2003). Retrieved February 25, 2004 from <http://www.ala.org/ala/acrl/acrlstandards/guidelinesdistancelearning.htm>.

Adams, K. E., & Cassner, M. (2002). Content and design of academic library Web sites for distance learners: An analysis of ARL libraries. In P. B. Mahoney (Ed.), *Conference Proceedings: Off-Campus Library Services Conference* (pp. 1-33). Mount Pleasant, MI: Central Michigan University.

Bao, X. (2001). Academic library homepages: Link location and database provision. *Journal of Academic Librarianship, 27*(1), 188-198.

Buckstead, J. R. (2001). Developing an effective off-campus library services Web page: Don't worry, be happy! *Journal of Library Administration, 31*(1), 93-107.

Connor, E. (2002). Real-time reference: The use of chat technology to improve point of need assistance. *Medical Reference Services Quarterly, 21*(4), 1-14.

Cote, D. (2001). The online college library: An exploration of library services to distance education students. *Community & Junior College Libraries, 10*(2), 61-77.

Dougherty, R. M. (2002). Reference around the clock: Is it in your future? The availability of 24/7 reference is less crucial than the capability to offer it. *American Libraries, 33*(5), 44-46.

Dunn, K., & Morgan, A. (2003). Going where the students are: Live/Web reference at Cal Poly Pomona. *The Reference Librarian, 38*(79/80), 201-213.

Gandhi, S. (2003). Academic librarians and distance education: Challenges and opportunities. *Reference & User Services Quarterly, 43*(2), 138. Retrieved February 26, 2004, from the InfoTrac OneFile database.

Goodson, C. (2001). *Providing library services for distance education students.* New York: Neal-Schuman Publishers.

Guidelines for library services to distance learners. Indian Library Association, Sectional committee on Distance Education. Retrieved February 26, 2004 from <http://uviclib.uvic.ca/dls/LSDL_Guidelines.pdf>.

Guidelines for library support of distance and distributed learning in Canada. (2000). Retrieved February 25, 2004 from <http://www.cla.ca/about/distance.htm>.

Heise, J., & Kimmel, S. (2003). Reading the river: The state of the art of real-time virtual reference. *Internet Reference Services Quarterly, 8*(1/2), 1-7.

Helfer, D. S. (2001). Virtual reference in libraries: Remote patrons heading your way? *Searcher: The Magazine for Database Professionals, 9*(2), 67-70.

Jerant, L. L., & Firestein, K. (2003). Not virtual, but a real, live, online, interactive reference service. *Medical Reference Services Quarterly, 22*(2), 57-68.

Jones, M. F. (2002). "Help! I'm the new distance librarian–Where do I begin?" In Mahoney, P. B. (Ed.) *Distance Learning Library Services: The Tenth Off-Campus Library Services Conference,* 397-410.

Jones, M. F. (2003). *Getting started: A guide for new distance learning librarians.* Retrieved February 25, 2004 from <http://caspian.switchinc.org/~distlearn/guidelines/getting_started.pdf>.

Katz, B. (Ed.). (2003). *Digital reference services* (2003). New York: The Haworth Press, Inc.

Kratzert, M., Richey, D., & Wassmann, C. (2001). Tips and snags of academic cyberreference. *College & Undergraduate Libraries, 8*(2), 73-82.

Library opens 24-hour reference desk. (2001). *Capper's, 123*(14), 10.

Linden, J. (2000). The library's Web site *is* the library: Designing for distance learners. *College & Research Libraries, 6,* 99-101.

Ludwig, L. (2002). *Essential library support for distance education.* Retrieved February 24, 2004 from <http://www.mlanet.org/government/positions/disteduc_2.html>.

Pease, B. G., & Power, C. J. (1994). Reference services for off-campus students and faculty. *The Reference Librarian, 43,* 43-62.

Shank, J. D., & Dewald, N. H. (2003). Establishing our presence in courseware: Adding library services to the virtual classroom. *Information Technology and Libraries, 22*(1), 38. Retrieved March 2, 2004 from the InfoTrac OneFile database.

Sloan, B. (2003). *Digital reference services: A bibliography.* Retrieved April 12, 2004 from <http://www.lis.uiuc.edu/~b-sloan/digiref.html>.

Stacy-Bates, K. K. (2000). Ready-reference resources and E-mail reference on academic ARL Web sites. *Reference & User Services Quarterly, 40,* 61-73.

Standards & guidelines by topic. (n.d.). Retrieved February 25, 2004 from <http://www.ala.org/ala/acrl/acrlstandards/standardsguidelinestopic.htm>.

Stormont, S. (2002). Here, there and everywhere–live virtual reference. *Collection Management, 26*(2), 79-87.

Sullivan, D. (2003). Characteristics of e-mail reference services in selected public libraries, Victoria, Australia. *The Reference Librarian, 41*, 85.

Academic Library Web Sites for Distance Learners in Greater Western Library Alliance Member Institutions

Mary Cassner

Kate E. Adams

SUMMARY. Through the library Web site, academic libraries present extensive resources and a suite of services to support distance learners. The Web site is a vital communication link between the distance student and the reference-based instructional component that the librarian provides. This article examines Web sites and distance learning library services pages of Greater Western Library Alliance members. *[Article copies available for a fee from The Haworth Document Delivery Service: 1-800-HAWORTH. E-mail address: <docdelivery@haworthpress.com> Website: <http://www.HaworthPress. com> © 2004 by The Haworth Press, Inc. All rights reserved.]*

KEYWORDS. Academic libraries, distance education Web pages, distance learners, distance learning library services, Greater Western Library Alliance

Mary Cassner (mcassner1@unl.edu) is Subject Specialist Librarian and Associate Professor, C. Y. Thompson Library, University of Nebraska-Lincoln, Lincoln, NE 68583-0717. Kate E. Adams (kadams1@unl.edu) is Coordinator for Distance Education and Undergraduate Services and Professor, Love Library, University of Nebraska-Lincoln, Lincoln, NE 68588-4100.

[Haworth co-indexing entry note]: "Academic Library Web Sites for Distance Learners in Greater Western Library Alliance Member Institutions." Cassner, Mary, and Kate E. Adams. Co-published simultaneously in *Internet Reference Services Quarterly* (The Haworth Information Press, an imprint of The Haworth Press, Inc.) Vol. 9, No. 3/4, 2004, pp. 33-42; and: *Internet Reference Support for Distance Learners* (ed: William Miller, and Rita M. Pellen) The Haworth Information Press, an imprint of The Haworth Press, Inc., 2004, pp. 33-42. Single or multiple copies of this article are available for a fee from The Haworth Document Delivery Service [1-800-HAWORTH, 9:00 a.m. - 5:00 p.m. (EST). E-mail address: docdelivery@haworthpress.com].

Available online at http://www.haworthpress.com/web/IRSQ
© 2004 by The Haworth Press, Inc. All rights reserved.
Digital Object Identifier: 10.1300/J136v09n03_04

INTRODUCTION

The library Web site is an important tool for distance learners. Often, the distance education home page is the student's main communication link with the library when accessing library resources and services. The purpose of this article is a review of library Web sites that serve distance learners. Of particular interest to the researchers are libraries' distance education Web pages, which describe library services and resources available to distance learners. The content of library Web sites can be examined to determine what reference information is conveyed as well as how it is presented.

The population studied is the Greater Western Library Alliance members, a consortium of 30 research libraries spanning states from the Mississippi River Valley to the Pacific coast. The mission of the Greater Western Library Alliance (GWLA) is "to deliver quality cost-effective services and resources required by clients of member institutions through joint action and collaboration." Members collaborate in resource sharing initiatives in interlibrary loan, electronic licensing, and cooperative collection development (Greater Western Library Alliance, 2004).

The research builds upon earlier studies of library Web sites and applies these methodologies to Web pages specific to distance learners. The content of library services and resources provided to distance learners is examined, with particular attention given to the broad scope of reference service offered. Data collected was tabulated to compare similarities and differences among the population studied.

It is essential that all students and faculty, regardless of on-campus or off-campus location, have access to quality library resources and services. The originating institution has the responsibility to provide library services and resources to distance learners and distance faculty. As libraries continue to shift into a digital emphasis, librarians have been reflecting on the best way to adjust services to a changing environment with new information needs.

Tenopir and Ennis (2002) found that a significant number of students, because they are comfortable searching the Web, are using the open Web to find information for their assignments rather than electronic periodical indexes which libraries pay for. Students view searching the library as less convenient than using commercial search engines. Jackson (2003, p. 36) stated, "Libraries must gear up to provide a competing level of convenience while retaining the authority and quality of information delivery for which they have been traditionally known."

Library patrons are becoming increasingly vocal in indicating their desire for simple, helpful self-service. Users indicate that they will request assistance only at point of need. Consequently, librarians' efforts should focus on self-help modes to improve and expand services for the student community. At the same time, human assistance still forms a key part of the library user support system (Han & Goulding, 2003).

The main role of reference librarians has not changed significantly over the years, although there have been substantive changes in the way they carry out the role. Information professionals have always been skilled at identifying users' information needs and recommending quality resources. However, rather than assisting patrons directly, a great deal of a reference librarian's time is now spent behind the scenes, invisible to users (Han & Goulding, 2003). Bunge and Bopp (2001) believe that rather than helping users personally, librarians will spend an increasing amount of time designing and engineering interface and help systems. This prospect can benefit distance learners.

Reference services within a digital library environment consist of multiple delivery modes such as face-to-face, e-mail, telephone, Webform, and other computer-based systems. The variety of methods offered is necessary to ensure that services are accessible and convenient for all library users. Each delivery mode has specific strengths and weaknesses, and digital reference is no different. Certain users, whether because of learning style or personal preference, will desire human help even more than online assistance. Others will opt to use an online method when requesting reference help (Lessik, 2000).

One of the newest modes for providing reference service is chat or digital reference. A survey by Janes, Hill, and Rolfe (2001) found digital reference is a most effective approach for repeat library users and to answer short ready reference questions. This mode of reference delivery has application for distance learners.

Kern (2004) noted that there are similarities and differences in providing virtual reference services to on-campus and distance users. Similarities occur in reference interview skills used, instruction in use of resources, and the need to troubleshoot electronic access. Kern identified differences in virtual reference policies and document delivery options.

Reference assistance is essential to meet the bibliographic, informational, and user needs of all learners, whether taking classes on campus or via distance education. Bunge and Bopp (2000) stated that activities comprising reference services fall within three groups. One group consists of information services such as ready reference questions, bibliographic verification, and interlibrary loan/document delivery options. Distance users frequently ask about how to request delivery of material, how to obtain an electronic version of a desired journal article, and what the procedures are for remote access and authentication.

The second group of reference services involves individual or group assistance related to class projects and assignments. The students who seek to locate journal citations on a specific topic or request dissertation consultation are examples. User instructions on a particular database is another example of informational service. Posting pathfinders or subject guides on Blackboard or WebCT in support of a class also falls into this category. All of these examples can serve both on- and off-campus students.

In contrast to the second group, the third group of reference services covers general information related to the libraries or the research process itself. This may involve individual or group instruction. Examples can be a session that introduces users to the libraries or an individual consultation with a graduate student on discipline-specific library research.

For decades, libraries have been collaborating in various venues, such as bibliographic utilities, collection development, and interlibrary loan. Peters (2003, p. 111) states, "Perhaps the question is not whether or not to collaborate, but how to collaborate and with whom." Subramanian (2002) discusses the role of consortia in providing support for distance education. Brunvand, Lee et al. (2001) discuss an academic library consortium in statewide Utah that serves distance learners, while Wittkopf (2002) describes one in Louisiana.

METHODOLOGY

The population for the study consisted of the Greater Western Library Alliance (GWLA) members, a consortium of Western and Midwestern research libraries. The GWLA Web site listed 30 institutions as of June 2004. Criteria for inclusion in the study were that the institution be an academic library, and that the library Web site has a distance education page. One GWLA member did not meet the first requirement, and eight GWLA libraries did not offer a distance education home page. Therefore, the library Web sites and distance education pages of twenty-one GWLA libraries were examined.

The authors were interested in knowing how reference service is presented to distance learners. The study focused on the content communicated on distance education pages and library Web sites, as reflected by hyperlinks. The authors adapted the general model used in their earlier study, "Content and Design of Academic Library Web Sites for Distance Learners: An Analysis of ARL Libraries" (Adams & Cassner, 2002). The authors developed a checklist of electronic resources and library services that are available to distance learners as links. Informational links such as contact information for the distance education coordinator and liaison librarians were included. Links to local policy, such as mission statement or definition of what constitutes a distance learner, were noted.

A spreadsheet enumerating the content elements was created with Excel. The presence or absence of each element was recorded. Data were compiled using raw numbers and percentages. Summary notes were prepared describing specific services, search paths, and creative presentations of library information.

RESULTS

There is great variety in the GWLA libraries' description of distance learning as a header on the distance education pages. The word "distance" is used in 13 of the headings, while "extended" is used by two libraries. Three libraries prefer "Distance Education" and three head the page "Distance Learning Services." Examples of other headings include "Distance Learners," "Distance Users," "Distance Learning Services," and "Distance Learning Support Services." In this article, the authors use several different terms interchangeably.

Nine GWLA library Web sites have a top link for distance education, so the page is reached after one click. In eleven instances, the distance education page is two clicks from the library Web site top page, and for one institution the distance education page is three levels down.

Each distance education page was examined for inclusion of several features. Fifteen (71%) of the distance pages provide a mission statement describing eligibility and scope of services offered to distance learners. One institution provides distance service to faculty, students, and staff who reside more than 30 miles from the institution's city. Another uses the "30 miles away" guide for faculty and students, and also includes students who commute irregularly. A third provides service for students in distance courses held at other system campuses, students who are studying abroad, and students taking correspondence courses. Another institution provides distance service to any affiliates who access library resources remotely, and are not necessarily enrolled in a distance course.

A link to a distance education coordinator or distance team is present on 17 (81%) of the distance education pages, and usually is a pop-up e-mail. Contact information with name, title, phone number, and e-mail address for the coordinator or team is provided in all cases. Only nine distance learning home pages (43%) show a link to liaison librarians.

Nearly half (10) of the distance pages have information on library services specifically for distance faculty. A link to the library's online catalog is present on 20 of the distance learning pages. In 17 cases (81%), a link to the university Web site is available. On only six distance learning pages is there a link to the university's services for distance learners. Eighteen of the 21 (86%) distance education pages contain freshness dates, with 11 pages updated during 2004.

. Navigation bars are present on 20 of the 21 distance education home pages. Seven distance pages use top, bottom, and sidebars. Several pages use one bar only, and several use two. Two distance pages have no bars.

Each library's Web site top page was studied for several features that present specific reference-related information to meet the needs of distance learners. A site search or site index is a link on 19 (90%) of the GWLA library home pages. Proxy instructions or remote access information do not typically appear on the library's home page; in only four instances (19%) is there a top page link. Links to Web search engines appear on only eight (38%) of the GWLA library home pages. The library's address is present on 18 (86%) of the library Web site top pages. Online catalogs for other institutions are links on 13 (62%) of the GWLA library Web sites.

Links to Blackboard or WebCT are present on the top page in three of the 21 library Web sites. This was surprising since distance courses have been delivered via courseware for the past decade.

The GWLA library Web sites were reviewed for instruction-related resources. All 21 have a link for library instruction. Sometimes this refers to site-based instruction, while in other instances instruction is available to remote users. One institution encourages distance faculty to arrange for chat or interactive video instruction sessions. Electronic tutorials are available on 17 (80%) of the 21 Web sites examined. Examples of tutorials include the library research process, a literacy tutorial, and how to use the library's online catalog.

Subject guides or pathfinders are present on 19 (90%) of the library Web sites, and guides to library research are available on 20 (95%) of the library pages. Other examples of instruction-related resources include online instruction on how to build search strategies and a Web search engine feature tip sheet.

Electronic resources are extensive. All of the GWLA library Web sites have links for electronic journals, and 20 (95%) offer an electronic journal finder. Electronic books are accessible at 17 (80%) of Web sites. All of the library Web sites have an article indexes and databases page that typically provides both a subject access list and a title list of databases. Eligibility for access to electronic resources is explained, and users are informed that they will need to provide their name and university identification and/or pin number.

Several GWLA libraries have federated searching or multiple database search capability. One library uses "multiple database search" as a link on the library's home page. Another library provides a link called "multiple indexes" as one of the options on the indexes to articles page, while one library labels the link as "search multiple databases."

Electronic reserves are available at all 21 of the Web sites studied. Each GWLA library Web site has a section of electronic reference materials. Examples include encyclopedias, atlases, almanacs, and dictionaries. Links to digitized collections are present on 17 (80%) of the Web sites.

Multiple access points to reference assistance are essential for distance users. Reference via e-mail or Web-form is available at all of the GWLA libraries. A phone number for reference service is provided in all instances. Eight GWLA libraries (38%) have a toll-free phone number. Consultation with a librarian is a service at all of the libraries. Twenty Web sites have a link to a list of liaison librarians on one of the lower pages, and not necessarily from the top page.

Chat or virtual reference is available at 15 (71%) of the GWLA libraries. Three libraries provide the service on a 24/7 basis, as a collaborative statewide effort. Two GWLA libraries offer chat service seven days a week, with hours of service during the afternoon through early evening. Ten libraries provide the service Monday-Thursday or Monday-Friday (but not on weekends), ranging from 20 hours to 65 hours weekly. Of these ten, hours of service usually begin at noon or 1 p.m. or 2 p.m., although one library staffs chat at 8 a.m. and two open the service at 10 a.m. Often, some kind of authentication is required for the service. While checking the Web sites for the study, the authors observed some changes in hours of chat service, presumably to better match the demand for service.

Delivery of books and articles from the home library's collection is typically available to distance users. State-wide or system-wide borrowing of books is an option for distance users at 15 (71%) of the GWLA libraries. However, state-wide or system-wide borrowing of articles is an option for distance users at only 11 (52%) of the libraries.

All of the GWLA libraries provide interlibrary loan request forms for distance users. At 20 libraries, interlibrary loan allows borrowing of articles, while at 19 libraries, interlibrary loan borrowing of books is an option for distance users. Options for article delivery are Web, USPS, and fax. Returnables are delivered using expedited delivery, with this service typically limited to users within the United States. Eight of the GWLA libraries are using ILLiad, and a registration form is usually required.

DISCUSSION

Through library Web sites and distance education pages, GWLA libraries provide extensive resources and a suite of services to support distance learners. Dew (2002) recommended certain components that should appear on Web pages designed to support distance learners. These included a statement of eligibility for distance service, links to electronic resources, remote access and authentication procedures, and information about document delivery services. Additionally, instruction-related resources such as library research tutorials, discipline-specific pathfinders, and electronic reference materials are vital elements of library service to distance students.

Increasingly, students expect to be able "to do it themselves" (self-service). They want to find what they need for class assignments or projects, through independent searching. Full-text library databases and off-campus access to the library catalog were found to be the most useful library services, according to a survey of distance students at the University of Maryland University College. Web-based library instruction was preferred over alternate methods of instruction. Students indicated a desire for Web-based information about library services versus other formats (Kelley & Orr, 2003).

Libraries provide multiple ways for users to obtain needed research materials by providing electronic journals, full-text and citation databases, e-books, digital collections, and Web-request forms. If the user cannot find the needed information or item from the library Web site, often that is when contact is made with a librarian. The librarian is the intermediary who provides the point-of-need instructional component, often directing the user back to a specific electronic resource or navigating the user through the steps for authentication or placing a request for delivery of library materials. It is the reference-based instructional component the librarian provides that is essential.

In the immediate future, it is likely that librarians will allocate more time and staffing resources to implementing and designing interface and help systems. In part, this will reflect librarians' dual desires to improve users' information skills and to encourage students to make full use of the digital library. In part, user demand for additional full-text resources and ease of library access has been growing and will continue to do so. Libraries are responding to these trends by creating or purchasing multiple database search capability and electronic journal finders. These provide the remote user with easy-access, one-stop, self-help information services, through a combination of Web surfing functionality and high quality library resources.

Another trend that libraries face is the rapid adoption of course management software by many universities. Relatively few libraries currently are taking advantage of Blackboard or WebCT capabilities. Examples of potential usage for libraries include mounting resources such as pathfinders, using course management systems as an assessment tool, and using them as another means of communicating with students. As more librarians develop instructional design skills, there is great opportunity for librarians to partner with faculty. Improved integration of course management software is fundamental to libraries reaching distance users.

Consortial collaboration allows libraries to manage and distribute costs of products and keeping staff expertise up-to-date. While a distance user may search the library catalog or database 24/7, library budgets are not adequate for such a level of staffing. Consortial collaboration is a way to leverage staff to meet user demand in a complex Web-based environment.

CONCLUSION

The library's Web site and distance education home page are key communication links for distance learners. These, combined with reference-based instruction and liaison librarian assistance, give the distance user access to numerous resources. As librarians add new services and electronic finding tools, the distance learner stands to benefit.

REFERENCES

Adams, Kate E. and Mary Cassner. "Content and Design of Academic Library Web Sites for Distance Learners: An Analysis of ARL Libraries," *Journal of Library Administration* 37 no. 1/2 (2002): 3-13.

Brunvand, Amy, Daniel R. Lee et al. "Consortium Solutions to Distance Education Problems: Utah Academic Libraries Answer the Challenge," *Journal of Library Administration*, 31 no. 3/4 (2001): 75-92.

Bunge, Charles A. and Richard E. Bopp. "History and Varieties of Reference Services." In *Reference and Information Services: An Introduction* (Englewood, CO: Libraries Unlimited, 2001): 3-25.

Dew, Stephen H. "Documenting Priorities, Progress, and Potential: Planning Library Services for Distance Education," *Journal of Library Administration* 37 no. 1/2 (2002): 217-243.

Greater Western Library Alliance [homepage] 1 July 2004, <http://www.gwla.org>. (23 July 2004).

Han, Lifeng and Anne Goulding. "Information and Reference Services in the Digital Library." *Information Services & Use* 23 (2003): 251-262.

Jackson, Mary E. "The Advent of Portals." *Library Journal* 127, no. 15 (2002): 36-39.

Janes, J., C. Hill, and A. Rolfe. "Ask-an-Expert Services Analysis." *Journal of the American Society for Information Science and Technology* 52 (2001): 1106-1121.

Kelley, Kimberly B. and Gloria J. Orr. "Trends in Distant Student Use of Electronic Resources: A Survey." *College & Research Libraries* 64 (2003): 176-191.

Kern, M. Kathleen. "Chat It Up!: Extending Reference Services to Assist Off-Campus Students." In *Eleventh Off-Campus Library Services Conference Proceedings: Scottsdale, AZ, May 5-7, 2004* (Mount Pleasant, MI: Central Michigan University, 2004): 161-168.

Lessick, Susan. "Transforming Reference Staffing for the Digital Library." In *Digital Reference Service in the New Millennium: Planning, Management, and Evaluation* (New York: Neal-Schuman, 2000): 25-36.

Peters, Thomas A. "Consortia and Their Discontents." *Journal of Academic Librarianship* 29 (2003): 111-114.

Subramanian, Jane M. "The Growing and Changing Role of Consortia in Providing Direct and Indirect Support for Distance Higher Education." *The Reference Librarian*, no. 77 (2002): 37-60.

Tenopir, Carol and Lisa Ennis. "A Decade of Digital Reference: 1991-2001." *Reference & User Services Quarterly* 41 (2002): 264-273.

Wittkopf, Barbara J. "Resource Sharing in Louisiana." *Resource Sharing & Information Networks* 16 (2002): 103-120.

Keep IT Simple:
Internet Reference Support
for Distance Learners

Marthea Turnage
Wade Carter
Randy McDonald

SUMMARY. Distance education students are often goal-oriented and task-driven. They do not appreciate roadblocks that prevent them from gaining access to the information or services they need to complete their course objectives. However, Web-based reference support sites are sometimes more frustrating than helpful. This article discusses some of the difficulties of accessing reference services faced by distance education students and examines ways in which librarians should "keep IT simple" when designing the tools and methods to access reference support. *[Article copies available for a fee from The Haworth Document Delivery Service: 1-800-HAWORTH. E-mail address: <docdelivery@haworthpress.com> Website: <http://www.HaworthPress.com> © 2004 by The Haworth Press, Inc. All rights reserved.]*

Marthea Turnage (mturnage@sfasu.edu) is Reference and Distance Education Librarian; and Wade Carter (wcarter@sfasu.edu) is Library Webmaster, both at Stephen F. Austin State University, P.O. Box 13055, SFASU Station, Nacogdoches, TX 75962. Randy McDonald (rmcdonald@sfasu.edu) is Director of the Office of Instructional Technology, Stephen F. Austin State University, P.O. Box 13038, SFASU Station, Nacogdoches, TX 75962.

[Haworth co-indexing entry note]: "Keep IT Simple: Internet Reference Support for Distance Learners." Turnage, Marthea, Wade Carter, and Randy McDonald. Co-published simultaneously in *Internet Reference Services Quarterly* (The Haworth Information Press, an imprint of The Haworth Press, Inc.) Vol. 9, No. 3/4, 2004, pp. 43-54; and: *Internet Reference Support for Distance Learners* (ed: William Miller, and Rita M. Pellen) The Haworth Information Press, an imprint of The Haworth Press, Inc., 2004, pp. 43-54. Single or multiple copies of this article are available for a fee from The Haworth Document Delivery Service [1-800-HAWORTH, 9:00 a.m. - 5:00 p.m. (EST). E-mail address: docdelivery@haworthpress.com].

Available online at http://www.haworthpress.com/web/IRSQ
© 2004 by The Haworth Press, Inc. All rights reserved.
Digital Object Identifier: 10.1300/J136v09n03_05

KEYWORDS. Distance education, support services, collaboration, Web design

It is amusing that many consumers continue to have problems using their VCR. The VCR has been around a long time and yet, its complexity is still a problem. Apparently, manufacturers and advertisers know and understand that consumers are still having trouble with the VCR features, hand-held remote, and complex hook-ups. So, they know and understand the characteristics of a portion of their users and yet, is there really a VCR that is easy to use? Is there no one trying to make them easier and more convenient to use? And why is it that the children who could program the VCR 10 years ago are the adults today who are having trouble? Many of the same problems exist regarding the technologies used in distance education.

Students acquiring their education through distance education are often goal-oriented and task-driven. They do not appreciate information technology (IT) roadblocks that prevent them from gaining access to the resources they need in order to be successful. Librarians play an important role in facilitating the convergence of the growing number of distance education students and the growing complexity of IT. To be successful in this role, librarians must know the characteristics of the distant education student population and must know the technical aspects of how those students gain access to online resources. Librarians must understand the interface design allowing access to library resources and how to facilitate research assistance in the online environment. We will examine ways in which librarians should "keep IT simple" when designing the interfaces and methods through which students gain access to information and reference support.

KNOW YOUR STUDENTS

Who are the distance education students? The typical distant learner has often been identified as a more mature student who is attempting to complete a degree from a location remote from campus. They are often less familiar with technology than their younger counterparts and because they have many simultaneous responsibilities in addition to their education goals, they are very focused and motivated. Sikora (2002) refers to a U.S. Department of Education-sponsored survey of students participating in distance education for 1999-2000 that reported distance education students as:

- tending to have more family responsibilities and limited time;
- more likely to be enrolled in school part time and to be working full time while enrolled.

The survey also reported that higher rates of participation in distance education among undergraduates were associated with students' family and work responsibilities (such as being independent, older, married, or having dependents).

As campus networks increasing reach "to the pillow" (and even beyond, via wireless), and as more students bring computers to campus, the more traditional students who are enjoying the campus-based experience are becoming a sort of pseudo distance education student–accessing Web-based courses and library resources from their dorm rooms. A review of the literature reveals many of the important characteristics we must know about these students that will aid in our attempts to appropriately use technology to meet their needs.

Sheesley refers to today's students as the 'Net generation–students who are growing up in a culture and society of instant information, global influences, and advancing technology (Sheesley 2002). In addition to Sheesley, other authors also document from several surveys the following compilation of 'net generation characteristics (Cannon 1991; Frand 2000; Lee 1996; Sheesley 2002). Even though some of the surveys are from the early 1990s, many of the characteristics still apply for these students:

- Prefer activity that entertains and stimulates them and is meaningful to them. They abhor boring work.
- Prefer concrete, specific information.
- Desire to learn leading-edge technology.
- Turn to the World Wide Web to get news and search for information and consider it the best source of most information.
- Accustomed to solving problems by trial and error rather than by what might be characterized as the scientific method.
- Prefer typing over handwriting and assume the ability to manipulate data.
- Consider advanced telecommunication connectivity to be a natural part of living.
- Have zero tolerance for delays.

- Are part of a culture that routinely blurs the distinction between users and creators of information.
- Prefer to use the library's resources remotely.
- Prefer to learn in the evening.

In one study for the Pew Internet and American Life Project, 754 teenagers were surveyed using probing questions that would profile how our teenagers use the Internet. The report provides a variety of information on how boys and girls, older teens and younger teens, and family deal with Internet issues. One of the not so surprising discoveries is teenagers' use of instant messaging. Not only do they use instant messaging for communicating with teachers and classmates about schoolwork or projects, but some teens say that "instant messaging allows them to stay in touch with people they would not otherwise contact–for instance, those who are only casual acquaintances, or those who live outside their communities" (Lenhart, Rainie, and Lewis 2001, 11).

How do they use the Internet for class work? The survey confirms that teens use the Internet instead of the library as their primary tool for doing research. When

> asked about the last big report they wrote for school, 71% of all online teens reported relying mostly on Internet sources for their research, 24% using mostly library sources. Students cite the ease and speed of online research as their main reasons for leaving the library behind, and also say that the Internet frees them and their parents from the hassle of getting to the library to find the information they need. (Lenhart, Rainie, and Lewis 2001, 35)

Teens appear to have little awareness of the wealth of information not available to them when they search using only a popular search engine. They also do not have a clear idea of how to find library information available using the Internet.

Another question posed by the survey pertained to the accuracy or quality of information teens found by searching the Internet. Teens are more aware now about inaccurate or bogus information on the Internet than most librarians are led to believe. Some teens will "double check with books or other Web sites on similar topics, and some go by whether a Web site has a good reputation or a trustworthy offline counterpart" (Lenhart, Rainie, and Lewis 2001, 36).

According to another survey by Kelley and Orr, "66% of their respondents reported that they 'seldom' or 'never' visited a library facility versus 32% who 'frequently' or 'often' used a library facility" (Kelley 2003, 179). In addition, another question asked was, "which library services do students perceive as important?" A majority responded that "off-campus access to full-text materials in the library's databases was the most useful service" (Kelley 2003, 180).

Also important to note is that upon examination of the survey, a large percentage of undergraduates were not aware of the availability of the library's online resources. Reference librarians spend a good portion of their time inventing ways to get the word out about the newer resources available with the strategies used to access them.

However gallant the efforts are, students and faculty still think of the library only at point of need. Should the efforts of librarians then focus on that point of need during assignments or when the student needs to access the library over the Internet? Kelly and Orr's findings also suggest that "students' usage of the library resources has more to do with the curriculum and course requirements than difficulties using the library facility" (Kelley 2003, 183).

When students responded to the questions on the survey regarding the library Web pages, "students prefer the ease of use going to the Internet and searching, regardless of the quality of the information even though the library may provide better resources because the library resources are more difficult to identify" (Kelley 2003, 185). The survey results also confirm that "students taking their courses online are more likely to use the library's databases and are using them more often than those students taking courses face-to-face" (Kelley 2003, 186).

When combined, the needs and characteristics of the more mature non-traditional student and those of the pseudo distance education students of the 'Net generation point to a necessity for librarians to provide and support fast and efficient access to a wealth of electronic information sources while making sure that the information technology components of the process do not impede connectivity, navigation, or service. Or in other words, librarians must work to "keep IT simple."

Because the library seldom controls the entire IT environment of an institution, academic librarians must work collaboratively with other members of the campus community to create innovative solutions designed specifically to meet the needs of distance education students. "The methods used by academic libraries to address these needs depend upon the types of human and material resources available on that campus, the types and amounts of funding available, computing support, and communication between all of the entities servicing distance education efforts" (McDonald 2003, 50). Information technology enters this equation at three points for the distance education student: getting network access and clearance to access the library databases; providing a search interface that is easy to navigate; and providing electronic access to reference assistance. How can librarians work collaboratively with other components of the campus to keep IT simple at each of these critical points?

A SIMPLE MEANS TO ACCESS THE NETWORK

As enrollments in distance education classes are increasing each semester, reference librarians have had to address ways to provide off-campus students with access to licensed library databases. Many libraries use software such as EZProxy or other authentication systems for this purpose. Often these systems require their own username and password login routine. Given that an off-campus distance education student may have already had to remember and enter one username and password to access the Internet, and a second username and password to access his/her course management system, having to remember and enter a third and usually different username and password to access library resources is quite aggravating. To simplify access, a growing number of higher education institutions are implementing portal systems that seamlessly interconnect all campus computing systems and provide a consistent interface and single sign-on experience. By working collaboratively with IT departments across campus, librarians can help to ensure that distance education students enjoy the benefits of this simplified access to the network and to library resources.

A SIMPLE (YET POWERFUL) SEARCH INTERFACE

Librarians rely heavily on library Web pages to relay information to their user groups: students, faculty, staff, and community. Many reference librarians have acquired the technological skills to design and develop library Web pages.

One type of page that has become popular on library Web sites is the course-specific page. Librarians have found that course-specific Web pages are a popular venue to help students with a specific need. Collaborating with faculty, librarians can create a library Web page that contains the resources and instructions addressing an assignment. Using a combination of paper resources, library databases, and images, the example below (see Figure 1) is concise with some interactivity.

Knowing that students use the Internet for the first place to answer a question, librarians should contribute to designs that are clear and simple, enticing students to use the library as their first choice on the Internet. At this time, Google gets a lot of attention from students, teachers, parents and the media. "Googlizing" is a phrase coined because of the popularity of the search engine. If a student compares the Web pages of Google, Excite, and Yahoo, Google is very simple to use. The homepage is a textbox with a lot of white space. Type a word in, and lists come back in a matter of nano-seconds. According to the Pew Internet and American Life Project Survey mentioned above, students are aware of bogus information on the Internet. However, even though students are aware that libraries would be most likely to have authoritative information, they chose not to use the library on the Internet because of the difficulty in doing so. Students want the shortest, quickest, and most interactive way to find authoritative information and the many library Web pages even today continue to use language that might be outdated or library jargon that the 'Net generation does not know or un-

FIGURE 1. English 132–Literary Criticism Course-Specific Web Page

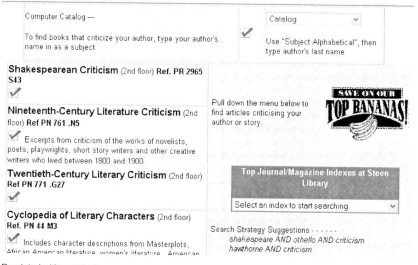

Reprinted with permission.

derstand. "Whether available on the library's Web site, in paper format in the library, or both, textual library information should look attractive and appealing, and should be limited to a single concise presentation of the most practical information" (Sheesley 2002, 38).

Historically, the librarians' primary focus has been to organize information in a meaningful way and secondarily to provide access to it. The information seeking processes for our students still remain the same whether they seek information in the physical-print or digital-Web-based library environment. The most significant difference between the environments is the ability for users to gather vast amounts of information quickly and then to evaluate the result of the queries meaningfully.

Librarians generally study other library Web sites to get ideas on designs. Raward noted in 2001 that "librarians have few tested principles to refer to when designing library Web sites. Librarians are often self-taught, Web design is usually additional to the librarian's job, and Web design is often driven by management, not the user" (Raward 2001, 125). Raward developed a "Usability Index Checklist for Academic Library Web Sites" that includes also disability access description and download speeds. Certainly, some common sense features should be apparent on academic library homepages. According to the Kelley survey, findings strongly suggest that "libraries need to ensure that their homepage is current, updated regularly, and provides information in a format that is helpful to students" (Kelley 2003, 185). College library Web pages should use images illustrating the physical building and real people that work in or use the library. Moreover, a library site should use common or popular text. For example, instead of Reference Department, use Library Research; instead of Electronic Resources use Find Articles, Find Books. Public service phone numbers should be prominently displayed on the home page with a street and mailing address.

Librarians at Stephen F. Austin State University recently released a new version of the Web site for the university's Ralph W. Steen Library. As with the previous site, the new site's cornerstone is its subject based access to resources determined by the areas of study at the university. However, the new site combines improved simplicity and functionality by providing users immediate access to all major resources directly from the homepage. Review of the library homepage usage statistics over several years informed these changes in navigation and architecture. Librarians in Steen's Web Development Office also collected data during a usability study that aided in the site's final design. The methodology for this informal study was adapted from a study at the University of Washington Libraries (http://www.lib.washington.edu/Usability/).

To conduct the usability study, participants were selected randomly from the library and were asked to use a prototype of the new interface to complete several online search tasks typical to distance education students. Examples of the tasks included:

1. Find a list of electronic indexes for a topic in Art.
2. Find material your instructor has placed on electronic reserve.
3. Find an interlibrary loan form to fill out over the Web to request an article from another library.

The Web site provides multiple access points to specific resources; thus, there are situations when various paths may take the user to the same destination. Observations made during our user test showed that many of the search questions required clicking deeper into the site. It was significant that participants did not use a link to a site index and only on a few occasions did they perform a site-specific search on a search engine for content. Moreover, one task, "Find a book review on a specific book," proved to be the most difficult for the participants. Observation of the use by participants of links made with graphics as opposed to underlined text-based links indicated that users are more attracted to the underlined format. Redundancy of the naming of the links was used to safeguard the site's design.

During the user test, librarians were interested in learning things such as how the students searched various sites from the library homepage and if they drilled deeper into the library site for specific subject-related content. Librarians were also interested in the ability of students to search the library catalog and its various indexes from the homepage. Timing the activity and observing the path the student took were used to confirm the difficulty of the task, the appropriateness of the title of a link, and the correlation to the navigability of the homepage to the task.

Based on the results of the usability testing, a new site was designed that included link names consistent with the old site. However, the overall navigation structure of the new site was flattened in order to require fewer clicks to find the information requested. The new site design also encompasses features that are now ubiquitous on the Web as well as enhancements that are unique to the Steen Web site, "Libweb." The result is an interface with the simplicity of Google and the richness of all of the traditionally expected library resources and services (see Figure 2).

FIGURE 2. New Ralph W. Steen Library Homepage

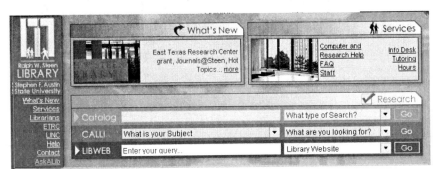

A SIMPLE MEANS TO ACCESS REFERENCE SUPPORT

Many reference librarians could be described as chameleons discovering every venue to meet the informational needs of students. "Many librarians have embraced changes in service delivery in numerous ways from developing online orientation and instruction tools to creating electronic services that facilitate distance learning" (McDonald 2003, 50). Internet reference help is available from most academic libraries in the form of e-mail usually designated as an Ask-a-librarian service. If the students are using the Internet, reference librarians will be there. However, some academic libraries will post restrictions on the type of question that can be posed, or the category of user who can pose the question, or the special hours that questions will be answered.

Commercial counterparts to the Ask-a-librarian service, such as Ask Jeeves, create a database searchable through a portal. Many academic libraries are using a knowledge base that might be searchable and also Q&A lists of the most popular inquiries. With all of the work related to creating a reference Internet service, placing the service on the library homepage would be imperative. Moreover, some libraries are moving to interactive reference services on the Web. If we know our students are using chat as a primary method of communication on the Internet, library reference chat would be a comfortable, even expected mode of use by our students.

Bao did a survey in 2001 investigating access to interactive reference services in academic libraries. Bao discovered that from "143 academic institutions surveyed, 46.9% offered Web-based interactive reference services while 53.1% did not" (Bao 2001). From those libraries that did offer Internet interactive reference service, "52.2% placed their reference links on the first level of the library home page, 37.3% on the second level and 10.4% on the third level down" (Bao 2001, 253). Eligibility restrictions were posted on 35.8% of those academic libraries whereas 62.7% had none. However, the study reported that "more research is needed to learn why the 'discussion forum' and 'chat room' methods of interactive reference services are underutilized. One reason that might explain the lack of popularity . . . is that the reference interview process is essentially an individual and private interaction" (Bao 2001, 255).

In addition to providing electronic tools and services, librarians may also make it simpler to access research assistance by collaborating with distance education support staff and faculty. At Stephen F. Austin State University, librarians play an important role in the training of faculty who are preparing to develop and teach distance education courses. During the workshop series designed to help instructors create a course in WebCT, instructors are introduced to their librarian and provided examples of how links to library resources may be designed into their course. During online chat sessions with the faculty, librarians discuss strategies for assisting their distance education students in using library information on the Internet. Collaborating in this has provided librarians a way to simplify access to library resources and reference assistance by weaving library access into the design process of distance education courses.

CONCLUSION

As distance education becomes more popular, reference librarians must continue to develop the technical skills to overcome any kind of roadblock that prevents students from gaining access to the information or services they need to complete their coursework. By maintaining constant and open dialog with distance education students and technical support functions on campus, librarians will be able to help bring about creative solutions to keep IT simple for distance education students.

REFERENCES

Bao, Xue-Ming. "A Study of Web-Based Interactive Reference Services via Academic Library Home Pages." *Reference & User Services Quarterly* (2003): 250-256.
Cannon, David. "Generation X: The Way They Do the Things They Do," *Journal of Career Planning and Employment* 51 (1991): 34-38.

Frand, Jason L. "The Information-Age Mindset," *Educause Review* 35 (Sept./Oct. 2000). Database online. Available from EBSCOHost, Academic Search Premiere, AN: 3560472. [34 paragraphs].

Kelley, Kimberly B. and Gloria J. Orr. "Trends in Distant Student Use of Electronic Resources: A Survey," *College & Research Libraries* (2003): 176-191.

Lee, Catherine A. "Teaching Generation X," *Research Strategies* 14 (Winter 1996): 56-59.

Lenhart, Amanda, Lee Rainie, and Oliver Lewis. "Teenage Life Online: The Rise of the Instant-Message Generation and the Internet's Impact on Friendships and Family Relationships." Report for PEW Internet & American Life Project 2001. <http://www.pewInternet.org/reports/pdfs/PIP_Teens_Report.pdf>.

McDonald, Randy, and Marthea Turnage. "Making the Connection: Library Services for Distance Education and Off-Campus Students." *Texas Library Journal* (2003): 50-53.

Raward, Roslyn. "Academic Library Website Design Principles: Development of a Checklist." *Australian Academic & Research Libraries* (2001) 123- . Database online. Available from Expanded Academic ASAP Plus.

Sheesley, Deborah. "The 'Net Generation: Characteristics of Traditional-Aged College Students and Implications for Academic Information Services." *College & Undergraduate Libraries* 9 (2002): 25-42.

Sikora, Anna C. "A Profile of Participation in Distance Education: 1999-2000." U.S. Department of Education, National Center for Education Statistics, 2002 (NCES 2003-154).

Ask a UT System Librarian:
A Multi-Campus Chat Initiative
Supporting Students at a Distance

Kimberly Chapman
Darcy Del Bosque

SUMMARY. University of Texas System libraries initiated a chat reference program to support distance learners enrolled at University of Texas component institutions, including the UT Telecampus Digital Library. Librarians at several geographically distant campuses staffed the collaborative chat reference service.

Librarians assisted students at other UT System campuses, in effect becoming "distance librarians" who must have thorough knowledge of both their own library resources and the resources available at other campus libraries.

Librarians at The University of Texas at San Antonio share their experiences with this collaborative chat reference service. *[Article copies available for a fee from The Haworth Document Delivery Service: 1-800-HAWORTH. E-mail address: <docdelivery@haworthpress.com> Website: <http://www. HaworthPress.com> © 2004 by The Haworth Press, Inc. All rights reserved.]*

Kimberly Chapman (kchapman@utsa.edu) and Darcy Del Bosque (ddelbosque@ utsa.edu) are Reference Librarians/Bibliographers, University of Texas at San Antonio, John Peace Library, 6900 North Loop 1604 West, San Antonio, TX 78249-0671.

[Haworth co-indexing entry note]: "Ask a UT System Librarian: A Multi-Campus Chat Initiative Supporting Students at a Distance." Chapman, Kimberly, and Darcy Del Bosque. Co-published simultaneously in *Internet Reference Services Quarterly* (The Haworth Information Press, an imprint of The Haworth Press, Inc.) Vol. 9, No. 3/4, 2004, pp. 55-79; and: *Internet Reference Support for Distance Learners* (ed: William Miller, and Rita M. Pellen) The Haworth Information Press, an imprint of The Haworth Press, Inc., 2004, pp. 55-79. Single or multiple copies of this article are available for a fee from The Haworth Document Delivery Service [1-800-HAWORTH, 9:00 a.m. - 5:00 p.m. (EST). E-mail address: docdelivery@haworthpress.com].

Digital Object Identifier: 10.1300/J136v09n03_06

KEYWORDS. Chat reference, digital reference, virtual reference, collaborative reference, University of Texas System, University of Texas at San Antonio, distance learners

LITERATURE REVIEW

Virtual or digital reference services include a wide variety of reference services delivered via the Internet, such as e-mail and chat reference.[1] While these types of services involve relatively new technologies, they have received a great deal of coverage in library literature. This article deals primarily with chat reference service implemented in a collaborative network, although other formats of providing virtual service are briefly addressed.

The library literature indicates that several aspects of chat reference have been covered, from the technical to the practical, although much more will be discovered as the technology and implementation of chat reference services becomes more prevalent. This literature review provides a brief overview of chat reference issues; however, other resources are available that provide a more comprehensive picture.

Bernie Sloan has written several articles on virtual reference and has a Digital Reference Bibliography available online that covers over six hundred different resources.[2] The Virtual Reference Desk, a project sponsored by the U.S. Department of Education, includes a newsletter and a link to conference proceedings.[3] Also included on the Website is a listing of resources about virtual reference compiled by Joann M. Wasik. OCLC, a creator of software for library chat reference, also provides a site dedicated to virtual reference.[4] In addition to articles and Websites, this Website includes a forum where people can comment on their own experiences and ask others for help. Rebecca Maddox has highlighted a much smaller and more targeted list of Websites that libraries considering implementing chat reference will want to review (Maddox 2003).

Articles about chat reference often focus on one aspect of the service. Frequently one of the first areas studied is how to implement virtual reference service. Part of the How-To-Do-It Manual for Librarian's series, *Starting and Operating Live Virtual Reference Services*, provides information for those needing background on chat technology, practical advice on choosing and implementing a software system, and information on evaluating and marketing the program (Meola and Stormont 2002). *Chat Reference: A Guide to Live Virtual Reference Services* will also help those at the beginning stages of planning chat reference (Ronan 2003).

Librarians at all types of libraries have written articles describing how their libraries have initiated virtual reference. Several articles in the April 2003 issue of *Computers in Libraries* address virtual reference. Roy Balleste and Gordon Russell discuss how Nova Southeastern University's Law Library and St. Thomas University's Law Library set up a joint venture in chat reference (Balleste and Russell 2003). Another article from this issue provides a public library viewpoint. Schaake and Sathan's "We Jumped on the Live Reference Bandwagon and We Love the Ride" explains how their libraries joined the 24/7 Reference collaborative chat service (Schaake and Sathan 2003). For an overview of a University's experience, consult Marianne Foley's "Instant Messaging Reference in an Academic Library: A Case Study," which describes the University of Buffalo's experiment with chat (Foley 2002). The examples listed demonstrate the types of articles available, but additional articles can be found with a quick search within library literature.

Librarians write about the type of software chosen for establishing a chat reference system and some of the technical necessities that arise when using chat reference software applications. Elias and Morrill describe testing various software programs and then discuss implementation of one program after it had been chosen (Elias and Morrill 2003). Steve Coffman takes a look beyond software that is currently available and describes the updates he feels are necessary to create better virtual reference software in "We'll Take It from Here: Further Developments We'd Like to See in Virtual Reference Software" (Coffman 2001).

After chat systems are implemented other issues arise. Marketing the service is often briefly addressed in articles focused on other chat reference issues. An example of this is Viggiano's "Distance Learners: Not Necessarily Distant," which concentrates on issues about distance learners, but mentions marketing virtual reference to those students (Viggiano 2003). Corey Johnson's Master's Paper, "Online Chat Reference: The Awareness of, Use of, Interest in, and Marketing of This New Reference Service Technology," also dedicates a portion to the aspects of marketing.[5] Only a few authors have focused primarily on marketing issues in their articles. Catherine Wells' "Location, Location, Location: The Importance of the Placement of the Chat Button" addresses the issue of low use of chat services and then undertakes a study that shows how placement of the chat button can increase use of the service (Wells 2003).

Quality standards for chat reference services are beginning to be addressed in the literature. Lankes, Gross, and McClure have written extensively about this topic. They and Pomerantz include a chapter in the book *Implementing Digital Reference Services: Setting Standards and Making It Real* that lists the literature dealing with quality of digital reference services (Lankes et al. 2001). Many of the same authors collaborated on the online manual, "Statistics, Measures, and Quality Standards for Assessing Digital Reference Library Services," which helps libraries find ways to assess pre-existing virtual library projects.[6] Lankes, Gross, and McClure have furthered this research by undertaking two studies that aim to assess digital reference services and develop standards that support these services, which resulted in "Cost, Statistics, Measures, and Standards for Digital Reference Services: A Preliminary View" (Lankes et al. 2003).

Other libraries have chosen to approach quality standards by performing content analysis of chat sessions and studies that quantify the accuracy of answers given via the service. Joanne Smyth presents three models that can be used in analyzing transcripts including the Eisenberg-Berkowitz Information Problem Solving Model, ACRL's Information Literacy Competency Standards, and a modified version of William Katz's model created by Joann Sears at Auburn University (Smyth 2003). Joann Sears' article is an example of literature dealing with one library's analysis of chat reference transcripts, in this case the analysis of one semester's chat reference transcripts from Auburn University (Sears 2001).

Many libraries begin implementation of chat reference as members of a consortium. These joint chat ventures often have to deal with additional issues. Peters takes a positive view of these efforts in "E-Reference: How Consortia Add Value." Peters discusses how consortia can be helpful to starting and operating chat reference, although he concedes they can also have some problems (Peters 2002). Steve Coffman takes the alternate view in "What's Wrong with Collaborative Digital Reference." He points out various problems, including the fact that start-up costs often outweigh the number of questions that are received (Coffman 2002).

"The Local Nature of Digital Reference" questions the ability of libraries to answer questions from patrons of a different institution, but concludes that fewer than 25% of questions require on-site handling (Berry et al. 2003). Other literature about consortial agreements recounts individual efforts in creating chat reference programs. "Collaborative Virtual Reference in Colorado" provides the reasoning behind the state's initiation of a chat reference service that includes participation from twenty public, fifteen academic, three special, and one school library (Bailey-Hainer 2003). Peter Bromberg discusses how New Jersey implemented its twenty-four hour collaborative service and how the service is managed in his "Managing a Statewide Virtual Reference Service: How Q and A NJ Works" (Bromberg 2001).

This article will discuss the implementation of a collaborative chat reference program within the University of Texas System and highlight benefits and concerns about the service.

UT SYSTEM

The University of Texas System, established by the Texas Constitution in 1876, consists of fifteen component institutions.[7] These components, nine general academic universities and six health institutions, awarded 30,723 degrees during academic year 2001-2002, and had a combined enrollment of more than 177,855 students in Fall 2003.[8]

In addition to distance learning courses offered at UT System campuses, the UT Telecampus was created in 1999 to deliver online education and online degrees from the University of Texas System component institutions.[9] An online collection of materials, the UT Telecampus Digital Library, provides library services to distance learners enrolled in UT Telecampus courses. Another resource, the UT System Digital Library, provides support to UT System libraries, including information about distance learning initiatives. The UT System Digital Library maintains a listserv called Offcamp, which disseminates information about distance learning resources to UT System libraries. Library administrators and librarians across the University of Texas System subscribe to the listserv. Information about the UT System Ask a Librarian Project submitted to the listserv was how the University of Texas at San Antonio Library first became aware of and involved with the chat reference project.

UT SYSTEM VIRTUAL REFERENCE

The UT System Digital Library was awarded an LSTA Library Cooperation Grant in FY 2003. The grant supported the hiring of a Virtual Reference Coordinator for "establishing and coordinating a collaborative virtual reference service for distance learners across the UT System."[10] UT System Libraries, while independent from one another, participate in various consortia. The UT System has consortial arrangements for many library services. In addition, UT System libraries participate in TexShare, a state-wide consortium of academic and public libraries.[11] As a result, the UT System libraries have many licensed electronic databases in common, which is particularly useful for assisting distance learners. Additionally, the UT System libraries have all developed Websites that address policies and procedures, and provide links to library catalogs, databases, online help, and other relevant information.

The literature indicates that when libraries contemplate embarking on virtual reference projects, a great deal of time and energy is spent on evaluating software products, organizing the virtual reference plan, and taking care of technical details. The Virtual Reference Coordinator directed these aspects of the collaborative service. UT libraries participated in software evaluation arranged by the Virtual Reference Coordinator during Spring 2003 and provided feedback. The Virtual Reference Coordinator handled the remainder of the background work, technical details, and implementation. Start-up and maintenance costs were funded centrally. The participating libraries were asked to contribute four hours of staffing per week, and to identify a librarian to serve as contact person or coordinator for each institution.

It is interesting to note that at the time, although all the libraries involved provided virtual reference services in the form of e-mail service and/or Web forms, only the UT Arlington library was offering chat reference service. UT Austin embarked on its own chat reference service in October 2003. Both UT Arlington and UT Austin continued to participate in the collaborative UT System Ask A Librarian service, as well as staffing their own libraries' chat services. The UT System Ask a Librarian service is the only chat reference service that other libraries involved in the project are using at this time.

The FY2003 LSTA grant funded the first part of the Virtual Reference Project, but an LSTA grant was not awarded for FY2004. UT Austin and UT System continued to supply funding for the project; however, the Virtual Reference Coordinator's position was modified, and the emphasis on UT Telecampus distance learners was shifted to include the broadest possible range of UT-affiliated students.

Five academic libraries and one medical library participated in the Fall 2003 Beta Test. The academic libraries were UT Austin, UT Arlington, UT Brownsville, UT Dallas, and UT San Antonio (UTSA). The medical library was the UT Health Science Center Houston, School of Public Health. UT Pan American, an academic library, joined the project in Spring 2004. All libraries continue to participate, and several other UT components have expressed an interest in joining the project at some point in the future.

UTSA LIBRARY

The UT System libraries support a diverse range of educational programs. The UTSA Library has three campus locations: the John Peace Library Building on the 1604 Campus, the Downtown Library, and the Archives in the Institute of Texan Cultures. The library has both physical and online collections of materials: more than 610,000 books, 2,500 current periodical subscriptions, access to over 30,000 periodicals online, and a variety of resources in other formats, including videorecordings, DVDs, CDs, microform materials, atlases, maps, and curriculum materials. The Public Services staff providing assistance at the Reference Desks includes nine full-time librarians, one part-time librarian, and several full- and part-time library assistants.

Staffing

The Ask a UT System Librarian Beta Test began on September 2, 2003.[12] The service was staffed on a rotating schedule and available to UT System affiliated users 28 hours per week, Monday through Friday. The service schedule of Monday through Thursday, 12:00 p.m.-6:00 p.m., and Friday, 12:00 p.m.-4:00 p.m., was in effect during both Fall 2003 and Spring 2004 semesters, and continues at this time.

Each participating UT library was asked to contribute four hours of staff coverage per week. The UTSA Library decided that staffing the service would be voluntary, not mandatory. The UTSA Chat Coordinator solicited volunteers from among the Public Services librarians available at both the 1604 and Downtown Campuses. Five UTSA librarians volunteered to staff the chat reference rotation in Fall 2003, with two new librarians joining the rotation in Spring 2004. The librarians had different levels of familiarity and experience with chat reference and distance learning issues.

UT System campuses have a variety of distance learning programs. Some campuses have very active distance learning programs, with appropriate library support. One of the emphases at UTSA is on the relationship between its own two campuses, the 1604 campus and the Downtown campus. The UTSA Library has programs in place, such as document delivery and a courier service, to support students at these two campus locations, but does not have a library support structure that easily accommodates other types of distance learners. Several UT System libraries have library Webpages describing library support for distance learners, and the UTSA Library can benefit from the models provided by other UT System libraries, as library support for distance learners develops. For example, UTA Libraries Online has a Webpage about Distance Education Services available at the UTA Libraries.[13]

Training

Prior to the initiation of chat reference, UTSA librarians received training from both the UT System Virtual Reference Coordinator and the UTSA Chat Reference Coordinator.

The UT System Virtual Reference Coordinator visited participating component libraries to provide training on both the QuestionPoint software application and chat reference techniques. The coordinator visited the UTSA Library in August 2003, providing the above training in addition to information about chat reference services, the development of the UT System Ask a Librarian Project, and the goals of the project in terms of serving all UT System users, including distance learners. The coordinator demonstrated the QuestionPoint software and provided real-time demonstrations with the software, followed by hands-on training with librarians working in pairs taking turns being both the patron and the librarian. Librarians were able to create their own "canned responses" for frequently used phrases, such as greetings; in addition, some standardized responses, such as a "Thank you" message that included a survey link, were discussed to ensure consistency among participating components.

Training included discussion of basic policies, including the policy not to send proprietary information from subscription databases directly to users due to copyright and licensing concerns. This was especially important because librarians had no way to verify if users who claimed to be affiliated with an institution were in fact affiliated with the institution. The coordinator also provided basic "best practice" guidelines for providing virtual reference service and directed librarians to Websites that supported distance learning. Another useful tool was a comprehensive Excel spreadsheet of subscription databases to help librarians determine if a library subscribed to a resource. These databases included

EBSCOhost and ProQuest products, WorldCat, and publisher packages such as JSTOR, Project Muse, ScienceDirect, Kluwer, and so on.

Training and communication updates have been a strong point of the Ask a UT System Librarian service since its inception. A separate listserv, Systemchat, was implemented during the Fall 2003 semester, specifically targeted at the librarians who were staffing the collaborative service. It is used for nuts-and-bolts types of questions, such as reporting software problems, notifying components about closing the service due to holidays or semester breaks, and so forth. Many Systemchat messages involved librarians needing to trade shifts due to scheduling conflicts. The UTSA librarians' experience has been that they have picked up several shifts for other components when needed, and the favor has been reciprocated when UTSA librarians were in need of assistance themselves. The quick response of UT librarians at one institution in assisting librarians at other UT institutions to ensure that chat hours were covered is an excellent example of cooperation and communication.

The UT System Virtual Reference Coordinator also provided periodic updates and PowerPoint presentations that summarized project results. During the Spring 2004 semester, statistical information about the Beta Test phase of the project was made available to components, and goals for the next phases of the project were articulated.

Communication was also enhanced by teleconferences arranged by the UT System Digital Library Distance Learning Task Force. One teleconference was dedicated to the Ask a Librarian project, where some components shared their marketing strategies. Additional marketing tools were provided on the project Website. Another teleconference provided a forum for discussion of distance learning issues and the role of the UT Telecampus Digital Library. Both teleconferences were useful ways for librarians to "meet" and exchange ideas about the distance learning services and the UT System Ask a Librarian Project.

While the Virtual Reference Coordinator provided the initial training and continuous information to coordinators to keep participants "in the loop," the UTSA Chat Reference Coordinator took responsibility for providing additional training and information to UTSA library staff.

The UTSA Chat Coordinator facilitated chat reference service by preparing a spreadsheet of URLs that assisted UTSA librarians with providing online reference to students of other libraries. This proved important because, during the Spring 2004 service period, a UTSA librarian assisted a UTSA student only once via chat reference. The UTSA librarians' other transactions involved students from other UT libraries. UTSA librarians needed to become familiar with other libraries' Websites in order to provide effective assistance to those students. The spreadsheet provided links to:

- Homepages
- Catalogs
- Databases Lists
- Electronic Journal Lists
- Subject Guides or Pathfinders
- Off-Campus Access Instructions
- Borrowing Privileges and InterLibrary Loan Policies
- E-mail Assistance and Web Forms
- Contact Persons
- Reference Desk Phone Numbers

This type of support was essential for finding information about other libraries' policies and services quickly. Several participating libraries updated their Websites during the Fall 2003 and Spring 2004 semesters, so the UTSA Chat Coordinator updated spreadsheet links each semester.

The UTSA Chat Coordinator held meetings with the UTSA librarians at the beginning of each semester to discuss any changes about the service and share information that had been provided via Systemchat or the Ask a Librarian Project pages. When the UT Telecampus began promoting the chat reference service to distance learners in Spring 2004, the UTSA Chat Coordinator provided UT Telecampus information to librarians, and information describing the types of support that Telecampus users expected. UTSA librarians spent time reviewing the UT Telecampus brochures and the definitions of "home campus," "host campus," and so on that were part of the distance learners' vocabulary.

Although the most extensive training was provided for the librarians participating in the chat rotation, it was also important for other Public Services staff to understand the new service being provided, and how it could affect them. Training provided an explanation to staff as to why some librarians were occasionally "tied to their desks" and were not available for traditional reference duties. The UTSA Chat Reference Coordinator briefed Public Services staff about the service during a regular meeting when the service was being tested. After the conclusion of the Beta Test and the subsequent decision to continue the service, a training session was held that provided more information about the service. The session was well-attended by several library departments, including Collection Development and Technical Services, and generated interest in the service among library staff.

LOCAL IMPLEMENTATION:
ASK A UT SYSTEM LIBRARIAN LINK

UT libraries participating in the collaborative service were asked to place a link to the *Ask a UT System Librarian* service on their Websites. This ensured that there would be a variety of access points to the chat reference interface. This also ensured equity by providing opportunities for students of each institution to use the service, which was important because the potential user group had been expanded to include any UT-affiliated user, not just distance learners. Some libraries placed the link on their home page, as did UT Brownsville.[14] Other libraries placed the link on second-level pages, as did UT Arlington.[15]

The UTSA Library had undergone an extensive Web redesign that was released in August 2003, and decided to place the link on its existing Ask a Librarian page.[16] Like many libraries, UTSA Library had e-mail and Web forms for assistance that were already in existence and used extensively. The UTSA Library page with these services was already called "Ask a Librarian." A decision was made to add the chat reference link to this page, rather than replacing this page entirely. The existing Web form was renamed "Ask a UTSA Librarian," and the chat reference link was named "Ask a UT System Librarian." The UTSA librarians involved felt that users would make little distinction between the UTSA Librarian and UT System Librarian designations, and that the format, Web form versus live chat, would influence the user to choose the format most convenient and available at the point-of-need. For example, if a user visited the Website in the morning, the user would choose the Web form, or another avenue of communication, such as phone reference, simply because chat was not available at that time of day.

The UTSA Library Ask a Librarian page is a second-level page, with a prominent link under the "Quick Links" section of the library homepage. The "Quick Links" section is placed on almost every page within the UTSA Library Website, so that the links in this section, including Ask a Librarian, are highly visible and easily accessible to users. As will be discussed later, despite the "same page" location of both links, the Web form service has continued to garner users, while the chat service has received comparatively few transactions from UTSA students.

LOCAL IMPLEMENTATION:
STAFFING

During the Fall 2003 Beta Test, UTSA librarians staffed the chat service on Wednesdays and Thursdays from 4:00 p.m.-6:00 p.m. Librarians staffed the chat rotation in addition to their regularly scheduled face-to-face reference desk duties. The UTSA Chat Reference Coordinator scheduled librarians for one- or two-hour shifts, checking with the face-to-face reference desk scheduler to avoid scheduling the same librarian for face-to-face reference and chat reference at the same time. In addition, librarian teaching loads, special projects, vacations, illness, and other factors influenced availability of librarians for chat staffing. The 4:00 p.m.-6:00 p.m. shift proved problematic, due to most librarians having regularly scheduled workdays from 8:00 a.m.-5:00 p.m. Matters were complicated further because three of the five librarians who volunteered for chat reference took turns working Wednesday and Thursday nights, and were thus unavailable from 4:00 p.m.-6:00 p.m. Despite these difficulties, the librarians were still able to staff the service.

The UTSA Library was able to trade chat times with another UT component for the Spring 2004 semester, staffing the service on Wednesdays 4:00 p.m.-6:00 p.m. and Thursdays 12:00 p.m.-2:00 p.m. This factor, in conjunction with two new librarians joining the staffing rotation, as well as adaptation of a new block scheduling system for reference staff, allowed more flexibility for scheduling and has been a better fit overall. UTSA Librarians have traded shifts when necessary, both among themselves, and with librarians at other component institutions. The willingness of component institutions to assist one another with staffing has been one beneficial aspect of the collaborative experience.

LOCAL IMPLEMENTATION:
MARKETING

During the Fall 2003 semester Beta Test period, UTSA librarians informed other library staff about the service and the service links on the UTSA Library Website, but did not market the service directly to faculty and students. Librarians did not want to build expectations by marketing a service that might not be available the following semester. Additionally, practical considerations such as heavy teaching loads did not allow librarians time to implement marketing strategies.

During the Spring 2004 semester, the UT System Virtual Reference Coordinator made a "Press Kit" of marketing materials available to component libraries.[17] Additionally, marketing was discussed at one of the teleconferences. With the idea that the Chat Reference service was "here to stay," three of the UTSA librarians informally marketed the service during Bibliographic Instruction sessions during the Spring 2004 semester. One librarian demonstrated the service, while other librarians mentioned it or handed out information about the service, as part of general encouragement to "Ask a Librarian" for assistance with library resources. One librarian, as a guest speaker at a faculty workshop that discussed distance learning, described the chat reference service to faculty members.

PRELIMINARY EVALUATION OF THE SERVICE: USERS SERVED

The UT System Virtual Reference Coordinator provided a brief analysis of the Fall 2003 Beta Test, but a similar analysis is not yet available for the Spring 2004 semester.[18] The authors of this article and the Virtual Reference Coordinator at UT Austin are beginning a thorough analysis of the chat reference transcripts from both the Fall 2003 and Spring 2004 semesters. Approximately 300 chat reference transcripts will be analyzed to determine the types of questions asked, reference, directional, technical, and so on, and to determine the number of questions that require referral. Determining referrals is challenging, because anecdotal evidence suggests that librarians both follow up with questions and refer questions outside of the QuestionPoint software application, partly because these features on the software are viewed as cumbersome. The transcript analysis will also study demographics about students, institutions, and distance learners using the service.

The UTSA Chat Coordinator collected some basic data during the Spring 2004 semester, in part to determine the impact of staffing chat reference on librarians' workloads. UTSA librarians staffed the collaborative chat reference service for a total of eighty hours in Spring 2004, exclusive of training time. This was an average of 11.4 hours per librarian during the semester, although some librarians had higher or lower hours due to scheduling considerations. During those eighty hours, thirty-eight users initiated sessions.

Not all sessions were full transactions with a reference interview, question, response, and follow-up. Some sessions were "disconnects" in which a user accesses the software, the librarian welcomes the user, but gets no response from the user, and the user never asks a question. "Disconnects" were a problem for the system as a whole, having been noted at a rate of 21% during the Beta Test period.[19] It remains unclear if the disconnects are a software problem, or the user just deciding he/she didn't really want to ask a question, or a combination of both those factors.

Of the thirty-eight sessions that UTSA librarians responded to, ten were "disconnects" and twenty-eight were successful transactions. One UTSA librarian received only one question during his staffing time the entire semester. Of the twenty-eight successful transactions, only one transaction involved a UTSA student. The other twenty-seven transactions involved students from other UT campuses, thus reinforcing the idea that UTSA librarians became "distance librarians."

Other data collected indicate that UTSA students used the chat reference service infrequently. The transcripts show that out of seventeen users identified as UTSA students, three students were "disconnected" and fourteen sessions resulted in transactions where the students received assistance. One patron was actively referred to the UTSA librarians, via e-mail, for additional assistance.

During the same time period, January 2004 through May 2004, the Ask a Librarian Form that is located on the same page as the Ask a UT System Librarian link generated 162 transactions, all of which were responded to by UTSA library staff. The disparity between usages of the Web form versus the chat reference service is especially interesting because both links are on the same page. There is not currently a method to determine why users chose one format over the other, and it will be interesting to see if this pattern changes as the Chat Reference service continues.

In order to gauge the impact on UTSA librarians participating in chat reference and to assess their attitudes about the service, two surveys were developed. SurveyMonkey.com was used to create the surveys, which were distributed to all participants in chat reference at UTSA, including the two authors of this article. The decision to include the authors in the survey resulted in part because so few librarians staff the service and as many opinions as possible were desired. Since the surveys hold no statistical significance, it was felt that including the authors would not skew the results. One survey consisted of seven fixed-response questions with one follow-up open-ended question, while the other survey consisted of eight open-ended questions. All librarians responded to the fixed-response survey, while one librarian failed to respond to the open-ended survey.

The responses of the UTSA librarians participating in chat reference provide an opportunity for honest feedback about the service. The responses provide insight into the perceptions of librarians participating in chat reference at UTSA and bring up some issues of concern regarding the program and the services it provides to both distance learners and students as a whole. The UT System Ask a Librarian project began with the goal of assisting distance learners, even though other factors have impacted that original goal. Although many of the survey questions address the use of chat reference to assist these students, other questions were asked to understand the impact of the service on the daily workload of librarians at UTSA and their attitudes about participating in the collaborative reference service.

Librarians were asked to "Describe the role that chat reference plays in overall library services" in order to learn how this group of librarians view chat reference service in relation to their other duties. Most librarians responded that chat reference is one component of reference services and that it plays a supplementary role to other duties. One librarian replied that he/she did not know how chat fit into overall library services, while another librarian replied that it was "Too soon to tell." These responses illustrate that most UTSA librarians view chat reference as an additional way to help students with their information needs, although it does not replace traditional methods of reference such as face-to-face, phone, or even bibliographic instruction.

Another question asked was whether or not librarians enjoyed staffing chat as part of their overall duties. A slight majority of librarians liked staffing chat reference as part of their overall duties. One librarian stated that he/she strongly liked staffing chat reference and three stated that they liked staffing chat reference. The remaining three respondents neither liked nor disliked staffing the service. This positive inclination could be influenced by the fact that staffing chat reference at UTSA is a voluntary service. Librarians disliking chat reference would not volunteer to take part in staffing the service.

Although most librarians were positively inclined towards participating in chat reference, there was some concern about the impact on their workloads. When asked the question, "I feel staffing chat reference is a productive use of my time," only one librarian stated that staffing chat reference was productive most of the time. Four respondents said that it was productive some of the time, while two said that it was productive almost none of the time. These responses may stem from the low use of the service, because when asked, "How does participating in this service impact your overall workload?" five out of six respondents stated that the impact was minimal. The one librarian who stated that her workload has increased, the coordinator of the service, must complete scheduling of the service, attend meetings with other UT System components, and provide training for the service. More than half of the librarians felt they were able to successfully accomplish other work while waiting for a chat user, but two librarians said it was difficult being tied to their computers. Several librarians commented about having to be ready for a chat question to pop up at any moment.

Some librarians have more anxiety when staffing chat reference than when working with patrons face-to-face at the reference desk. When librarians were asked to compare their anxiety levels in face-to-face reference with those in chat reference, two librarians responded that they had more anxiety, one librarian responded that he/she had some anxiety, three librarians responded that they had neither more nor less anxiety, and one librarian stated that he/she had less anxiety. There are several possible reasons for anxiety. It could stem from software and dealing with new technologies, or it could be because traditional cues used in face-to-face reference transactions, such as facial expression and body language, are absent in chat reference transactions.

Another possible source of anxiety is the "grab bag" of possible users; it is unlikely that librarians will get a chat reference question from a UTSA student, and must be mentally prepared to assist another institutions' users. Anxiety could stem from the pressure of having to locate information about the other institutions quickly, while letting the user know the question is being investigated. Additionally, anxiety may also stem from concerns about whether the question can be answered with the information that the UTSA librarians have, or will need to be referred to the user's home institution. Remembering that it is appropriate to refer questions that cannot be answered with online resources to the home institution can reduce anxiety.

Training for chat reference has been continuous and has covered technical aspects of the project, resources available at other UT libraries, and tips for effectively answering questions in the chat format. Questions about training received the most positive feedback on the survey. All participants felt that the training they received before the implementation of the service was adequate to prepare them for providing chat reference service, with two librarians saying that the training was more than adequate to prepare them for providing service. Librarians also indicated satisfaction with the amount of periodic training and informational updates provided, with all seven librarians indicating that training and updates meet their needs.

In addition to assessing the impact of chat reference on librarians, it was also an aim of the surveys to assess the opinion of UTSA librarians towards the effectiveness of chat reference as a tool and also its ability to serve distance learners and our own students. These questions were addressed because the attitudes of participants often affect the outcome of a program. It was found that four UTSA librarians viewed chat reference as an effective way to answer questions only some of the time, while three of them stated that it is an effective way to answer questions most of the time.

Librarians were asked, "Can you answer questions as effectively through chat reference as in face-to-face reference? Why or Why not?" Half of the respondents stated, "It depends on the question." Two librarians responded "No," with one person commenting, "I can only type so fast" and the other stating "No. With face-to-face reference it is easier to conduct a reference interview, you have other cues such as body language and such to go on when determining what a person really needs, and people are more willing to spend some time." One librarian stated he/she could answer questions as effectively with chat, "but only because I make a conscious attempt to use language that conveys what I would normally do through my voice, tone, eye contact, body language, etc." This librarian also mentioned that being a fast typist was helpful. Answers to these questions show that most librarians did not feel that they were as effective in providing chat reference as in providing face-to-face reference services. However, at the same time, most librarians mentioned that there were questions that were suitable to be answered via chat, and that it was only in cases when "the question gets really in-depth and multi-faceted" that chat is not an effective method of delivering assistance to users.

One aspect of collaborative reference work indicated in the literature is that patrons are frequently not users of your own institution. This proved true for UTSA librarians providing the service: 27 out of 28 transactions involved users from another institution. The original goal of the Ask a UT System Librarian service was to help distance learners enrolled in UT Telecampus courses; however, this was not necessarily the outcome. Librarians were asked, "This service was started in support of distance learners. Do you feel distance learners benefit from the service?" Most librarians responded that they didn't know what type of patrons they were assisting, but that they doubted many of them were distance learners. Many librarians see the benefit of chat reference for distance learners, but feel that these students underused the service.

Some cited the hours of service as being a possible reason that distance learners were not using the service in large numbers. One respondent stated, "From what I know about distance learning, a lot of distance learners might be non-traditional students who work all day and then work on their coursework in the evening or the weekends. Since we don't offer chat when they might actually be working on their assignments, I don't know how effective the service is." Other librarians questioned if the service was adequately marketed to distance learners. Currently, each UT component is responsible for marketing to its students and there is no joint effort to market to distance learners. Users are asked to self-identify with a specific campus when logging onto the service, but they do not indicate if they are distance or local learners. Unless they are enrolled with the UT Telecampus it is difficult for librarians to determine if they are assisting a distance learner.

Since all but one of the students who were assisted by UTSA librarians came from different institutions, another question asked was, "How do you feel spending your work time helping students from other institutions via chat?" Four librarians felt it was fine to be helping students from other institutions, especially since other institutions are helping our students. However, they did have some reservations about the level of service they could provide to patrons of other libraries. The remaining two respondents expanded on these reservations and worried that they could not provide appropriate help for students of a different institution. One librarian stated, "I find it somewhat stressful because I am concerned that they will ask me something I will not be able to answer as quickly as a librarian from their own institution, due to not using their system on a day-to-day basis. I think we would really be making better use of our time if we provided chat service only to students at UTSA." The other response also questioned the quality of the service: "It is often vexing, because often we have to try and answer questions that are best handled by on-site librarians. Then, I feel that the patron might think our service to be lousy because we can't help them in those instances." These responses indicate that the underlying issue may not be with the effort it takes to help students from another institution, but the fear that the information to help these students is not readily available and that patrons might not get an accurate answer from UTSA librarians, despite their best efforts, simply because they do not have "local" knowledge that may be appropriate to answer the question.

When asked the previous question, there seemed to be a consensus that helping students from other institutions could be difficult because of institution-specific information, but when asked, "Describe your comfort level with the resources available at other participating UT component libraries," half of the responding librarians responded positively. Many cited the spreadsheet of UT library Websites created by the UTSA Chat Coordinator for providing them with enough information to get by. One librarian felt comfortable with databases, but stated, "Policies are harder to deal with, especially if the Websites are not in-depth or are poorly organized. It does take time to figure out who has what and where to lead the student. Usually they are patient while I dig around, but I could help a UTSA student more quickly." Another librarian echoed the problem of speed saying, "I'm concerned about the student waiting while I try to find the answer on another's Web page." Other librarians were concerned about not being aware of institution-specific problems, such as an Internet outage or subscription resource problems. Some librarians felt very comfortable with resources available at other institutions and when they encountered a problem they felt they "have good judgment in referring students back to their home institution when appropriate."

Despite the issues mentioned previously, five librarians felt they can answer non-UTSA students' questions effectively via chat most of the time and two felt they can answer the questions effectively some of the time. Interestingly, only three librarians responded that non-UTSA librarians could assist UTSA students effectively via chat most of the time, while four librarians responded that non-UTSA librarians could only answer UTSA students' questions effectively some of the time.

In an open-ended question that asked, "Do you feel that chat is an effective way to serve UTSA students?" most respondents replied yes, but many of them provided stipulations to this positive answer. Three librarians mentioned that they had not received questions from UTSA students and thought it was not a method students were using to ask for help. A different respondent stated that better hours could have been chosen for the service and that the service might get more use once the campus becomes wireless-access ready. Two librarians mentioned that chat could be effective for some types of questions, but that it cannot replace face-to-face reference and is not appropriate for other types of questions. One librarian, who was unsure of the benefits of chat reference, said, "I'm concerned that we have less control over answers given to UTSA students by someone from another institution." This statement may provide clues as to why librarians felt other institutions could not help UTSA students, although they felt they could help students from other UT System components.

The surveys illustrate that, although the majority of the participants like staffing chat, they have concerns about its use and effectiveness as is currently implemented. The majority of librarians, five respondents (one person responded to this question twice, for a total of eight responses), felt that the UT System Chat Service is only somewhat worthwhile. Two librarians answered that the service is not very worthwhile at all, and only one person responded that the service was very worthwhile. When asked to list any comments of why they like or dislike chat reference five librarians commented. Three stated that use was low, making chat reference "a drain on the librarian's time."

One librarian summed up the frustration by saying, "While I am enthusiastic about the potential of chat reference as another method of interacting with users and reaching our students, I am disappointed that the service gets such little use, by either UTSA students or other UT System students. It doesn't seem like the investment of time and resources that librarians have invested is having any significant service outcome, in terms of numbers of patrons using the service, compared with the energy being put into staffing the service." Another librarian suggested revising the hours of the service in order to increase the number of patrons using the service. Two librarians questioned the ability of librarians not working at a student's institution to answer questions.

The answers to the survey questions show that although most of the volunteers for this service see a positive use for distance education students, there are still many issues that need to be addressed before the program can become effective for both the library and for the patrons it strives to serve. Collaborative virtual reference will continue in the future and the UTSA Library will remain an active participant. Although currently few of our own students are using the service, other students are being served and the amount of questions continues to climb. It is clear that chat reference, especially collaborative chat reference, cannot be used for all questions. However, it is an effective way to reach out to users and to refer them to the appropriate sources. UTSA librarians are at a point at which they can assess the outcomes of the service thus far, and decide how best to market the service to UTSA students in upcoming semesters.

NOTES

1. Reitz, Joan M., "ODLIS: Online Dictionary for Library and Information Science," Libraries Unlimited, http://lu.com/odlis/odlis_d.cfm#digitalref (accessed June 30, 2004).

2. Sloan, Bernie, "Digital Reference Services Bibliography," Graduate School of Library and Information Sciences, University of Illinois Urbana-Champaign, http://www.lis.uiuc.edu/~b-sloan/digiref.html (accessed March 13, 2004).

3. Virtual Reference Desk, "The Virtual Reference Desk: Supporting Internet Q&A," Virtual Reference desk, http://www.vrd.org/ (accessed March 13, 2004).

4. OCLC Online Computer Library Center, "Topics and Trends: Virtual Reference," OCLC, http://www.oclc.org/community/topics/virtualreference/default.htm/ (accessed March 13, 2004).

5. Johnson, Corey, "Online Chat Reference: The Awareness of, Use of, Interest in, and Marketing of This New Reference Service Technology," University of North Carolina School of Information and Library Science, http://ils.unc.edu/MSpapers/2755.pdf/ (accessed June 21, 2004).

6. McClure, Charles R., David Lankes, Melissa Gross, and Beverly Choltco-Devlin, "Statistics, Measures, and Quality Standards for Assessing Digital Reference Library Services: Guidelines and Procedures," Information Institute of Syracuse, http://quartz.syr.edu/quality/Quality.pdf (accessed June 21, 2004).

7. "What is the University of Texas System?" The University of Texas System, Office of Public Affairs & Communications, http://www.utsystem.edu/news/ReportersToolkit2.htm (accessed June 25, 2004).

8. Ibid.

9. "UTTC FAQs," The UT Telecampus, http://www.telecampus.utsystem.edu/index.cfm/4,0,85,92,html (accessed June 25, 2004).

10. Dobbs, Joseph W., "Offcamp: Collaborative Virtual Reference Service," UT System Offcampus Library Services Support, http://www.lib.utsystem.edu/offcamp/vrs/VRS_grants.html (accessed June 30, 2004).

11. "Welcome to TexShare," Texas State Library and Archives Commission, http://www.texshare.edu/ (accessed June 25, 2004).

12. Dobbs, Joseph W. "Ask a UT System Librarian," PowerPoint presentation. Offcamp Collaborative Virtual Reference Service, http://www.lib.utsystem.edu/offcamp/vrs/index.html (accessed June 30, 2004).

13. Distance Education Services, UTA Libraries Online, http://www.uta.edu/library/distance/ (accessed June 30, 2004).

14. "Arnulfo L. Oliveira Memorial Library Online," The University of Texas at Brownsville, http://library.utb.edu/ (accessed June 27, 2004).

15. "Ask Us! UTA Libraries Online," The University of Texas at Arlington, http://www.uta.edu/library/askus.html (accessed June 27, 2004).

16. UTSA Library, "Ask a Librarian," The University of Texas at San Antonio, http://www.lib.utsa.edu/Forms/asklib.html (accessed June 27, 2004).

17. "Press Kit," Offcamp Collaborative Virtual Reference Service, http://www.lib.utsystem.edu/offcamp/vrs/index.html (accessed June 24, 2004).

18. Dobbs, Joseph W. "Ask a UT System Librarian," Offcamp Collaborative Virtual Reference Service, http://www.lib.utsystem.edu/offcamp/vrs/index.html (accessed June 24, 2004).

19. Dobbs, Joseph W. "Ask a UT System Librarian," Offcamp Collaborative Virtual Reference Service, http://www.lib.utsystem.edu/offcamp/vrs/index.html (accessed June 24, 2004).

BIBLIOGRAPHY

Bailey-Hainer, Brenda. "Collaborative Virtual Reference in Colorado." *Colorado Libraries* 29, no. 1 (Spring 2003): 15-18. Library Literature <http://vnweb.hwwilsonweb.com/>.

Balleste, Roy and Gordon Russell. "Implementing Virtual Reference: Hollywood Technology in Real Life." *Computers in Libraries* 23, no. 4 (April 2003): 14-16. Library Literature <http://vnweb.hwwilsonweb.com/>.

Berry, Teresa U., Margaret M. Casado, and Lana S. Dixon. "The Local Nature of Digital Reference." *The Southeastern Librarian* 51, no. 3 (Fall 2003): 8-15. Library Literature <http://vnweb.hwwilsonweb.com/>.

Bromberg, Peter. "Managing a Statewide Virtual Reference Service: How Q and A NJ Works." *Computers in Libraries* 23, no. 4 (Apr 2003): 26-ff. Academic Search Premier <http://search.epnet.com/>.

Coffman, Steve. "We'll Take It from Here: Further Development We'd Like to See in Virtual Reference Software." *Information Technology and Libraries* 20, no. 3 (2001): 149-53. ABI/Inform Complete <http://proquest.umi.com/>.

Coffman, Steve. "What's Wrong with Collaborative Reference?" *American Libraries* 33, no. 11 (December 2002): 56-58. Academic Search Premier <http://search.epnet.com/>.

Elias, Tana and Morrill, Stef. "Our Virtual Reference Training Camp: Testing the Players Before Signing Them On." *Computers in Libraries* 23, no. 4 (April 2003): 10-12, 70-72. Library Literature <http://vnweb.hwwilsonweb.com/>.

Foley, Marianne. "Instant Messaging Reference in an Academic Library: A Case Study." *College & Research Libraries* 63, no. 1 (January 2002): 36-45.

Lankes, David, Charles R. McClure, Melissa Gross, and Jeffery Pomerantz, Eds. *Implementing digital reference services: Setting standards and making it real.* New York: Neal-Shuman, 2001.

Lankes, David, Melissa Gross, and Charles R. McClure. "Cost, Statisics, Measures, and Standards for Digital Reference Services: A Preliminary View." *Library Trends* 51, no. 3 (Winter 2003): 401-413. Library Literature <http://vnweb.hwwilsonweb.com/>.

Maddox, R. Internet Review: "Virtual Reference Desks." *Kentucky Libraries* 67, no. 2 (Spring 2003): 21-23. Library Literature <http://vnweb.hwwilsonweb.com/>.

Meola, Mark and Sam Stormont. *Starting and Operating Live Virtual Reference Services: A How-To-Do-It Manual for Librarians.* New York: Neal Shuman, 2002.

Peters, Thomas A. "E-Reference: How Consortia Add Value." *The Journal of Academic Librarianship* 28, no. 4 (Jl/Ag 2002): 248-250. Library Literature <http://vnweb.hwwilsonweb.com/>.

Ronan, Jana. *Chat Reference: A Guide to Live Virtual Reference Services.* Englewood, CO: Libraries Unlimited, 2003.

Schaake, Glenda and Eleanor Sathan. "We Jumped on the Live Reference Bandwagon, and We Love the Ride." *Computers in Libraries* 23, no. 4 (April 2003) 20-22, 24-25. Library Literature <http://vnweb.hwwilsonweb.com/>.

Sears, Joann. "Chat Reference Service: An Analysis of One Semester's Data." *Issues in Science and Technology Libraries*, Fall 2001. Directory of Open Access Journals <http://www.doaj.org/>.

Smyth, Joanne. "Virtual Reference Transcript Analysis." Searcher 11, no. 3 (March 2003): 26-30. Library Literature <http://vnweb.hwwilsonweb.com/>.

Viggiano, Rachel. "Distance Learners: Not Necessarily Distant." *The Southeastern Librarian* 51, no. 3 (Fall 2003): 31-34. Library Literature <http://vnweb.hwwilsonweb.com/>.

Wells, Catherine A. "Location, Location, Location: Placement of the Chat Request Button." *Reference & User Services Quarterly* 43, no. 2 (Winter 2003): 133-137. Library Literature <http://vnweb.hwwilsonweb.com/>.

APPENDIX

Survey #1 Open-Ended Questions

1. Describe the role that chat reference plays in overall library services.
2. Do you feel that chat is an effective way to serve UTSA students?
3. How do you feel spending your work time helping students from other institutions via chat?
4. Describe your comfort level with the resources available at other participating UT component libraries.
5. How does participating in this service impact your overall workload?
6. Are you successful in accomplishing other work when there are no chat users during your shift?
7. This service was started in support of distance learners. Do you feel that distance learners benefit from the service?
8. Can you answer questions as effectively through chat reference as in face-to-face reference? Why or why not?

Survey #2 Fixed-Response Questions

1. As part of my overall duties I
   1. strongly like staffing chat reference
   2. like staffing chat reference

APPENDIX (continued)

3. neither like nor dislike staffing chat reference
4. dislike staffing chat reference
5. strongly dislike staffing chat reference

2. In comparison to the way I feel when involved with face-to-face reference, with chat reference I have
   1. more anxiety
   2. some anxiety
   3. neither more nor less anxiety
   4. less anxiety
   5. no anxiety

3. I feel staffing chat reference is a productive use of my time
   1. always
   2. most of the time
   3. some of the time
   4. almost none of the time
   5. none of the time

4. I feel chat is an effective way to answer questions
   1. all of the time
   2. most of the time
   3. some of the time
   4. almost none of the time
   5. none of the time

5. I feel I can answer non-UTSA students questions effectively via chat
   1. all of the time
   2. most of the time
   3. some of the time
   4. almost none of the time
   5. none of the time

6. I feel non-UTSA librarians can answer UTSA students effectively via chat
   1. all of the time
   2. most of the time
   3. some of the time
   4. almost none of the time
   5. none of the time

7. The training I received before staffing chat service was
   1. more than adequate to prepare me
   2. adequate to prepare me
   3. neither adequate nor inadequate to prepare me
   4. inadequate to prepare me
   5. very inadequate to prepare me

8. Periodic training and informational updates
   1. exceed my needs
   2. meet my needs
   3. meet some needs, do not meet other needs
   4. meet few of my needs
   5. do not meet my needs

9. I feel the UT System Chat Service is
   1. very worthwhile
   2. somewhat worthwhile
   3. neutral
   4. not very worthwhile
   5. not worthwhile at all

Please list any comments of why you like or dislike the service.

HawkHelp:
From Chat to a Student Services Portal

Nancy J. Burich
Frances A. Devlin

SUMMARY. This article describes the factors that influenced the design of a chat reference service that meets the needs of distance learners as well as traditional students. Emphasis is placed in the importance of collaborative projects, evaluation of software, and planning the organizational structure. An innovative "peer and tier" staffing initiative may extend hours and free reference librarians to concentrate on research and in-depth questions. Finally, a planning effort by information services may lead to a one-stop shopping service that will include student services that often are problematic for the distant learner (counseling, enrollment, financial aid, etc.). *[Article copies available for a fee from The Haworth Document Delivery Service: 1-800-HAWORTH. E-mail address: <docdelivery@haworthpress.com> Website: <http://www.HaworthPress.com>* © 2004 by The Haworth Press, Inc. All rights reserved.]

KEYWORDS. Distance learning, chat, electronic reference, collaboration, student services, Convey Systems, Inc.

Nancy J. Burich (nburich@ku.edu) is Coordinator for Distance Learning Information Services, University of Kansas Libraries, Edwards Campus, 12600 Quivira Road, Overland Park, KS 66213-2402. Frances A. Devlin (fadevlin@ku.edu) is Virtual Reference Librarian, University of Kansas Libraries, Watson Library, 1425 Jayhawk Boulevard, Lawrence, KS 66045-7544.

[Haworth co-indexing entry note]: "HawkHelp: From Chat to a Student Services Portal." Burich, Nancy J., and Frances A. Devlin. Co-published simultaneously in *Internet Reference Services Quarterly* (The Haworth Information Press, an imprint of The Haworth Press, Inc.) Vol. 9, No. 3/4, 2004, pp. 81-98; and: *Internet Reference Support for Distance Learners* (ed: William Miller, and Rita M. Pellen) The Haworth Information Press, an imprint of The Haworth Press, Inc., 2004, pp. 81-98. Single or multiple copies of this article are available for a fee from The Haworth Document Delivery Service [1-800-HAWORTH, 9:00 a.m. - 5:00 p.m. (EST). E-mail address: docdelivery@haworthpress.com].

Available online at http://www.haworthpress.com/web/IRSQ
© 2004 by The Haworth Press, Inc. All rights reserved.
Digital Object Identifier: 10.1300/J136v09n03_07

INTRODUCTION

Distance learning by its very nature requires that those using services do not need a physical presence in a library. Consequently, librarians serving this group of users often have led the way in developing and providing electronic services. In the past, distance learners who need reference assistance could either call a librarian (and hope that someone was available to answer the phone) or send an e-mail query. Today, e-mail reference services are common in academic libraries (Stemper and Butler, 2001, p. 184; Lipow, 1999, *Serving the Remote User*; and Moyo and Cahoy, 2003, pp. 284 and 287).

However, the reference interview using this form of communication often requires days to complete, delaying an answer considerably. This is unacceptable to today's student who values convenience and a rapid response (Abram and Luther, 2004). Chat, or threaded discussion, is a feature in most course management systems used to deliver distance learning, so the concept is familiar to students taking such classes. As a result, chat has gained popularity in distance learning circles, because questions and responses can occur quickly. According to Anne Lipow, it is we librarians who are remote, not the users. We need to go where they are (Lipow, 1999, *Serving the Remote User*).

Distance learners, like other students, need a broad array of services. But because distance learners may never visit a campus, they have special difficulty in interpreting the organizational structure and jargon of a university (Burnett, 2002, p. 11). In addition, various units within the university operate separate help desks. How is the user able to choose the right one? The array of possibilities is daunting (Stemper and Butler, 2001, p. 173). It is no wonder that learners may be confused and insecure so that their needs compound and frustration grows.

The University of Kansas (KU) developed a branch campus in Overland Park in 1976 to meet the educational needs of adult students in the Kansas City metropolitan area. Consequently, the KU Libraries have developed many services to meet the needs of these students at a distance from the main campus. As Web-based courses grew in number, the use of these services has spread to include all students. These services include the development and testing of an electronic request form to request the delivery of materials from the main campus.

We have also implemented a centralized e-mail reference service that consolidates smaller unit-based services to simplify requests for assistance by those unfamiliar with our units. Next, we made electronic reserve a standard service for all KU courses. Our most recent project involves the addition of chat to our other modes of delivering reference–in person, by phone, and by e-mail. With today's students, it is important to use their "devices of choice" to reach them, including chat (Abram and Luther, 2004).

THE CHARGE

In the fall of 2002, the University of Kansas (KU) Libraries formed a task force to implement a chat reference service to complement its existing e-mail reference service. The charge given by the libraries' administration was to review chat reference software packages available on the market and to recommend one to test with public service staff for implementation no later than spring semester 2003. The Coordinator for Distance Learning Information Services (Burich) and the Virtual Reference Services Librarian (Devlin) were appointed as Co-Chairs to lead the project.

Access to the chat service would not be limited to distance learners. Indeed, our experience indicates that all students are becoming distance learners. On campus our students take Web-based courses along with traditional classes. Our students move between branch campus courses and on-campus courses easily and often. As the needs of these two groups of students converge, it is no longer practical to provide different services for students based on the course delivery mechanism or a student's location. This is a common phenomenon elsewhere, too (Burich, 2004; Moyo and Cahoy, 2003, 284).

LITERATURE SEARCH

Once the task force received its charge, members began to gather information. We began by conducting an extensive literature review to gather information about the chat software that was available on the market and to learn from other institutions' experiences. The chart developed by KANAnswer, the pilot chat service developed by the Kansas State Library (see p. 84), indicated which features each software package had, along with an evaluation of the software and costs proved extremely useful (see Addendum). Bernie Sloan's "Digital Reference Services Bibliography" <http://www.lis.uiuc.edu/~b-sloan/bernie.htm> and Alexander Slade's *Library Services for Distance Learning: The Fourth Bibliography* <http://uviclib.uvic.ca/dls/bibliography4.html> provided valuable starting points in our review. A review article about changes in the technology that supports digital reference was very useful (Penka, 2003). Previous VRD Conference Proceedings also provided a wealth of information on chat-case studies, managing, staffing and training, and many other issues. The Co-Chairs attended the 4th Virtual Reference Desk 2002 Conference in Chicago to meet with various vendors and to view demonstrations of their chat software packages.

Next we gathered information about chat service organization and documentation. Once again, the KANAnswer service provided valuable guidance. Task force members also searched ERIC and Expanded Academic ASAP databases for recent reports (Broughton, 2001; Maxwell, 2002; Sears, 2001). The Abram and Luther article (2004) gave us a good perspective on the aspects of behavior among the current generation of teens as well as the implications for library services, including the use of chat and instant messaging.

Three examples of management models helped ensure that we considered all aspects of administering and managing a chat service (Lipton, 2002; MacAdam and Gray, 2000; and Stemper and Butler, 2001). Other valuable sources of information were Web pages of successful services mentioned in the literature such as the University of Wisconsin <http://www.library.wisc.edu/libraries/reference/>, University of California at Irvine <http://www.lib.uci.edu/services/ask/ask.html>, and Washington State University <http://www.wsulibs.wsu.edu/24-7/ask.html>.

The Slade bibliography and the Proceedings of the last three Off-Campus Library Services Conferences provided information about chat services that were developed for or used by distance learners.

Finally, we searched for examples of collaborative reference services in ERIC and Expanded Academic ASAP. We were fortunate to find a counterpart to KANAnswer in the Statewide Virtual Reference Project that is supported by the Washington State Library.

KANAnswer

As we began giving serious consideration to chat, the library had the opportunity to participate in a statewide chat service that was being developed as a pilot project by the Kansas State Library. This service is called "KANAnswer" <http://skyways.lib.ks.us/KSL/KLNB/KANAnswerWeb/> and its development was at least six months ahead of our own project. We knew that we could gain insight into developing and operating our chat service by participating in its. In addition, as the leading research library in the state, it was politically advantageous for KU to provide leadership through our participation.

The Co-Chairs of the task force received training in the use of that service's software (LivePerson) and were assigned service hours as operators. We, in turn, trained other operators at KU so that additional staff members could become experienced in providing chat reference service. Through our participation in this service, we gained access to their software selection process (a spreadsheet that listed more than two dozen products, software features, and thorough evaluations; see Appendix). We also received copies of service guidelines and other documentation. A discussion list was created so that KANAnswer operators could share information. When the service was implemented, it became clear that adjustments and clarifications were needed to training and to service guidelines. As the new service grew, it was improved as operators gained valuable experience. Eric Hansen's presentation at the 2003 Virtual Reference Desk Conference provides additional details about this project (Hansen, 2003).

When the term of the pilot project was completed, Burich chaired a Best Practices Task Force for the chat reference service. The report that resulted consolidated a large body of experiential information in order to recommend next steps for the project <http://skyways.lib.ks.us/KSL/KLNB/KANAnswerWeb/KANAnswerBestPractices.htm>. The report also made it clear to Burich which parts of the project we wanted to emulate at KU and those elements we wanted to approach differently.

THE VISION

The number of electronic resources available to the KU community has increased dramatically in recent years and will continue to grow. The number of online courses and traditional courses with a Web component expanded dramatically once the university began to support the use of the Blackboard course management software. With the advent of electronic reserves, federated searching and an anticipated array of digital repositories to be included in the KU Digital Library, we wanted to provide KU students and faculty access to "help" of all types quickly, electronically, and without leaving their homes or offices.

SOFTWARE SELECTION

Although the new chat service at KU was intended for the use of all students, there were several distance learning considerations that were included in its design. The first step was to determine what software features were more important so that they could guide our selection process. Because many distance learners use their telephone lines to connect to their computers, voice over-IP (voice over Internet Protocol) can be very useful in answering questions about database searching. This feature allows the user to connect to help from within the application. There is no need to disconnect and try to remember where the problem occurred. A software package that provides service at the point of need was important.

Push-pull technology is important so that the user and librarian can share Web pages. But even more important is the ability to provide contextual help by sharing an application. Not only can a user ask for help from within a database, but the librarian can see the page where help is needed and can guide the user through the solution. Experience has shown that a significant number of the requests for help from distance learners involve technical support. A University of Tennessee survey supports our experience. It found that 23% of the questions coming to their chat service requested assistance with technical issues (Berry, Casado, and Dixon, 2003, p. 9). Consequently, it would be highly desirable for application sharing in the software package we choose to include access to the desktop to determine problems involving hardware settings and software configurations, along with the ability to change those settings remotely to resolve the problem.

Because courses include a wide range of subject matter, any librarian may need to consult with colleagues to answer detailed questions. Here, the ability to transfer a call is essential. In addition, it would be highly desirable to be able to include a transcript of the conversation to the new operator. It should not be necessary for a user to repeat a request for help, especially if the call needs to be transferred more than once.

Research into effective delivery of distance learning has indicated the value of personal contact (Chou, 2001, 79; Chickering and Ehrman, 1996, 1; Mendels, 1999; Phipps and Merisotis, 1999, "Forward"). A recent study shows that social presence in a distance learning setting can contribute to the success of the course (Gunawardena and Zittle, 1997). Librarians often make one visit to a class to introduce research tools. This face-to-face contact makes a student more comfortable in contacting that librarian for future assistance. For instances in which such visits are not practical, the use of audio and video technologies within chat can be useful to put a voice and a face to the librarian providing help. In addition, the ability for the user to view video (especially streaming video tutorials) expands the usefulness of the software.

After evaluating the software features that met the needs of our students (including distant learners), we recommended Convey Systems' OnDemand software <http://www.conveysystems.com>. Contractual arrangements between Convey and OCLC to support the enhanced version of their chat service, QuestionPoint, prohibits Convey from supplying software to a library to support a chat-only service. But because we wanted it to support distance-learning applications and to offer desktop support in addition to providing a more traditional chat service, Convey agreed to work with us. For additional details about features of the Convey software, see the review by Devlin and Burich (2004).

OPERATIONAL ISSUES

One of the first issues we encountered was to name the service so that the "brand" was recognizable to users. We settled on the name "HawkHelp" because it is associated with the Jayhawk, the university's mascot. A service button was designed featuring a Jayhawk using his wing to tap a computer keyboard. The button can be placed on any Web page that is associated with the service. When users click on the service button while on a Web page, they are connected with the help desk associated with that page. In other words, clicking on the HawkHelp button from the Libraries' Distance Learning Information Services (DLIS) page connects the user with the Coordinator for Distance Learning to chat.

Similarly, clicking on the button from the online catalog connects the user to the reference service. This arrangement addresses the issue of providing service at the user's "point of need . . . where they are when they have a question" (Lipow, 1999, *Serving the Remote User;* Penka, 2003; Moyo and Cahoy, 2003, p. 289). It also provides a centralized service not obviously related to a specific service unit (Stemper and Butler, 2001, p. 175).

However, almost immediately, the service expanded beyond library chat. We provided a link to the KANAnswer statewide service mentioned earlier (see p. 84) for those not served by our service as well as to Instructional Development and Support (IDS) for those needing assistance with Blackboard courses <http://www.ku.edu/~ids/blackboard.

shtml>. Since KANAnswer does not use Convey software and IDS is not using chat at all, we simply provided links to the services they provide. We decided that all sorts of help (telephone, e-mail, chat, in-person) would fall under the umbrella of HawkHelp and use that button. The chat service became HawkHelp *LIVE*.

Once the Convey software was selected, our next step was to develop service policies and procedures, both for the students using the service and for the personnel who were staffing the service. We decided to limit the service to KU students, faculty, and staff and to authenticate our users at the point where they downloaded a small companion plug-in needed to connect to the service. This strategy would ensure that use of licensed databases met the terms of our contracts that limit access to members of the KU community.

With the assistance of our Library and Information Technology Services (LITS) staff, we designed the user interface and Web pages for the HawkHelp service <http://www2.lib.ku.edu/hawkhelp/> that outlines the various ways to request help from library staff (i.e., online, e-mail, telephone and in-person). FAQs and technical instructions were included to provide information to users about the service (e.g., scope and level of service, intended audience, scheduled hours, how to download the plug-in, types of questions that could be asked, confidentiality of transcripts, etc.). Finally, alternative Web-based reference services were listed and linked. They would provide assistance when the service was not available or when non-affiliated users needed help.

STAFFING AND TRAINING

Training staff is a key element in operating a successful online chat service. They not only need to become familiar with the software capabilities, but also need to have a basic level of computer literacy skills to feel comfortable in the online environment. Keyboarding skills and the ability to multi-task are essential. Operators also needed to absorb the culture of chat, especially the need to send frequent messages to the user to maintain contact and the use of short and simple sentences. Since the person asking the question is not visible, the operator needs to compensate for the lack of visual clues that are customary in a face-to-face interview. Books written by Lipow (2003), Ronan (2003), and Meola and Stormont (2002) offer excellent advice on training staff for chat. They provide guidelines for chat etiquette and several examples of neutral questioning for the online reference interview.

At KU, members of the task force were the first to receive training in using the Convey software. This involved a two-hour "virtual" overview and demonstration of features by the Convey technical staff. This group became the "more experienced" chat operators and served as desk-side coaches during subsequent training sessions with the rest of the library staff who were serving as operators. As more staff members were trained, several practice sessions were scheduled to provide opportunities to become familiar with the Convey software capabilities.

Training strategies employed were:

- assigning coaches or mentors to work individually with each trainee following the initial training session
- holding monthly drop-in practice sessions with training exercises
- online practice (staff would call in as users to ask a question)
- setting up an operator listserv for discussion, asking questions, and sharing experiences with the software
- providing handouts outlining chat etiquette, technical tips, and an overview of the software features
- developing pre-scripted messages for use by the operators

HawkHelp *LIVE* was launched on March 31, 2003 and was staffed 18 hours per week, Monday-Thursday from 12:30-4:30 p.m. Operators had 1 1/2 hour shifts and staffed the service in their own offices, away from the reference desk. However, anticipating that many distance education students work during the day and need research assistance after work, we soon expanded our chat schedule to include evening hours. Since its implementation, scheduled hours of operation have continued to increase and, during the spring semester 2004, the service was staffed approximately thirty hours per week.

However, staff members generally viewed chat as an added burden to already full schedules, and there was resistance to expanding hours further (see discussion by Lipton, 2002, p. 21). In the summer of 2004, in response to staff criticism of this added burden, the libraries' public services units began moving to a new service model with trained student peer assistants acting as the initial contact at the information and reference desks in Watson and Anschutz libraries. With the addition of the student assistants to staff the chat service, we will be able to expand our scheduled hours even further (MacAdam and Gray, 2000). By restructuring staffing for reference within our buildings, we can use librarians' time more productively to answer more difficult questions, thus improving access to library services and resources (Coffman, 2001, p. 25).

ASSESSMENT

Now that we have one year of usage statistics, we are starting to see some interesting trends. Data are stored on the Convey customer support Web pages and are accessible only to the Digital Reference Services Librarian (Devlin). Analysis of the data over the past year has indicated a steady increase in use since the implementation of the service. Counts of the number of "hits" to the HawkHelp LIVE Web pages outside the scheduled hours of service show interest by our users in accessing the service from 9 p.m.-midnight. A user survey has recently been added to the HawkHelp LIVE Web page to obtain additional feedback.

Continuing assessment and further evaluation will determine the extent to which the HawkHelp service is meeting its goal to provide convenient access to research assistance and other kinds of help for students and faculty in an online environment. Sears (2002) provides an example of the kinds of analysis that are possible and what might be learned from it.

AN EXPANDED VISION AND NEXT STEPS

The capabilities of Convey Systems' OnDemand software presented us with an opportunity to provide coordinated online help for several departments across campus. In effect, we wanted to use the Convey software to create an online support framework for a newly designed student services portal <https://students.ku.edu> (see also MacAdam and Gray, 2000).

The concept of a broad help service is needed because the requests we receive for help may not be connected to library services. An inability to open a library database may instead be connected to an employer's firewall protection, the institution's network, a registration problem, blocks to an account due to unpaid fees, or even to an admissions problem. The library cannot solve these problems, even if librarians are able to diagnose them. Why not include some of these other units in the service? The inability to print from a Blackboard course is also problematic and the primary reason we sought the link with the IDS Blackboard help desk. But it would be even better for IDS staff to see the problem on the screen and direct the student to the solution.

The ability to transfer a call within the Convey software to another unit would bring us closer to providing a unified help desk gateway or portal (MacAdam and Gray, 2000). Another reason to look for partners beyond our walls is that those who choose the convenience of online courses (distance learners) often are unable to locate student services such as advising, enrollment and fee payment in the same format. The Western Cooperative for Educational Telecommunications supported the development of a "Guide to Developing Online Student Services" for institutions that want to develop such services. The trend toward service consolidation and an extensive list of institutions offering varying levels of one-stop shopping are included in the "Guide" (see Krauthe and Carbajalm, 2000).

The Co-Chairs made several presentations to other units on campus that share a need to be able to communicate with remote users. Instructional Development and Support (IDS) is responsible for all Blackboard courses. Instructors are required to attend training sessions before they can begin working on a Blackboard course. However, students are given no instruction in the use of the software beyond what the instructor tells them. As a result, the library receives many requests for help in accessing materials linked to the course and for printing them. Instead of struggling to provide assistance or asking students to call IDS for help (using the link on the HawkHelp page), it would be much more efficient for the user to contact them from within their Blackboard course using the Convey software.

Another major distance learning provider is our Division of Continuing Education. Here, too, students are likely to be far from campus. The fact that the Continuing Education budget is separate from those of academic units adds to authentication problems, especially as they relate to the use of third-party databases. Some courses are for academic credit and others are not; some of their students are enrolled in degree programs, while many want a single course. Depending on the course, students may need access to library services. Students need access to Continuing Education staff members when they have questions or problems. After a demonstration of the capabilities of the software, there was keen interest among Continuing Education administrative staff in using Convey to communicate with and to help their students.

A presentation was also made to employees of other units within Information Services. In addition to the Libraries, these units include academic computing services as well as networking and telecommunications. Another presentation was made to the Vice Provost for Student Success. Units in this division include resident life, enrollment, financial aid, and the writing center. Typically, each unit has an independent help desk. Many individuals in both divisions saw the possibilities for improving student services using the Convey software.

Based on these presentations and conversations with staff members, the vision for chat expanded to include an array of service offices under an umbrella called HawkHelp. Chat reference became HawkHelp *LIVE*, and it was added to walk-in, phone, and e-mail (Ask-a-Librarian) services <http://www2.lib.ku.edu/hawkhelp/>.

Another opportunity for collaboration within Information Services appeared when the IS units began a major examination and reorganization of its operations. The planning project is called "High Velocity Change Through High Volume Collaboration: HVC^2" <http://www.ku.edu/~hvc2/>. The goal is to become more student-centered and more efficient in providing our services. To that end, several working groups have been charged with developing strategies for establishing a Quality Service Model (including Student Services, Scholar Services, and Decision-Maker Services), Collaborative Learning Spaces, and Digital Preservation. Several of these groups have recommended a centralized help desk that would serve all units while presenting a single gateway to users (see also Burnett, 2002, p. 7 and the table on p. 9). This dovetails nicely with our vision of an expanded HawkHelp service beyond the Libraries. KU is not alone in proposing this gateway approach. Burnett indicates that student services at many institutions are moving toward one-stop service centers (Burnett, 2002, p. 4).

Because of the work of HVC^2, we are considering hosting the software server on our campus so that we can control patron records. With a lease arrangement, the transcripts of all chat sessions are archived on a server at Convey. Because of the number of potential users of Convey on the KU campus, we have proposed buying an enterprise version of Convey. This arrangement provides a pool of operator "seats" that can be used by operators of the service simultaneously. Another thought being considered is purchasing information kiosks. In this way, collaborative learning spaces and places where students congregate (e.g., the union, residence halls, the administrative building) could provide help without the user having a computer handy. New features of the Convey software under development will make it even more attractive. These include secure wireless and instant messaging capabilities and a one-to-many connection for distance learning instruction that allows an instructor to interact with up to five students at a time.

BEYOND KU

KU Libraries has recently formed a partnership with Kansas State University (K-State) Libraries to provide a collaborative chat service to the users of both institutions. If the pilot project proves successful (set for the 2004 summer and fall semesters), it is anticipated that Emporia State University Library, along with other interested state academic institutions, will be brought into the collaborative service at a later date. By developing partnerships with other institutions in the State of Kansas, we will be able to expand our knowledge base and subject expertise, while providing additional hours of availability to an expanded group of users.

Another collaborative possibility being evaluated is through our membership in a library consortium called the Greater Western Library Alliance (GWLA). We have been participating in a Digital Reference Task Force to investigate the possibility of establishing a chat reference collaboration among GWLA members. With a membership of thirty academic libraries and several different types of chat software already in use, the task force is recommending that member institutions form "clusters" or small groups currently using the same software to develop partnerships. Our work with K-State (also a member of GWLA) will form such a "cluster."

As HawkHelp *LIVE* evolves into a mature online information service, the development of these and other collaborative partnerships will continue to bring a new set of challenges and rewards.

CONCLUSION

The nature of distance learning, that students and instructor are separated by time and/or place, has often forced librarians to explore ways to provide assistance electronically. This has included answering reference questions and requests for research assistance. These are the same services provided to traditional students in person, but using a different mode of delivery. When the technical capabilities of chat software improved sufficiently to provide reasonable expectations of a viable service, often it was distance learning librarians who began to experiment with the software. For instance, two years ago at the Virtual Reference Desk Conference in Chicago, many distance learning librarians who attended were searching for successful models of supplying chat services to our users.

This does not mean that "traditional" on-campus users would not benefit from chat reference service; they simply have other options readily available to them. But as institutions have developed their distance learning programs (often to stabilize or increase enrollments), this new student component provided extra urgency to the development of chat reference. It is interesting that the two partners so far identified for an expansion of HawkHelp beyond KU (K-State and Emporia State) have important distance learning programs.

The concept of providing a centralized portal for all student services using chat software will make those services available to distance learners in a coordinated fashion never before provided. By clicking on the HawkHelp button, one will receive contextual help at the point of need. It is expected that the student services portal will contribute significantly to the success of all students, including distance learners.

REFERENCES

Abram, Stephen, and Judy Luther. 2004. Born With the Chip. *Library Journal* 129, no. 8:34-37.

Berry, Teresa U., Margaret M. Casado, and Lana S. Dixon. 2003. The Local Nature of Digital Reference. *The Southeastern Librarian* 51, no. 3:8-15.

Black, James et al. 2002. *Innovation in Planning for Student Services Models That Blend High Touch With High Tech.* Ann Arbor, MI: Society for College and University Planning.

Broughton, Kelly. 2001. Our Experiment in Online, Real-Time Reference (Company Operations). *Computers in Libraries* 21, no. 4:26.

Burich, Nancy J. 2004. The Changing Face of Distance Learning: Implications for Distance Learning Librarians. *Journal of Library & Information Services in Distance Learning* 1, no. 1:99-104.

Burnett, Darlene J. 2002. Innovation in Student Services: Best Practices and Process Innovation Models and Trends. In *Innovation in Student Services: Planning for Models Blending High Touch/High Tech.* Ed. by Darlene J. Burnett and Diana G. Oblinger. Ann Arbor, MI: Society for College and University Planning, p. 3-14.

Casado, Margaret M. 2001. Delivering Library Services to Remote Students at the University of Tennessee. *Computers in Libraries* 21, no. 4:32-38.

Central Michigan University. 2000. *Ninth Off-Campus Library Services Conference Proceedings. Portland, OR, April 26-28, 2000.* Ed. by P. Steven Thomas. Mount Pleasant, MI: Central Michigan University.

Central Michigan University. 2002. *Tenth Off-Campus Library Services Conference Proceedings. Cincinnati, OH, April 17-19, 2002.* Ed. by Patrick B. Mahoney. Mount Pleasant, MI: Central Michigan University.

Central Michigan University. 2004. *Eleventh Off-Campus Library Services Conference Proceedings. Scottsdale, AZ, May 5-7, 2004.* Ed. by Patrick Mahoney. Mount Pleasant, MI: Central Michigan University.

Chickering, Arthur W., and Stephen C. Ehrmann. 1996. Implementing the Seven Principles: Technology as Lever. *AAHE Bulletin*. October:3-6. Available at: <http://www.tltgroup.org/programs/seven.html>.

Chou, C. Candace. 2001. Model of Learner-Centered Computer-Mediated Interaction for Collaborative Distance Learning. In *Annual Proceedings of Selected Research and Development [and] Practice Papers Presented at the National Convention of the Association for Educational Communications and Technology (24th, Atlanta, GA, November 8-12, 2001)*: 74-81.

Coffman, Steve. 2001. Distance Education and Virtual Reference: Where Are We Headed? *Computers in Libraries* 21, no. 4:20-25.

Convey Systems. Available at: <http://www.conveysystems.com/>.

Devlin, Frances and Nancy J. Burich. 2004. Convey System OnDemand™. *Journal of Library & Information Services in Distance Learning* 1, no. 1:122-125.

Gunawardena, C.N, and F.J. Zittle. 1997. Social Presence as a Predictor of Satisfaction within a Computer-Mediated Conferencing Environment. *American Journal of Distance Education* 11:8-26.

Hansen, Eric. 2003. KANAnswer: A Kansas Collaborative for Virtual Reference. *Virtual Reference Desk Conference 2003, San Antonio, Texas, November 17-18, 2003*. Available at: <http://www.vrd2003.org/proceedings/presentation.cfm?PID=157>.

Kansas Library Network Board. 2004. KANAnswer. Available at: <http://skyways.lib.ks.us/KSL/KLNB/KANAnswerWeb/>.

Kansas Library Network Board. 2003. KANAnswer Best Practices. Available at: <http://skyways.lib.ks.us/KSL/KLNB/KANAnswerWeb/KANAnswerBestPractices.htm>.

Krauthe, B., and Carbajal, J. 2000. *Guide to Developing Online Student Services*. Washington, D.C.: Western Cooperative for Educational Telecommunications. Available at: <http://www.wiche.edu/Telecom/resources/publications/guide1003/guide/wfdigest.htm>.

Lipow, Anne G. 1999. *Serving the Remote User: Reference Service in the Digital Environment*. Keynote Address at Information Online & On Disc 99, Sydney, Australia, 19-21 January 1999. Sydney, Australia: Australian Library and Information Association. Available at: <http://www.csu.edu.au/special/online99/proceedings99/200.htm>.

Lipow, Anne G. 2003. The Librarian Has Left the Building–But to Where? *Internet Reference Services Quarterly* 8, no. 1/2:9-18.

Lipow, Anne G. 2003. *The Virtual Reference Librarian's Handbook*. Berkeley: Library Solutions Press in association with Neal-Schuman Publishers.

Lipton, Saundra. 2002. Administration and Management. *Library Technology Reports* 38, no. 4:15-48.

MacAdam, Barbara, and Suzanne Gray. 2000. *A Management Model for Digital Reference Services in Large Institutions*. Edited by Abby S. Kasowitz and Joan Stahl. Seattle, Washington: ERIC Clearinghouse on Information & Technology.

Maxwell, Nancy K. 2002. Establishing and Maintaining Live Online Reference Service. *Library Technology Reports* 38, no. 4:1(76).

Mendels, Pamela. 1999. Courses That Teach How to Learn Online. *New York Times On the Web* October 6, 1999. Available at: <http://www.nytimes.com/library/tech99/10/cyber/education/06education.html>.

Meola, Marc, and Sam Stormont. 2002. *Starting and Operating Live Virtual Reference Services: A How-To-Do-It Manual for Librarians.* New York: Neal-Schuman Publishers.

Moyo, Lesley M., and Ellysa S. Cahoy. 2003. Meeting the Needs of Remote Library Users. *Library Management* 24, no. 6/7:281-290.

Penka, Jeffrey T. 2003. The Technological Challenges of Digital Reference: An Overview. *D-Lib Magazine* 9 no. 2. Available at: <http://www.dlib.org/dlib/february03/penka/02penka.html>.

Phipps, Ronald A., and Jamie P. Merisotis. 1999. *What's the Difference? A Review of Contemporary Research on the Effectiveness of Distance Learning in Higher Education.* Washington, D.C.: Institute for Higher Education Policy.

Ronan, Jana. 2003. *Chat Reference: A Guide to Live Virtual Reference Services.* Westport, Conn: Libraries Unlimited.

Sears, JoAnn. 2001. Chat Reference Service: An Analysis of One Semester's Data (computer file). Auburn University. *Issues in Science & Technology Librarianship* no. 32. Available at: <http://www.istl.org/01-fall/article2.html>.

Slade, Alexander. 2004. *Library Services for Distance Learning: The Fourth Bibliography.* Available at: <http://uviclib.uvic.ca/dls/bibliography4.html>.

Sloan, Bernie. 2002. Digital Reference Services Bibliography in Graduate School of Library and Information Science, University of Illinois at Urbana-Champaign. Available at: <http://www.lis.uiuc.edu/~b-sloan/digiref.html>.

Sloan, Bernie, and Sharon Stoerger. 2004. Library Support for Distance Learning. 2003. Available at: <http://alexia.lis.uiuc.edu/~b-sloan/libdist.htm>.

Stemper, James A., and John T. Butler. 2001. Developing a Model to Provide Digital Reference Services at the University of Minnesota-Twin Cities. *Reference Services Review* 29, no. 3:172-188.

University of Kansas. Libraries. 2004. Distance Learning Information Services. Available at: <http://www2.lib.ku.edu/~public/distlearn/>.

University of Kansas. Libraries. 2004. HawkHelp. Available at: <http://www2.lib.ku.edu/hawkhelp/>.

University of Kansas' Information Services. 2004. High Velocity Change High Volume Collaboration (HVC^2). Available at: <http://www.ku.edu/~hvc2/>.

University of Kansas. 2004. KYou Portal. Available at: <https://students.ku.edu>.

Viggiano, Rachel G., and Meredith Ault. 2001. Online Library Instruction for Online Students. Florida Distance Learning Reference and Referral Center. *Information Technology and Libraries* 20, no. 3:135-138.

Washington State Library. 2004. Statewide Virtual Reference Project. Available at: <http://www.secstate.wa.gov/library/libraries/projects/virtualRef/>.

APPENDIX

Virtual Reference Software Comparisons (First Cut)

Compiled November 11, 2002

After careful consideration of several virtual reference software packages, we narrowed the field to four vendors: 24/7 Reference (MCLS), Convey, DigiChat (eLibrarian), and Docutek. Then we rated each on the following criteria:

FUNCTIONALITY PROVIDED

Chat
Push pages
Send active embedded URLs
Queue management
Librarian-initiated termination
Call alert
Preset answers for FAQs
E-mail chat transcripts
Reports/statistics
Redirection or message when closed
Co-browsing/escorting
Form sharing
Call transfer
Pull pages
Searchable transcript database
Built-in survey/evaluation
Persistent buttons to "brand" service
Video
Voice over IP
Remote control
Traffic monitoring

USERS' NEEDS

No special software needed
Supports multiple browsers
Proxy compatibility
No need to register with third party
Adaptive technology compatible
Ease of use (intuitive)
Response time

APPENDIX (continued)

STAFF SUPPORT

Vendor support
Handles advanced html features (frames, Java)
Customization capabilities
Documentation
Training tools provided
Co-operation opportunities
Ease of use
Number of simultaneous operators with purchase

TECHNICAL ISSUES

Software on local or remote server?
Web or client/server local software?
Identifies patrons by IP address (re tracking and history)

COST

What is included
Cost of extra seats
Extra costs for training

LIBRARIES USING THE SOFTWARE

MISCELLANEOUS NOTES

COMPANY URL

PROS

CONS

OTHER USEFUL INFORMATION

RECOMMENDATION

One School's Experience
with Virtual Reference

Carol J. Tipton

Vanessa J. Earp

SUMMARY. In 2004, ten libraries in the Texas A&M University System began AskNow, a collaborative pilot project offering a chat-based virtual reference service to patrons. This article attempts to describe one of these libraries' experience with implementing virtual reference service. *[Article copies available for a fee from The Haworth Document Delivery Service: 1-800-HAWORTH. E-mail address: <docdelivery@haworthpress.com> Website: <http://www.HaworthPress.com> © 2004 by The Haworth Press, Inc. All rights reserved.]*

KEYWORDS. Virtual reference, chat reference, collaborative projects, academic libraries

INTRODUCTION

The latter part of the 20th century saw a rapid growth and evolution of distance learning in higher education. The need to provide access to

---

Carol J. Tipton (c-tipton@tamuk.edu) is Head of Media Services; and Vanessa J. Earp (kfvjd00@tamuk.edu) is Instructor and Reference/Education Materials Center Librarian, both at the James C. Jernigan Library, Texas A&M University-Kingsville, Kingsville, TX 78363-8202.

[Haworth co-indexing entry note]: "One School's Experience with Virtual Reference." Tipton, Carol J., and Vanessa J. Earp. Co-published simultaneously in *Internet Reference Services Quarterly* (The Haworth Information Press, an imprint of The Haworth Press, Inc.) Vol. 9, No. 3/4, 2004, pp. 99-114; and: *Internet Reference Support for Distance Learners* (ed: William Miller, and Rita M. Pellen) The Haworth Information Press, an imprint of The Haworth Press, Inc., 2004, pp. 99-114. Single or multiple copies of this article are available for a fee from The Haworth Document Delivery Service [1-800-HAWORTH, 9:00 a.m. - 5:00 p.m. (EST). E-mail address: docdelivery@haworthpress.com].

Available online at http://www.haworthpress.com/web/IRSQ
Digital Object Identifier: 10.1300/J136v09n03_08

students at a distance has been identified as a top priority for many universities and colleges. According to Green (1997), this is linked to the increased demand for access to higher education, the rising cost of higher education, the growth of information technology, and increased competition from private enterprises. As universities embraced distance learning as a means of increasing access, they frequently overlooked the importance of student access to library services. Meanwhile, academic libraries struggled with rapidly changing technologies, increasing copyright restrictions, decreasing buying power, and the growing needs of distance learners. Initially, many libraries failed to meet the needs of the distance learner; however, academic libraries recognized the impact of providing service to this emerging group of students and continue to adapt themselves.

Typically students enroll in distance learning programs because the time and/or distance constraints in their lives make it difficult, if not impossible, to attend classes on campus. Many distance students, like on-campus students, require library services to complete their course assignments. The same constraints that restrict their ability to attend class on-campus also inhibit their ability to access library resources. Students in distance learning programs need to be able to access library services the same way they access instruction–from a distance and at times that fit their schedules (Toby Levine Communications, Inc. 1992). If distance-learning programs are to be credible and successful, the distance-learning student must have the same access to library support services as the on-campus student (Lebowitz 1997).

Although the libraries recognized this need, they continue to struggle with how to best meet it. An early effort implemented by the libraries at the University of Texas tested a prototype remote reference assistance, which allowed librarians to assist distance users in real-time by remote intervention in the online search process. Despite problems with the technology used, Billings, Carver, Racine, and Tongate (1994) reported that this mode of providing reference assistance could be a model for future services.

In the 1990s, libraries began experimenting with e-mail reference. Although some patrons find response time less than desirable, numerous libraries have had e-mail reference for several years. While e-mail reference service has its benefits, i.e., a user may ask a question without going to the library, it also has a downside, i.e., the response can take anywhere from a few minutes to a few days. It is also very difficult to conduct a reference interview via e-mail.

The advent of instant messaging offered libraries an alternative to e-mail. According to Heise and Kimmel (2003), "Instant messaging, or chat, is the online tool *du jour* for millions of Americans." A recent survey conducted by Pew Internet & American Life Project found that 53 million American adults use instant messaging. Of these, 62% were born in 1977 or later (Shiu and Lenhart 2004). Many libraries use chat technology as a method to provide reference service to offer "live" or synchronous library help.

In recent years virtual or digital reference services has become a hot topic in library literature. Han and Goulding (2003) redefined the paradigm of reference services and argue that a systematic process is needed to meet the information needs of patrons. Wells (2003) determined that expanding the number of pages on which the chat request button was located increased the use of this service. Additionally, Wells stated, "It is clear that the chat request button needs to be on all heavily used Web pages and the more the better" (136). Results of a survey conducted by Johnson (2004) found that awareness and use of the online chat reference service by respondents was relatively low; however, respondents predicted that the service would be one of the most heavily used in ten years. Tennant (2003, 38) suggests the need for further study in the following:

> Many early adopters of this technology are concerned about the generally low usage levels of online reference. The problem is that it may be too early to tell whether the reason is lack of awareness on the part of the community being served, or a lack of interest. . . . we need more experiences and better measurers before we can determine where the problems lie.

VIRTUAL REFERENCE

What exactly is virtual reference? Is virtual reference the same as digital reference? And where does e-mail reference fit in? Many people have tried to define digital reference, which encompasses e-mail and virtual reference, but each definition is slightly different. When conducting a keyword search using *Wilson's Library Literature full text* and *LISA* (Library and Information Abstracts) for the term *virtual reference*, the oldest entries found are from 1990 and 1994. When searching for the term *digital reference* using *Wilson's Library Literature full text* and *LISA*, the oldest entries are from 1994 and 1997. Interestingly, neither term is listed in either database's thesauri. Is it any wonder that there may be some confusion or misunderstandings in conversations involving the terms *virtual* or *digital reference,* especially when working with university officials?

According to Janes (2003), digital reference is the provision of direct, professional assistance to people who are seeking information, at the time and point of need. That definition can be broken down even further. There are two types of digital reference: synchronous service and asynchronous service (Janes 2003). Synchronous service is generally defined as live, instantaneous interaction with a librarian via a computer, typically using chat-based software. Virtual reference is an example of synchronous service. An asynchronous service is generally defined as slower services, such as e-mail reference or Web forms.

How are libraries providing digital reference services? Numerous libraries have had e-mail reference for several years. You might say that libraries started digital reference services by offering e-mail reference in the late 1990s. However, in the past few years, the virtual reference craze has swept many libraries. Perhaps virtual reference evolved because e-mail reference services were slow, or due to numerous ways to miscommunicate, were not pleasing to all patrons. With virtual reference, the patrons get real time responses, which, in today's "google-fied" world, seems to be what patrons want (Janes 2003). Fortunately for libraries, the technology has evolved for us to provide this service.

This technology can include features like co-browsing, where a librarian can control what the patrons see on their screen. It also allows librarians to "push" Web pages. Pushing is going to a specific URL on the librarian's computer, and then sending it to the patron's computer. While co-browsing is almost instantaneous, pushing involves more steps and does not have the same instructional value. It is interesting to note that these technologies were not created by a demand for the technology from libraries; they were borrowed from the private sector. Retail companies invented these technologies for interactive online support, or similar needs.

There are many issues involved in deciding whether or not to provide virtual reference service. Libraries must consider the cost, staffing, and patrons' willingness to use the service. While the technology now exists to provide instantaneous interactions with patrons, it is anything but cheap. Cost may be one reason that libraries are opting to provide collaborated virtual reference services. The collaboration is in having a number of libraries get together and share the costs and resources involved in having a virtual reference service. The state of Colorado launched a state-wide collaborative virtual reference project, made up of public and academic libraries, titled "AskColorado" on September 2, 2003 (Colorado Virtual Library). Ohio has a collaborative virtual reference service through OhioLINK, and many other states now have similar services.

While many think that collaborative virtual reference services are the way to go, others, including Steve Coffman, raise some very interesting issues. In his article "What's Wrong with Collaborative Digital Reference," Coffman (2002) states that collaboration means compromise. Sometimes collaborating for virtual reference negatively influences local practices. You must also remember that not all libraries are created equal. If a student from a university asks a detailed reference question while a librarian from a smaller institution is on the virtual reference desk, the librarian may not be able to answer the question, and would have to refer the question to another librarian, which takes away the instantaneousness of virtual reference. When virtual reference is part of collaboration between libraries of varying sizes, it could be argued that the smaller libraries benefit far more than a large library.

TEXAS A&M UNIVERSITY SYSTEM VIRTUAL REFERENCE COLLABORATIVE

In 2003 the Texas A&M University System received a Telecommunications Infrastructure Grant (TIF Grant). The goal of this grant was to create a baseline across all Texas A&M University System Libraries for automating selected core services in support of multi-institutional collaborations. The project objective that falls into the scope of this article is the identification and provision of a virtual reference system. Additional objectives of this grant were to identify and provide a serials management system and electronic interlibrary loan capabilities.

The Texas A&M University System librarians came up with sixteen issues they wanted to discuss about virtual reference software. Those issues were:

1. What statistics was the software capable of collecting?
2. Did the software offer voice-over capabilities?
3. Could the software push Web pages?
4. Could the software push canned scripts?
5. Did the software have escort capabilities?
6. Could it provide videoconferencing?

7. Could you have multiple people in simultaneous session?
8. Was it capable of archiving questions and responses?
9. Was it ADA compliant?
10. What would the system requirements be for the library and for the patron?
11. What about upgrades?
12. Could it be customized?
13. Were training materials available?
14. What were the capabilities for privacy/patron identification?
15. What were the scheduling capabilities?
16. What was the pricing model?

The A&M System chose the Virtual Reference Toolkit®.[1] In September 2003, representatives from the System libraries attended a virtual reference planning retreat. At this retreat, the ground work was done for providing integrated virtual reference services. Many questions were addressed including such issues as authentication of patrons, the breadth and depth of the questions to be answered virtually, and how the project would be evaluated.[2] The librarians who volunteered to provide virtual reference were trained in January 2004 and the participating System libraries went live with virtual reference later that month. Ten A&M System libraries chose to participate in the AskNow Virtual Reference pilot project:

- Texas A&M University
- Texas A&M at Galveston
- Prairie View A&M University
- Tarleton State University
- Texas A&M International University
- Texas A&M University-Commerce
- Texas A&M University-Corpus Christi
- Texas A&M University-Kingsville
- Texas A&M University-Texarkana
- West Texas A&M University

All participating schools had three days of training via teleconference with a representative from Tutor.com. The training was very beneficial; it mixed PowerPoint© presentations with hands-on activities which were extremely helpful. We went live a few weeks later. Each campus was assigned a specific "shift" on the virtual reference desk. Librarians from the A&M System were to provide coverage from 7:00 a.m.-7:00

p.m. with the librarians from Tutor.com providing coverage from 7:00 p.m.-7:00 a.m. Each library placed a link on its Web page to the AskNow site.

At Texas A&M University-Kingsville, we launched our e-mail reference service at the same time as virtual reference. Upon publicizing both services, we had our administrators question what exactly the difference was. This led to having the Associate Vice President who supervises the Library pay a visit. We set up our A.V.P. on one computer in our library instruction room as a patron, while I used another computer to log onto virtual reference. By demonstrating virtual reference this way our A.V.P. was able to see simultaneously both the patron and the librarian screens. He was very impressed, and better able to explain and "sell" the new services around campus.

We do not want to give the impression that everything was rosy with the implementation of virtual reference at our campus. We did have some technical issues that had to be worked out. We'll be the first to admit that we were slightly apprehensive about joining a collaborative virtual reference project. For example, how were the librarians on one campus supposed to know what all the other campuses held? A&M Systems does not have a unified catalog. In fact, some of the campuses use different library systems. While we do share some databases, we also have individual subscriptions to others. This led to licensing issues with the database vendors, but the problem was resolved relatively quickly. We let patrons know up front that librarians from different system schools were participating in the project and they might not get a librarian from their particular school. We also stated that some questions would have to be forwarded to another library. Patrons were encouraged not to ask campus-specific questions, such as which computer labs are open 24 hours. As illustrated in Figure 1, these announcements were made right on the AskNow log-on screen along with the technical requirements.

The other big problem we had was figuring out how to allow the students to see the databases that were available to them. At our campus we added a step in which students had to authenticate before they log onto virtual reference, which allowed the student to access the database with the librarian.

So what happens when starting a shift on the virtual reference desk? We first log on via a Web page, each librarian having a unique username and password, so that statistics for both individual schools and individual librarians are available for review. After logging on, the campuses to

FIGURE 1. AskNow Log-On

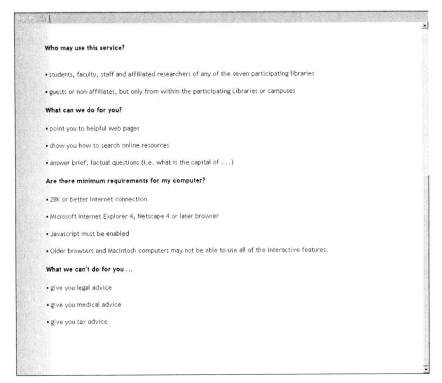

be monitored are selected. The display the librarian sees on the computer lists all of the queues (schools) being monitored (see Figure 2).

Students get a log-on page that asks for their e-mail address and question. Figure 3 shows the student log-on screen. After the student logs on, his or her school name will flash and the librarian's computer will sound an alert. A very nice feature is that each librarian can set up individual preferences on how his or her notification system works, so one librarian may like it to ding only once, while another may want it to ding every time the student sends a new message. When students come online, a simple click on their name and a window pops up indicating where the individual is from, his or her IP address, if he or she has ever used the system before, and what their question is (see Figure 4).

FIGURE 2. Queue Monitor Page

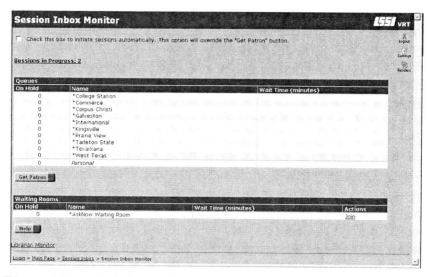

FIGURE 3. AskNow Student Log-On Screen

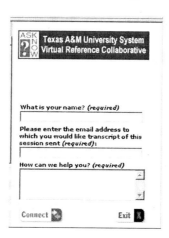

FIGURE 4. Patron Information Window

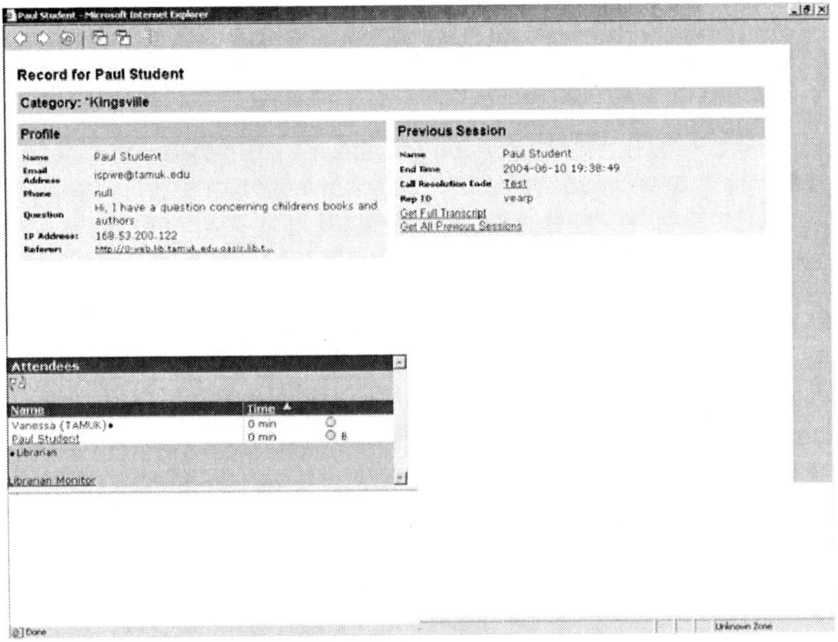

When students log on, there are two types of sessions they can enter. One is a basic session that does not allow a librarian to co-browse Web pages, and most of the interaction will involve the librarian pushing pages to the student. Patrons who use Macs or have an older operating system get put into basic sessions. The interactive session will allow their computer to co-browse. The librarian knows which type of session he or she is in by the icon that displays next to the student's name (see Figure 5). It is important to note that students are put into either basic or interactive session based on their individual computer's technology. Neither the librarians nor students can change from a basic session to an interactive session. However, the librarian can change from an interactive session to a basic session.

It is very important for librarians to always type in what they are doing before pushing Web pages or co-browsing. It is very easy to lose a student in the process. One thing we learned early on was to tell the student not to click any links. If students in a basic session click on links,

FIGURE 5. Librarian's Page When a Patron Has Logged On

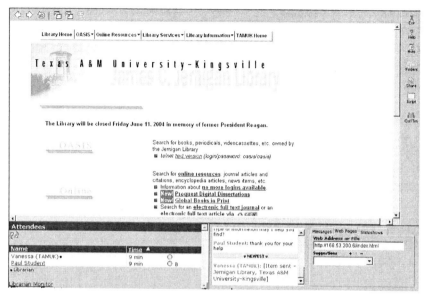

This screen is the property of Tutor.com and may not be copied or used without the permission of Tutor.com. Tutor.com is the sole provider of the Virtual Reference Toolkit for virtual reference software.

they will navigate away from the page already pushed to them. The librarian will not be able to see the screens and will not know that the student is not where he or she should be. In an interactive session, any link students click on changes not only their screen but also the librarian's screen. The session could take anywhere from 2 minutes to 20, all depending on the student's question. When the session is over, the librarian closes out of it and is asked to select a resolution code (see Figure 6). This gives the librarian the opportunity to enter how the transaction went. After the transaction is complete, both the student and librarian are sent transcripts, complete with URLs of visited Web pages (see Figure 7).

EFFECT OF VIRTUAL REFERENCE ON DISTANCE LEARNING

We are unsure how virtual reference affects our distance students. We do have statistics because Tutor.com provides many statistics. We are just not sure which students using virtual reference are distance stu-

FIGURE 6. Resolution Code Page

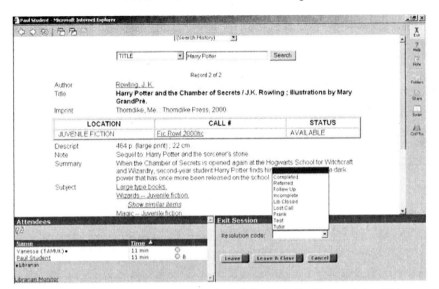

This screen is the property of Tutor.com and may not be copied or used without the permission of Tutor.com. Tutor.com is the sole provider of the Virtual Reference Toolkit for virtual reference software.

dents. One could argue that any student off campus is a distance learning student to the library because he or she is not physically in the building. When students who are affiliated with our campus (Texas A&M University-Kingsville) want to use Virtual Reference they must authenticate; one benefit of this is that we can run reports by user's IP range and see how many of our students have used the system. From January through June 2004, a total of 15 Texas A&M University-Kingsville students logged on to Virtual Reference.

While we are not sure how implementation of virtual reference impacted our distance learning students specifically, we know it has the potential to be extremely useful in the future. The Texas A&M University System offers distance learning courses worldwide. Additionally, the System operates the Trans Texas Video Network (TTVN), a two-way, multi-point digital videoconferencing system with classrooms at 11 System campuses and a variety of other locations. In addition to TTVN, Texas A&M University-Kingsville also has a branch or off-campus site in San Antonio, Texas A&M University-Kingsville System Center San Antonio. Currently this site is located at the Palo Alto Community Col-

FIGURE 7. AskNow Virtual Reference Session Transcript

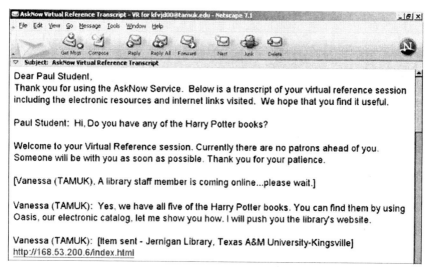

lege campus and System Center students use the library at Palo Alto Community College. While the Palo Alto librarians provide wonderful service to our students, we cannot expect them to provide detailed instructional services and assistance, and we have identified this as something we have to devote more time and energy to.

Virtual reference is a first step in providing stronger support and more immediate assistance over a long distance that we had not easily been able to provide before. Having A&M System librarians available daily to assist these students makes them feel that they are truly a part of the A&M University Kingsville campus. We should keep in mind that while students may log on to virtual reference for a quick answer to a question, it is also an opportunity for librarians to provide instruction. This is similar to the quick instruction provided when students approach the Reference Desk with a research question. Many of us have answered the phone at the reference desk to find a student on the other end unable to find something or access the online databases. This is a common telephone reference question on our campus. This can be frustrating for students if they don't have a cell phone to call us with or DSL so they cannot actually do the steps while we are talking to them. If they log on to Virtual Reference, this is no longer a problem. They not only get our typed instructions, but they also see on their computer screen what we are doing. Our software even has the capability of letting the students see what we are typing into the search box in the OPAC or databases as we are typing it. At the end, students even get e-mailed a transcript of their Virtual Reference session that they can refer to the next time they have a question. This software opens up the possibility of doing online training with these students. Before January, this wasn't even a dream. The current software for online teaching, WebCT and Blackboard, really are not structured for one or two short sessions of library instruction; they are geared more for a semester-long class or self-paced instruction.

This service has not caught on at our university. Our hope is that in the future these students will benefit from our virtual reference service, not just by being able to talk with a librarian in real time, but also by allowing us more flexibility with our teaching of distance learning students. Although some studies are suggesting that patrons would rather use e-mail reference than virtual reference (Lankes and Shostack 2002), our belief is that there has not been a strong and concerted effort to advertise and explain the service. Perhaps we are offering a service the students do not really want or need. We see all the potential and possibilities, but only time will tell if it will succeed or fail.

While the A&M System purchased and implemented the Virtual Reference Toolkit, each institution has had to deal with problems as they arise. A virtual reference coordinator at College Station is in charge of the project while each school has a virtual reference manager who coordinates the virtual reference at their site. Before each new semester, the participating A&M System libraries send the virtual reference coordinator the names of the librarians who will be providing virtual reference service, the total number of hours they can commit to virtual reference, and which hours they would prefer to be scheduled. The virtual reference coordinator takes all this information and creates the system's virtual reference schedule for the semester. The virtual reference shifts last from two to four hours depending on what each school can handle. The librarians at College Station provide the most coverage.

The librarians providing virtual reference service from the different institutions communicate via e-mail and telephone. Additionally, we set up a listserv to provide for exchanging ideas and posting questions. When one library has a problem it contacts the virtual reference coordinator. If the coordinator cannot solve the problem, the library with the problem contacts Tutor.com.

One thing that has made this project difficult is the autonomy maintained by each institution. The Texas A&M University System is a loosely coupled system with each institution retaining a lot of independence in daily operations and the ability to choose to participate in System initiatives to some extent. Each institution has different technologies in place. Indeed, the libraries within the System have different integrated library systems and network technology; this has led to the different schools having unique issues while implementing virtual reference.

The most recent problem that most schools encountered involved the use of SFX when in a virtual reference session. When a librarian was in a virtual reference session and clicked on the SFX link the patron would be lost. That problem has been solved; however, what the librarian does in the SFX pop-up screens cannot be viewed by the patron.[3]

A persistent concern is finding appropriate resources to help students from other A&M System Schools. While we do have some consortium agreements for certain resources, there are other resources that are specific to each school. This also arises when a patron asks a question specific to a particular library or institution, such as what computer labs on campus are open 24 hours a day. While the librarian can answer this question, it might take some time to navigate around to find the appropriate answer.

From January through June 2004, A&M Virtual Reference received a total of 1,451 questions. Of these, librarians at Texas A&M University-Kingsville received 115. Librarians at College Station received the majority of questions followed by Tarleton State and West Texas. Monday through Friday seemed to be the busiest with an average of 245 questions asked on those days from January to June of 2004.

At this point it would be premature to try to interpret how virtual reference has impacted the A&M System and its students. Perhaps after a full year of providing Virtual Reference Service, an in-depth study could be undertaken to see just how much impact Virtual Reference has had on the students and librarians in the Texas A&M University System.

NOTES

1. Tutor.com is the sole provider of the Virtual Reference Toolkit. Tutor.com, 40 Fulton Street, 9th Floor, New York, NY 10038. All screens in this article reprinted by permission of Tutor.com.

2. Wendi Arant-Kasper, e-mail message to Vanessa J. Earp, May 11, 2004.

3. Wyoma vanDuinkerken (Administrator for Virtual Reference Texas A&M Concortia), e-mail message to Vanessa J. Earp, September 17, 2004.

REFERENCES

Billings, H., I. E. Carver, J. D. Racine, and J. Tongate. 1994. Remote reference assistance for electronic information resources over networked workstations. *Library Hi Tech* 12 (1): 77-86.

Coffman, S. 2002. What's wrong with collaborative digital reference? *American Libraries* 33 (11): 56-58.

Colorado Virtual Library. "AskColorado–Anytime! Collaborative Virtual Reference Service from Colorado's Libraries," <http://www.aclin.org/reference/> (Accessed June 12, 2004).

Green, K. C. 1997. Money, technology, and distance education. *On the Horizon: The Environmental Scanning Publication for Educational Leaders* 5 (6): 1-16.

Han, L. and A. Goulding. 2003. Information and reference services in the digital library. *Information Services and Use* 23: 251-262.

Heise, J. and S. Kimmel. 2003. Reading the river: The state of the art of real-time virtual reference. *Internet Reference Services Quarterly* 8 (1/2): 1-7.

Janes, J. 2003. *Introduction to reference work in the digital age*. New York: Neal Schuman.

Johnson, C. M. 2004. Online chat reference: Survey results from affiliates of two universities. *Reference & User Services Quarterly* 4 (33): 237-247.

Lankes, R. D. and P. Shostack. 2002. The necessity of real-time: Fact and fiction in digital reference systems. *Reference & User Services Quarterly* 41 (4): 350-355.

Lebowitz, G. 1997. Library services to distant students: An equity issue. *The Journal of Academic Librarianship* 23: 303-308.

OhioLINK Ohio Library and Information Network, <http://www.ohiolink.edu> (Accessed June 12, 2004).

Shiu, E. and A. Lenhart. 2004. *How Americans Use Instant Messaging*. Pew Internet and American Life Project: Washington, D.C. Available at <http://www.pewinternet.org/pdfs/PIP_Instantmessage_Report.pdf> (Accessed: September 17, 2004).

Tennant, R. 2003. Revisiting digital reference. *Library Journal* 128 (1): 38-39.

Texas A&M University System Virtual Reference Collaborative. "AskNow Texas A&M University System Virtual Reference Service" <http://vrl-live01.lssi.com/wcscgi/CDM.exe/tamus?SS_COMMAND=CUST_SUP&Category=COLLEGE STATIONINTERACT> (Accessed June 12, 2004).

Toby Levine Communications, Inc. 1992. *Going the distance: A handbook for developing distance degree programs using television courses and telecommunications technologies*. Alexandria, VA: Annenberg/CPB Project and Public Broadcasting Service, Adult Learning Service. (ERIC Documents Reproduction Service No. ED 356 760).

Wells, C. A. 2003. Location, location, location: The importance of placement of the chat request button. *Reference & User Services Quarterly* 43 (2): 133-137.

Does Anyone Need Help Out There?
Lessons from Designing Online Help

Judith M. Arnold
Floyd Csir
Jennifer Sias
Jingping Zhang

SUMMARY. In order to provide online help for distance students, as well as the increasing number of on-campus students who regularly access library resources, a team of librarians from the Marshall University Libraries created an online library assistance site (HELP). This site brings together traditional print handouts, FAQs, online subject guides, course-specific guides, learning modules, and instructional videos in one central location where users can get assistance with library-related questions at their point of need. This article discusses the rationale for developing the site, the process of creating it and incorporating user input, ongoing content development, the impact upon the Libraries' Web site, and future development plans. *[Article copies available for a fee from The Haworth Document Delivery Service: 1-800-HAWORTH. E-mail address: <docdelivery@haworthpress.com> Website: <http://www.HaworthPress.com> © 2004 by The Haworth Press, Inc. All rights reserved.]*

Judith M. Arnold (arnoldj@marshall.edu) is Reference and Extension Services Librarian; Floyd Csir (csir@marshall.edu) is Web Librarian; Jennifer Sias (sias3@marshall.edu) is Reference and Instruction Librarian; and Jingping Zhang (zhangj@marshall.edu) is Digital Resources and Automation Librarian, all at Drinko Library, Marshall University, 1 John Marshall Drive, Huntington, WV 25755.

[Haworth co-indexing entry note]: "Does Anyone Need Help Out There? Lessons from Designing Online Help." Arnold, Judith M. et al. Co-published simultaneously in *Internet Reference Services Quarterly* (The Haworth Information Press, an imprint of The Haworth Press, Inc.) Vol. 9, No. 3/4, 2004, pp. 115-134; and: *Internet Reference Support for Distance Learners* (ed: William Miller, and Rita M. Pellen) The Haworth Information Press, an imprint of The Haworth Press, Inc., 2004, pp. 115-134. Single or multiple copies of this article are available for a fee from The Haworth Document Delivery Service [1-800-HAWORTH, 9:00 a.m. - 5:00 p.m. (EST). E-mail address: docdelivery@haworthpress.com].

KEYWORDS. Online help, Web site design, streaming video, FAQs

INTRODUCTION

Assistance to online users, whether they are distance learning students or campus users who do not physically visit the library, is an important dimension of a library's service. Whether that assistance involves answering a specific question or delivering a strategy for finding that answer (reference service), or teaching the user how to use a library resource (instruction), the goal is the same: to help users find the information they are seeking. Increasingly, a library's Web site is assuming a greater role in the reference/instruction transaction between the library and the user, and for online users, it is often their sole means of interacting with the library.

Because many of these primarily online users may use the Web site and a library's resources physically removed from in-person assistance, we have a responsibility through the Web site to offer them a way of obtaining online reference help or instruction. Not surprisingly, "Help" is a feature found on most Web sites, and common components of a library's online help often include Ask a Librarian (frequently an interactive opportunity with a librarian through e-mail and/or chat reference service) or more static help designed for independent use, such as FAQs, tutorials, subject and course guides, citation style guides, virtual tours and maps, library videos, and database searching help.

Library literature indicates that users want to be independent, self-reliant, and empowered to help themselves. In an article discussing interviews that contributed to development of the LibQUAL instrument, Cook and Heath report the significance of self-reliance to users;[1] similarly, the national LibQUAL norms for 2003 reveal that Personal Control–the desire to be an independent user–claims the highest desired mean among all of the study's dimensions.[2] A recent LibQUAL study (2003) at Marshall University supports these findings. The Personal Control responses (ability to navigate library resources independently) to survey items "A library Web site enabling me to locate information on my own" and "Easy-to-use access tools that allow me to find things on my own" and "Making information easily accessible for independent use" received desired means of 8.18, 8.16, and 8.16 respectively (on a 9-point scale), and were among the highest user priorities in the study.[3] While valuing independence, if users do choose to seek assistance, the literature has shown that they want it at their point of need, not well ahead of time.[4]

Another expression of the desire to be an independent user may be a reluctance to seek help. Recent articles on the usability of library Web sites have supported the experience of Trevor Grayling in "Fear and Loathing of the Help Menu: A Usability Test of Online Help" by observing that users will avoid help menus at all cost.[5] When designing their help pages, the University of Arizona named them "Tips" to avoid the term "Help" because it suggests that the user has failed.[6] Similarly, Battleson, Booth, and Weintrop (2001) studied usability of the University of Buffalo Libraries' site and found that "while there was little direct feedback as to why 'Need Help' was not regularly selected, it was apparent that when this link was chosen, students were not at all satisfied with the information obtained."[7]

A survey by Liu and Yang (2004) at Texas A&M University revealed that for distance education students, the availability of help ranked at the bottom of the factors that these users considered important when they selected information sources.[8] Referring to user behavior in the library, Barbara Fister writes of the "Fear of Reference," describing avoidance of help and the reference desk,[9] recalling the earlier findings of Constance Mellon's 1986 study on library anxiety where students avoided asking for help because they feared they would show their ignorance of the library.[10]

Despite this evidence that users prefer to be independent and tend to avoid help, libraries invest a great deal of time and other resources into making Web-based help available and attractive. While there are abundant discussions on developing and establishing many of these help components, such as virtual reference, subject guides, and tutorials, there is little in the literature that addresses the overall design or effectiveness of Help sites. Grayling (1998), mentioned earlier, found that his users (Ph.D. chemists) preferred popup and dialog boxes for help.[11] Faiks and Hyland (2000) demonstrate card sorting as a method to establish the organizational framework for an online help system. In their initial study, the project team found the avoidance phenomenon at work and while the team "realized that it could not change aversion to online help in general, it could try to create a more user-friendly system."[12] Through the card sort technique, they were able to create the Table of Contents structure for their Help pages. An earlier article by Byrne et al. (1996) addresses the difficulties in creating help documentation both in print and online by suggesting guidelines for writing help documentation.[13]

THE BIRTH OF HELP CENTRAL

Marshall University, a Master's College and Universities I institution, has a student population of approximately 16,000 students, with as many as 1,500 students taking online courses in this highly rural state. Following a re-design of the Libraries' home page in summer 2003, a Marshall University Libraries' team, consisting of the Web Librarian, Digital Resources and Automation Librarian, Instruction Librarian, and Reference and Extension Services Librarian identified the need to organize all existing reference and instructional assistance into a single location on the Web site. Perhaps falling into the "librarians know best" syndrome described by Dickstein and Mills,[14] the team envisioned a centralized Help page as an effective way to consolidate all types of help and offer a convenient, one-stop method of accessing it. They targeted first-year students and online users as primary audiences. The team hypothesized that these groups would appreciate the ease of finding a variety of help in one single, predictable location.

The impetus for creating a Help section on the Libraries' Web site was partially influenced by a decision to create an FAQ (Frequently Asked Questions) Web site. The FAQ site offers a menu of 11 categories that provide quick answers to commonly asked questions. Examples include "How long can I check out a book?" and "What are the library's hours?" The FAQ resides in an SQL database that can be edited by librarians; however, this model is structured around library functions so does not lend itself to learning situations where students need more in-depth knowledge.

The developing Help site was also influenced by an existing html page that had listed links to several pages of "General Research Help." Beginning with these established pages of subject guides, print handouts, and Library FAQs as a base, the development team formulated a long-term plan to transform this basic Help page into an online assistance site with learning modules and streaming video.

Experience with students shows that most do not have general research questions, so using the phrase "General Research Help" did not seem likely to appeal to them. Most students have specific needs, so a centralized sub-Web site made more sense. The site was initially titled "Help Central" and linked from a Help button in the Assistance category on the Libraries' homepage. Plans for development included these steps:

1. Identify all current online content that could serve as Help
2. Identify print content (handouts, pathfinders, etc.) that could serve as Help
3. Convert print content to digital format
4. Organize content into categories
5. Develop a graphically pleasing Web site
6. Expand content to include mini-tutorials and streaming video
7. Refine, re-categorize, and redevelop as needed

During implementation of these steps, a format problem arose. Because some Help content was in PDF as well as html format, signaling the difference posed a challenge. Providing a link to a PDF handout or a Web-based subject guide without indicating format could prove troublesome for users without Adobe Reader software, and Web courtesy requires displaying the format type so that users are not surprised or frustrated after clicking. For some topics, the same content was available in different formats to allow for varying student needs and purposes. Distinctive graphical buttons were created to clarify the mode of accessing Help content in PDF, Web (html) and video (wmv) formats. The new Help page, Library Help Central ("Get Your Library Questions Answered Here"), used these graphical buttons (WEB VIDEO PDF) to define the available formats of ten categories of Help, such as Database Guides, Subject Guides, and Evaluating Sources, among others. The design featured a bright yellow background with black accent bars, a color scheme that demanded attention like traffic caution signs.

With categories and all help topics crowding a single page, excessive scrolling and information overload quickly prompted a redesign in January 2004. With fewer choices and interactive mouse-over effects (see Figure 1), users could move the cursor across different headings and see the corresponding information displayed in the center panel.

DESIGN REFINEMENTS

While this design was an improvement and momentarily satisfying, the team's continuing desire to improve the appeal of the page and to accommodate the rapidly developing video and tutorial content prompted them to re-think the Help page design once again; in June 2004 a newly designed Help page (see Figure 2) re-organized and re-labeled many of the original components.

FIGURE 1. Help Central Revised

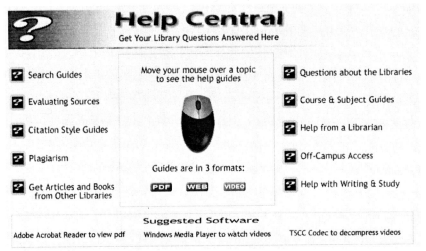

Labels that more clearly represented the evolving content and that employ terms that students recognize were substituted. Two headers, each with four subcategories, replaced the listing of 10 randomly organized categories. "Quick Answers" was added as a way for students to get brief instructions, such as "Citing Papers" and "Frequently Asked Questions." The second header, "Learn More," leads to more in-depth research assistance offered by subject guides and mini-tutorials.

Soothing earth-tones replaced the "cautionary" yellow and black color scheme to convey a welcoming atmosphere. A half-circle background was placed beneath the left navigation menu to emphasize it and to make it more inviting. In the center, several rotating professional stock photos display generally happy people with outstretched arms (as if they didn't know the answer) to convey to students that not having the answer and asking for help are acceptable.

At this point, though aware of the advisability of usability testing, librarians were nonetheless still dictating both design and content for students. An article, "Going Mental: Tackling Mental Models for the Online Library Tutorial," by Veldorf and Beavers (2001) caught their attention and presented a compelling argument for re-examining the "librarian knows best" model. This article explores the disconnect between student and librarian mental models and analyzes how the disconnect affects the

FIGURE 2. Current Help Page
http://www.marshall.edu/library/help/default.asp

Reprinted with permission.

effectiveness of library tutorials. Through a series of tests, Veldorf and Beavers found, as one example, that "while students tend to view library research as a means to an end, librarians tend to teach research as if it is an end in itself."[15]

In an effort to diminish this disconnect, in June 2004 the development team solicited student input through an informal survey of five questions about use of online or Web-based help. Responses from 14 students provided guidance in refining the design of the page. Almost all of the students preferred face-to-face interaction with a librarian rather than using e-mail, live chat, telephone, or online help on the Web, a revelation that underscored the importance of including Reference hours and contact information that would lead to live assistance. Student feedback supported the page and site terminology; the labels "Help," "How do I . . . " and "Ask a Librarian," the various terms used to lead into the Help page and topics, were ones that students preferred. The most popular topics for help suggested by the survey respondents were: "How to search for articles," "How to search for books," "How to evaluate sources," and "How to cite sources," topics that are already covered in the Help site. In response to preferred format for the help, students verified the need for Web-page guides, tutorials, printable handouts, and videos.

When asked about the "best" and "worst" of the page, a sampling of responses praised the simplicity and look: "Looks easy and helpful," "Many different topics in help–very helpful!" "It is easy to find the information that you have questions about." The "least liked" features included a few unappealing graphics, which were subsequently removed. Comments also suggested annoyance with the graphical format buttons (WEB VIDEO PDF) and a need to simplify the display even more. The buttons were very colorful, but in the context of this latest design they contrasted too much with the more subdued earth-tones. As a result, simple text links replaced the graphical format buttons.

This newly re-designed Help site has already shown a substantial increase in use. In June 2004, there were 577 page views for the Help homepage. For February 2004, at a time when considerably more students were using the Libraries' Web site, only 418 page views were recorded.

IMPACT ON WEB SITE DEVELOPMENT

A need to display this new Help page more prominently prompted modifications to the Libraries' homepage (see Figure 3). A link to Help was added to the Libraries' homepage in the top navigation bar that resides on all pages, replacing FAQ (Frequently Asked Questions), since FAQ was moved into the Help site. In addition, a new "How do I . . ." button was added under the "Assistance" category. Major help topics, such as "use databases off campus" and "cite books and articles," along with several others, are offered in a pull-down menu; each of these selections links into the appropriate portion of the Help site.

Linking the Help pages more prominently from the newly revised homepage redesign led to considering ways to embed Help links within other areas of the Web site. Future refinement of the database pages will involve inserting links to Help topics that pertain to specific databases, a strategy recommended in an article by Wells (2003) on the importance of the location of the chat button.[16] The goal is to catch the attention of students at their point of need for citation or searching help by placing help links next to a database URL.

According to a sampling of Web statistics and usability testing from various academic libraries, Reeb and Gibbons (2004) reveal that due to mental models that differ from those of the librarians designing the subject guides, students fail to connect their information queries with them.[17] To be truly useful, the article suggests, the guides must be la-

FIGURE 3. Marshall University Libraries' Homepage
http://www.marshall.edu/library

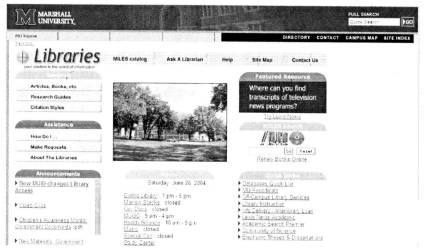

Reprinted with permission.

beled with meaningful terminology and available through a variety of access points within contexts where students are likely to need assistance; linking guides from appropriate database listings could increase their value.[18] Re-examining the role of subject guides in the Help site has also prompted the development team to revise the subject guide template and standardize content guidelines as well.

Other ways to extend the functionality of the Help site can be extrapolated from recommendations by Reeb and Gibbons; these include embedding Help topics in the online catalog, in databases, and in online course environments such as WebCT or Blackboard.[19] The ability to search the Help site specifically would also add significantly to its functionality. Continued student interviews and usability testing should keep the design on track.

CONTENT DEVELOPMENT

As the site's appearance evolved, so did its content. Employing the unique ability of the Internet and using a Web page to continually update and refine content and design, Marshall University Libraries' Help site continues to be a work in progress. Starting with some of the traditional forms of help–reference service, pathfinders transformed into Web-based subject guides, mini-tutorials in the form of online learning modules–the site began developing some of the common components of an online Help site.

VIRTUAL REFERENCE

Marshall University had already begun to offer online reference assistance, with an e-mail service that began in 1996. This Ask a Librarian e-mail page set the precedent for the centralized Help site, and in 2003 a Chat Reference component was introduced. Advertising Chat Reference was done through a text graphic on the Libraries' homepage in May 2003, and in spring 2004 an animated Flash advertising replaced the graphic.

Much of the literature on virtual reference is devoted to discussions of specific systems, surveys of use, case studies of individual libraries setting up digital reference, privacy issues, and analyses of the types of questions.[20] An entire issue of *The Reference Librarian* (Issue 79/80) is dedicated to the concerns of virtual (or digital reference) and explores issues such as the history and future of the service, communication strategies, and evaluation and analysis of use, as well as several case studies.[21] Many articles focus on the differences/similarities between virtual and traditional reference and how it is being implemented at various libraries; there is limited discussion of the service as a form of "help" and how to design it so that it is apparent to users.

One exception is an article by Duncan and Fichter (2004), who point out that few articles report user involvement in the creation of the service. In their article they discuss how, inspired by the model of the National Cancer Institute, they solicited user feedback to help label and locate a virtual reference service. Through preference testing they found that the term "Ask a Librarian" was the most recognizable to users.[22] After having placed links to the live reference service "on many pages of the Web site, particularly those where users might experience difficulty"[23] they experienced some success in usability testing when three out of five users actually found and clicked on the Ask a Librarian service; a fourth user saw the button but refused to use it, demonstrating the avoidance of help phenomenon.[24] Their article offers many excellent lessons on user behavior as well as a good model for applying usability studies in the design of online systems.

Organizing the virtual reference component of the Help site required consolidating all forms of reference service into a single entry point, giving users the option to select the mode for their reference question: phone, e-mail, or chat. The Ask a Librarian page (see Figure 4) was a redesign of a much simpler Reference Department page that had listed librarian e-mail addresses and phone numbers. To it was joined the existing Ask a Librarian e-mail service, and with the development of the FAQ and the promotion of Chat with a Librarian service emerged a need to bring these services under one umbrella. The Ask a Librarian page functions as a companion to the Help page, in that it offers the services the Librarians provide directly to students while the Help page features stand-alone assistance.

The major goals for this page included: no scrolling so information is not hidden; an appealing and easy to use interface; and professional and friendly looking graphics and photos. "Effective customer service" was the message to be conveyed. Macromedia Fireworks MX was used to create the site with rollover images. Important links to e-mailing a librarian and chat with a librarian were featured on the opening screen.

Since Help and Ask a Librarian function as companion pages, offering both side by side on the top navigation bar signals their importance to students. Both terms are generally used in libraries, so choosing them meant students were more likely to understand their purpose, a principle

FIGURE 4. Current Ask a Librarian Page
http://www.marshall.edu/library/help/default.asp

Reprinted with permission.

that the student feedback verified. Adding them to all of the Libraries' Web pages was made easy by Server Side Includes (SSI) for the standard header and footer, originally set up in the summer of 2003 during a site-wide restructuring. (In order to implement SSI, all of the pages needed their extensions changed from .htm or .html to .asp.) Each page points to one html file to pull the header and footer information, thereby making it easier to make changes across the site.

SUBJECT GUIDES

Web-based subject guides, a variant of the print pathfinder, are another popular help component that can assist online users. In a 2000 survey by Morris and Grimes, 88% of librarians responding reported having Web-based guides available[25] and feel that subject guides help students begin their research with quality print and Internet resources even while librarians may not really know if or how students are using them.[26] Some libraries have transformed the Web-based subject guide from a static html format to database-driven Web sites where users can select or type in topics and receive a customized listing of resources, such as the Research Wizard at the University of Nebraska-Omaha described by Hein and Davis (2002);[27] however, as a 2003 article by Magi reports, these research tools also introduce a complexity that students may find more difficult and less helpful to use than a print pathfinder.[28] In her study of Canadian university subject guides, Dahl (2001) argues for guidelines and cautions that to be useful the guides need to be easy to find on the library's Web site,[29] a point reinforced by Reeb and Gibbons (2004), who also emphasize that many usability studies show that students do not use them.[30]

Like most libraries, the Marshall University Libraries have offered numerous paper pathfinders on a wide variety of subjects, providing concise, directed information about library-based resources in specific subject areas. Updating the pathfinders, however, has always been an issue, particularly with the inclusion of Internet-based resources, URLs, and suggested Web sites. Transforming pathfinders into Web-based subject guides enabled an easy and more affordable way to update as well as a way to assist students in new ways by embedding hyperlinks, a particularly important feature for distance students who can simply click on the link to be taken to an important resource.

The Libraries' subject and course guides range from general ones, such as how to determine if a periodical is popular or scholarly, how to do research in biological sciences using the Libraries' resources, and how to find literary criticism to course-specific guides such as SFT630: Current Literature & Research in Occupational Safety & Health. At present the site offers nearly fifty guides with more in development. In addition to the appropriate database links, these guides lead students to pre-configured subject searches in the catalog, to significant online journals, valuable Web sites, and relevant print resources. Contact information for the appropriate librarian is also a standard component of the subject or course guide. In addition to serving as online help, these guides are frequently used in library instruction sessions.

TUTORIALS AND LEARNING MODULES

Librarians also sought ways to assist and instruct off-campus students, often at remote sites that lacked the requisite technology to show students how to access and search library databases and other scholarly resources. That need and challenge gave birth to another method of developing and delivering instructional assistance: the learning module.

Web-based tutorials are a popular and burgeoning area of online assistance. The LOEX site registers over 60 examples,[31] and a recent article by Hollister and Coe identifies online tutorials as one of the three current topics in the library instruction literature.[32] Though not exactly identical to a help page, where the user looks for quick answers, tutorials contain a curriculum and a sequenced plan.[33] Most tutorials are developed as instruments of information literacy instruction and are often designed to be assigned, rather than a stand-alone tool for the independent user seeking help on how to do research.

Nancy Dewald examined nineteen tutorials for "good practice" and found that 68% could be used independently, but she noted that "students will have more incentive to study the tutorial carefully when they know they will be required to produce something as a result of what they have learned."[34] In their usability testing of their QuickStart tutorial, Veldorf and Beavers (2001) also found that "Unless incorporated into a course curriculum, grading, and instructor expectations, the majority of student testers made it clear that they would not likely use the tutorial."[35] While doing usability testing for a tutorial on searching for books, Tempelman-Kluit and Ehrenberg (2003) noted that "we learned that our users were not interested in committing much time to lengthy tutorials, and wanted succinct information on how to use the library quickly."[36] So, while the idea of a stand-alone tutorial for help may be appealing, it would require a highly motivated user to take advantage of it. Tutorials seem best suited to be assigned in combination with classroom or other instruction. Instruction librarians surveyed by Hollister and Coe agree. While they consider online tutorials effective instructional tools, they add that tutorials need to be supported with other instructional methods.[37]

The concept of a learning module using a Web-based PowerPoint slide show offers a shorter, more specifically focused tool that students can use with a minimum investment of time. The team developed a series of PowerPoint slide shows that were easily transformed into Web slide shows. Rather than the usual text-heavy slide shows, these modules are highly visual, using numerous screen shots, photos, and graphics to present small pieces of information simply. Topics such as renewing an ILL book or retrieving online articles are some examples of the learning modules that were developed.

Another form that the learning module took was the video demo. When librarians worked in off-campus instructional settings without live connectivity, they were challenged to create presentations that showed students how to search databases. The software SnagIt captured live screen shots showing how to access and search databases and other resources via the Marshall University Libraries' Web page; these short video clips were then embedded within a PowerPoint slide show. These presentations could be saved to CD, shown to classes meeting at remote centers, and even mass produced for distribution to students who wished to review them from home or office computers. As with traditional paper guides, however, updating these instructional videos on CDs became a legitimate concern. Even if librarians produced revised CDs, there would be outdated information on the CDs still in the hands of students who attended earlier sessions.

BEGINNING WITH INFORMATION DELIVERY

Nevertheless, working with video captures whetted the appetites of librarians looking for other means to offer effective online instruction and assistance. This experience opened doors, possibilities, and minds. Librarians began to consider offering short, "how-to" video demos online via the Libraries' Web site.

Information delivery service (IDS)–the topic of frequent queries from distance students and an "unknown" service for most undergraduates (particularly freshmen)–was selected as the first Help area to be expanded. Working in collaboration with the IDS staff, the development team identified topics to be addressed:

- How to set up an IDS account
- How to order items from IDS
- How to retrieve online articles from IDS
- How to renew interlibrary loan books

In deciding how to present the information, the team considered the advantages of offering a range of media to attract different learning styles and to compensate for a variety of users and equipment. The first topic, setting up the account, was created using Camtasia Studio software in December 2003 as a video demo consisting of video screen captures enhanced with audio and annotation. For those who might not be able to access video, this topic was also available as a PowerPoint slide show, and as a printable handout in PDF format. The remaining topics were produced as PowerPoint slideshows, and are gradually being created as video demos using Camtasia. In the development process, it was discovered that creating the slideshows first streamlined the video demo production by offering a "readymade" script for taping.

However, the creation of the Information Delivery Services video demo introduced still more challenges:

- Screenshots and videos of less than ideal Web pages, although helpful, still force students to interact with these inadequately designed pages after the video is over.
- Redesigning the Web pages would build a better interface, which should diminish the need for help.

The impetus for re-design of the IDS homepage was born out of this realization. The original design of the IDS homepage was a confusing mix of bright colors and too many text instructions. This made it difficult to know where to begin. Thus, creating a large "First Time User Registration" button was a top priority. A photo of an approachable student working on the computer was incorporated to welcome visitors.

Tangential evidence suggests that this new design has made a difference for the better. The IDS office has seen a 50% reduction in telephone calls due to providing a range of media to attract different learning styles and redesigning the Web page. (The office now receives only two to three telephone calls a week from students and faculty needing customer service.) In addition, more off-campus students are using the service, but it is not known if this is directly due to the page redesign or some other factors, such as a cessation of some full-text journals. Compared to the previous spring semester, IDS requests from distance students more than doubled in the spring 2004 semester.

TRANSITION TO STREAMING VIDEO

The next step, to add library-themed short films to the Help site, was logical and exciting! The team of librarians worked with student assistants and graduate assistants to develop short videos focused on library situations that undergraduate students often encounter. Librarians wrote scripts and shared them with the team of students, who edited them and inserted language that would be more natural and believable to the typical undergraduate. Librarians became directors and camera operators who had to consider lighting, sound, and spatial issues, and who also had to learn to appreciate the intricate, sometimes tedious, and time-consuming work of the video editor as they toiled for hours on editing what would become a three-minute video. Videos were shot with a Canon Elura 20 MC Digital Video Camcorder and a Panasonic PV-GS50S Digital Video Camcorder, which use MiniDV cassettes. Microsoft Windows Movie Maker was used for editing and Smart Sound Movie Maestro added intrigue and enhanced scenes with music.

Throughout the video development process, librarians tried to keep the main audience in mind: undergraduate students, specifically first-year students who are just getting acquainted with the university setting and research and writing expectations. Videos needed to be short and concise (5 minutes, maximum), not just for the sake of attention spans, but also with respect to the requisite computer processor speed and the type of connectivity (high speed, not dial-up) these videos would require. In fact, alternate versions of the information covered in these videos were also proposed–PowerPoint versions and even copies of scripts for users who may not have the connectivity or means to view the short films.

Early in the project, the development team envisioned this type of instruction as a series, not unlike a television series, with episodes devoted to pertinent library and research-based issues in a university setting. The 1980s series *Dallas*, with its legendary opener, inspired the team. Ideas ultimately coalesced into *CSI: Confused Students Investi-*

gate Marshall University Libraries (http://www.marshall.edu/library/ help/list.asp#vide).

As noted earlier, the team's first video undertaking focused on an episode devoted to Information Delivery Services (IDS), which was designed as a way to extend to freshmen the topics in the already completed PowerPoint slideshows and Camtasia video demo. In the video, three students discuss an upcoming assignment, and two of them remark with frustration that they could not find the books and articles they need in the campus Libraries. One student, who is "in the know," shows her friends how to use IDS to obtain the materials they need. In this episode, as in the ones produced afterwards, scripts depict students helping and teaching other students. Classroom teachers have long recognized that in many situations students learn more comfortably and more effectively when taught by peers and the team wanted to incorporate this learning strategy in library-themed videos.

"MILES to Go Before We Read," the second episode in the series, used the same cast of students and depicted one student showing her friends how to search the Libraries' catalog (MILES) for the books they needed and telling them about other materials the catalog contains. The episode "Periodically Puzzled," focuses on a student's frustration trying to find articles on a particular subject for a paper she needs to write. Once more the scenario of "students helping students" becomes the theme as the confused student is assisted/bailed out by her friends, who discuss various ways to find articles using the Libraries' resources and where friendly help can be found at the Reference Desk.

Other episodes in the series are under development and include topics devoted to plagiarism, cell phone use in the Libraries, and a number of other relevant, library-focused issues and resources. The entire series is conceived as a fun, non-threatening way to introduce undergraduate students to the essential facts that they need to know about Marshall University Libraries to be successful and information-literate students. These short, focused episodes can serve as discussion starters in classes embarking on research and dealing with the issue of academic integrity, but they might also appeal to individual students visiting the Web site. Because the videos convey information in an entertaining and involving way, they enable the off-campus student (or any student not working face to face with a librarian) to have a more personalized exchange with the Libraries. Certainly, the videos will appeal to visual and auditory learners and learners who like material explained to them by another person.

CONCLUSION

Statistics confirm that students at Marshall University do access on-line help, so the effort involved in designing an attractive online Web-based Help site seems likely to pay off. In the period from August 2003 through April 2004, the Help pages recorded over 3,000 page views. Combined with the course and subject guides, the Help pages were viewed almost 13,000 times, or about 3% of the Libraries' Web site to-tal page views (adjusting out the home page views), and the course and subject guides consistently ranked in the top 10-20. The citation guides ranked in the top 50 documents viewed in February and April 2004. In this 2003 survey of the Libraries' Web site users, 7.3% reported "read-ing research guides" or "learn about library research" as reasons to go to the Libraries' Web site; 3.6% indicated that they go to the site to "get help." Results from this survey also revealed that reading research guides and looking at the Libraries' Web site have been helpful for users in need of assistance.

The Libraries plan to market the video series and other elements of the Help site to the university community through numerous means, including showing the Help site in library instruction sessions; sug-gesting it as a focal point for University and Honors 101 classes, a freshman orientation course that has a library instruction session built into the curriculum; advertising it prominently on the Libraries' home page; publicizing it in the school newspaper; and sending infor-mational postcards to professors encouraging them to use it with their students.

The process of developing a Help site has offered both challenges and lessons, not the least of which is that users tend to avoid help at all costs. Unwilling to let that stop the impulse to offer help, the develop-ment team persisted and in the course of developing the Help site real-ized that creating an attractive, inviting, and effective site is an iterative process. In order to create a truly workable site, design must originate in a combination of "librarian and student know best." While librari-ans may have a better concept of all that students need to know, stu-dents have valuable input to share on how to make that information attractive, understandable, and functional. Another realization is how much impact the help features of a Web site have upon the overall or-ganization of a library's Web site. In order for online help to be effec-tive, it must be fully integrated into the functioning of a library's Web site and available at the user's point of need. The reality is that once that integration process begins, it impacts the design and function of the rest of the site. What may begin as a simple vision inevitably evolves into a more far-reaching project that involves modifications to the entire Web site.

NOTES

1. Colleen Cook and Fred Heath, "Users' Perceptions of Library Service Quality: A LibQUAL+ Qualitative Study," *Library Trends* 49, no. 4 (2001): 553-57.

2. See LibQUAL "2003 Survey Highlights" at mhtml:http://www.libqual.org/documents/admin/ExecSummary1.1_locked.pdf.

3. Marshall University LibQUAL results are available at http://www.marshall.edu/library/libqual/assess_2004.mht!assess_2004_files/frame.htm.

4. Verlene J. Herrington, "Way beyond BI: A Look to the Future," *The Journal of Academic Librarianship* 24, no. 5 (1998): 383-84; Virginia M. Tiefel, "Library User Education: Examining Its Past, Projecting Its Future," *Library Trends* 44, no. 2 (1995): 335.

5. Trevor Grayling, "Fear and Loathing of the Help Menu: A Usability Test of On-line Help," *Technical Communication* 45, no. 2 (1998): 168-79.

6. Ruth Dickstein and Vicki Mills, "Usability Testing at the University of Arizona Library: How to Let the Users in on the Design," *Information Technology and Libraries* 19, no. 3 (2000): 149.

7. Brenda Battleson, Austin Booth, and Jane Weintrop, "Usability Testing of an Academic Library Web Site: A Case Study," *The Journal of Academic Librarianship* 27, no. 3 (2001): 193.

8. Zao Liu and Zheng Ye (Lan) Yang, "Factors Influencing Distance-Education Graduate Students' Use of Information Sources: A User Study," *The Journal of Academic Librarianship* 30, no. 1 (2004): 27.

9. Barbara Fister, "Fear of Reference," *The Chronicle of Higher Education* 48, no. 40 (June 14, 2002): B20.

10. Constance A. Mellon, "Library Anxiety: A Grounded Theory and Its Development," *College & Research Libraries* 47 (March 1986): 163.

11. Grayling, "Fear and Loathing," 172.

12. Angi Faiks and Nancy Hyland, "Gaining User Insight: A Case Study Illustrating the Card Sort Technique," *College & Research Libraries* 61, no. 4 (2000): 350.

13. Christina Byrne, Patricia Carey, Betsy Darrah, Karen Eliasen, Theresa Mudrock, and Louise Richards, "Help! Challenges of Creating Useful Online and Print Documentation in a Changing Electronic Environment," *Technical Services Quarterly* 14, no. 2 (1996): 1-17.

14. Dickstein and Mills, "Usability Testing at the University of Arizona Library," 144.

15. Jerilyn Veldorf and Karen Beavers, "Going Mental: Tackling Mental Models for the Online Library Tutorial," *Research Strategies* 18, no. 1 (2001): 10.

16. Catherine A. Wells, "Location, Location, Location: The Importance of Placement of the Chat Request Button," *Reference & User Services Quarterly* 43, no. 2 (2003): 137.

17. Brenda Reeb and Susan Gibbons, "Students, Librarians, and Subject Guides: Improving a Poor Rate of Return," *portal: Libraries and the Academy* 4, no. 1 (2004): 124-26.

18. Reeb and Gibbons, "Students, Librarians, and Subject Guides," 127-28.

19. Reeb and Gibbons, "Students, Librarians, and Subject Guides," 128.

20. See Olivia Olivares, "Virtual Reference Systems," *Computers in Libraries* 24, no. 5 (2004): 25-29; Corey M. Johnson, "Online Chat Reference," *Reference & User Services Quarterly* 43, no. 3 (2004): 237-47; Melanie E. Sims, "Virtual Reference Service: The LSU Libraries' Experience," *The Reference Librarian*, no. 79/80 (2002/2003): 267-79; Paul Neuhaus, Connie Van Fleet, and Danny P. Wallace, "Privacy and Confidentiality in Digital Reference," *Reference & User Services Quarterly* 43, no. 1 (2003): 26-36; and Joanne Smyth, "Virtual Reference Transcript Analysis," *Searcher* 11, no. 3 (2003): 26-30.

21. See *The Reference Librarian,* no. 79/80 (2002/2003) for over 20 articles devoted to virtual reference, including overviews by Bill Katz (pp. 1-17) and Diane Kresh (pp. 19-34).

22. Vicky Duncan and Darlene M. Fichter, "What Words and Where? Applying Usability Testing Techniques to Name a New Live Reference Service," *Journal of the Medical Library Association* 92, no. 2 (2004): 219-20.

23. Duncan and Fichter, "What Words and Where?" 221.

24. Duncan and Fichter, "What Words and Where?" 223.

25. Sara E. Morris and Marybeth Grimes, "A Great Deal of Time and Effort: An Overview of Creating and Maintaining Internet-Based Subject Guides," *Library Computing* 18, no. 3 (2000): 213.

26. Morris and Grimes, "A Great Deal of Time and Effort," 216.

27. Karen K. Hein and Marc W. Davis, "The Research Wizard: An Innovative Web Application for Patron Service," *Internet Reference Services Quarterly* 7, no. 1/2 (2002): 1-18.

28. Trina J. Magi, "What's Best for Students? Comparing the Effectiveness of a Traditional Print Pathfinder and a Web-based Research Tool," *portal: Libraries and the Academy* 3, no. 4 (2003): 671-686.

29. Candice Dahl, "Electronic Pathfinders in Academic Libraries: An Analysis of Their Content and Form," *College & Research Libraries* 62, no. 3 (2001): 237.

30. Reeb and Gibbons, "Students, Librarians, and Subject Guides," 124-26.

31. See http://www.emich.edu/public/loex/islinks/tutlinks.htm.

32. Christopher V. Hollister and Jonathan Coe, "Current Trends vs. Traditional Models: Librarians' Views on the Methods of Library Instruction," *College & Undergraduate Libraries* 10, no. 2 (2003): 52.

33. Veldorf and Beavers, "Going Mental," 14.

34. Nancy H. Dewald, "Transporting Good Library Instruction Practices into the Web Environment: An Analysis of Online Tutorials," *The Journal of Academic Librarianship* 25, no. 1 (1999): 30.

35. Veldorf and Beavers, "Going Mental," 15.

36. Nadaleen Tempelman-Kluit and Ethan Ehrenberg, "Library Instruction and Online Tutorials: Developing Best Practices for Streaming Desktop Video Capture," *Feliciter* 49, no. 2 (2003): 89.

37. Hollister and Coe, "Current Trends," 56-57.

If You Build It,
They Will Come, but Then What:
A Look at Issues
Related to Using Online Course Software
to Provide Specialized Reference Services

Linda L. Lillard
Mollie Dinwiddie

SUMMARY. A superior learning environment provides students with an opportunity to benefit from the knowledge and experience of an instructor and to engage in research into the subject matter. Librarians can collaborate with faculty in online courses to enhance the learning environment. The authors describe a project that enabled a librarian to have direct interaction with students in online courses. Responses from students regarding this project were gathered each semester for five years and are the basis for suggestions for continued experimentation and assessment of this model of information literacy instruction. *[Article copies available for a fee from The Haworth Document Delivery Service: 1-800-HAWORTH. E-mail address: <docdelivery@haworthpress.com> Website: <http://www.HaworthPress.com> © 2004 by The Haworth Press, Inc. All rights reserved.]*

Linda L. Lillard (lillardl@emporia.edu) is Assistant Professor, School of Library and Information Management, Emporia State University, 1200 Commercial Street, Emporia, KS 66801. Mollie Dinwiddie (dinwiddie@cmsu1.cmsu.edu) is Interim Dean of Library Services, James C. Kirkpatrick Library, Central Missouri State University, 600 South Missouri Street, Warrensburg, MO 64093.

[Haworth co-indexing entry note]: "If You Build It, They Will Come, but Then What: A Look at Issues Related to Using Online Course Software to Provide Specialized Reference Services." Lillard, Linda L., and Mollie Dinwiddie. Co-published simultaneously in *Internet Reference Services Quarterly* (The Haworth Information Press, an imprint of The Haworth Press, Inc.) Vol. 9, No. 3/4, 2004, pp. 135-145; and: *Internet Reference Support for Distance Learners* (ed: William Miller, and Rita M. Pellen) The Haworth Information Press, an imprint of The Haworth Press, Inc., 2004, pp. 135-145. Single or multiple copies of this article are available for a fee from The Haworth Document Delivery Service [1-800-HAWORTH, 9:00 a.m. - 5:00 p.m. (EST). E-mail address: docdelivery@haworthpress.com].

Available online at http://www.haworthpress.com/web/IRSQ
Digital Object Identifier: 10.1300/J136v09n03_10

KEYWORDS. Online instruction, Blackboard, collaborative instruction, specialized reference services, information literacy, library instruction

Attempting to meet the Guidelines set forth by the Association of College and Research Libraries (ACRL) for the provision of distance learning library services has brought forth a myriad of unique technology-based solutions. Because the Guidelines (Association of College and Research Libraries, 2004) require that the services provided are equivalent to those offered on campus, librarians have been struggling to alter services to fit the online course environment. Along with offerings of remote access to libraries' electronic resources comes remote access to other library services such as reference. ´

Today most academic libraries provide specialized Web pages with information for the distance learning community while e-mail reference and Ask-a-Librarian services that build on Internet-based chat software are becoming prevalent. The popularity of Web-based course software programs that attempt to mirror the traditional classroom environment such as WebCT and Blackboard provide another venue for providing library services for distance learners. Campus adoption of the Blackboard course software led librarians at Central Missouri State University to design services for the distance learning community that used this platform.

LIBRARY SERVICES
VIA WEB-BASED COURSE SOFTWARE

A 2002 article by Cox on the use of Blackboard to extend one-shot library instruction mentioned that only one article had been written to date on the subject of using courseware to deliver library instruction, yet a team of librarians at Central Missouri State University were experimenting with the presence of a librarian in the Blackboard online classroom since fall of 1999. In order to get this idea into the mainstream, this experiment became the topic of many conference presentations by this team from 1999 to 2002, including the Annual Conference on Distance Teaching and Learning.

Consistent with the proactive role promoted by contemporary library schools (Grover & Hale, 1998), the team of librarians at Central Missouri State not only provided online students with access to full-text databases, document delivery, and statewide library cards, but also provided select classes with a personal librarian who had the same virtual 24/7 availability to students as their course instructor. Furthermore, the librarian also had the same access to students as the course instructor and could make announcements, send messages to individual students, add content, and possibly mediate into the entire student learning experience. The librarian was available to the instructor for course planning and was actually listed as a co-instructor in the online classes with all the technical privileges with the software that entailed (Dinwiddie & Lillard, 2002).

REVIEW OF THE LITERATURE

Though a late 2001 editorial asks the question, "Course Management Software: Where Is the Library?" a review of the literature reveals that during this time period other libraries have also examined the possibility of using online course software to support distance learning in some way. In 2001, Ruey L. Rodman (2001) reported on the results of a model for library support for distance education at The Ohio State University. The course software used was WebCT and a library icon on the main course page directed students to specifically selected subject related resources. Of particular note was a document delivery request page designed to be used for the three online courses in the project. Gary Roberts (2003) at Alfred University in Alfred, New York, adapted the information literacy tutorial, Searchpath, for integration into Blackboard. He created a central course in which all students could be enrolled for information literacy instruction, though Roberts mentioned it might be better to import the tutorial into a subject-classroom course so that it could more easily be related to course requirements.

Librarians at Stetson University (Lenholt, Costello & Stryker, 2003) worked with content instructors and integrated library instruction handouts into course specific online classes offered through Blackboard. Burns integrated library instruction into courses delivered via the eCollege.com delivery system at Pace University, while Getty at University of California Riverside and Piele at University of Wisconsin Parkside integrated tutorials into Web-Course-in-a-Box and WebCT courseware respectively. At Regent University, Burd used the Blackboard course software to provide a required pass/fail information literacy course. Burd's team is very concerned with meeting the needs of their distance learners and considered using the virtual classroom feature of Blackboard to provide synchronous lessons. As did the team at Central Missouri State, Burd's team realized it would involve much extra time and effort, but they believed it was worth it to meet the needs of their distance learners (Getty, Burd, Burns & Piele, 2000).

Using Prometheus course management software at Rochester Institute of Technology (RIT), "subject specialists are encouraged to offer library expertise in their respective topical areas to either input the information for faculty into Prometheus or demonstrate the resources for faculty to post annotated links or other materials themselves" (Buehler, Dopp & Hughes, 2004, p. 56). Among services provided by RIT librarians are persistent links to e-books and writing and literature resources, librarian contact information, and participation in monitoring and contributing to a discussion board topic on plagiarism and other related topics. Consequently, as this review of the literature indicates, while libraries are dabbling in different approaches to using the course management software for the delivery of library services, nobody has arrived at a definitive model of the best way to make use of this resource.

THE PROJECT AT CENTRAL MISSOURI STATE

Consistent with the idea of one-to-one relationship management advocated by Keating and Hafner (2002), the team at Central Missouri State not only provided services for the class as a whole, but also used the online class access to broaden knowledge of the individual students' needs and preferences. With this knowledge, they were able to provide library services customized to meet the needs of individual students within the class.

Throughout the five years the team worked on this project with Criminal Justice and Nursing students at Central Missouri State University, several questions guided the process:

1. How will students use the librarian's expertise given 24/7 access?
2. What kind of library services and research assistance do distance learners really want from a librarian?
3. Do distance students feel that the librarian is helpful to their research process?
4. Is librarian mediation throughout their entire research process something that distance learners will embrace enthusiastically?

5. Will the students take advantage of this new role for the librarian in such close proximity and request more mediation into their research process (Dinwiddie & Lillard, 2002)?

STUDENT EXPECTATIONS
OF A DISTANCE LEARNING LIBRARIAN

Student expectations from a librarian at a distance are not unlike what they hope to receive in a face-to-face interaction. In a solicitation for opinions regarding what support students expect or desire from a distant librarian, twenty Nursing students completed an open-ended question, "What services do you expect from a librarian?" Some of their responses demonstrate how naive some students are about what they may reasonably expect. In general, students respond that they need fast, easy access to specific information, preferably one-stop shopping. They also want librarians to coordinate with faculty regarding specific reading assignments and have these readings available at their fingertips. They expect technical support when they are trying to access materials from off-campus and easy telephone access to information. Furthermore, students expect to have their e-mail questions answered immediately! Among the twenty responses to a question about the service/support that would be ideal, one student even indicated he wanted all librarians on the same Web page with the same format listing all services and providers.

The current mélange of different catalogs, databases, and Web pages appears to be very confusing to students. Today's busy part-time students would prefer that there be one online resource that can be used to deliver information required in the precise same formats and on any topic that might be needed. The Open-URL resolver products that are currently being marketed may come close to providing the sort of one resource research that students would truly prefer.

RESULTS

Though student comments regarding the presence of the librarian in the online classroom and her offer of personalized services were extremely positive and students were grateful for a library presence in their online class, it has been very discouraging to note that few took advantage of the opportunity to receive this personalized assistance. It is possible that the course research demands were not substantive enough to stimulate a need for this type of assistance or that the class-related resources provided by the librarian in Blackboard were sufficient to allow students to navigate on their own. An increase in requests for face-to-face assistance from on-campus students who were also taking the online courses was noted, however, leading to the possible conclusion that students who are in the library and have a research problem are more likely to seek out the librarian with whom they are familiar from the online course. While this is not the result the team was hoping to attain, it is a positive result nonetheless.

CHALLENGES FOR OUTREACH TO DISTANCE LEARNERS

In the experiments with Blackboard as a tool for providing library research assistance and instruction to distance learners at CMSU a number of challenges have been identified. Distance learners are far less likely to be able to find a human to assist them than are face-to-face students who may visit the library and ask for help. The first challenge is to make sure the students know that a service exists and that there is someone available to help. If a librarian has access to students via Blackboard courses that permit her to create library content for the course, participate in the discussion boards, post announcements, post information in the staff directory, and send e-mail to students, there is automatically a mechanism for reaching out to the students.

Whether the librarian is involved with a course taught by a faculty member or whether some mechanism exists for the librarian to create a "course" and have selected majors enrolled therein, once library content is added and an effort has been made to reach out to the students via the Blackboard tools available, another challenge is to maintain the integrity of the content, keeping it both fresh and current. This requires the librarian involved with Blackboard to monitor the library-related content, track statistics on the use of the specific areas that relate to library research and content, and continue to reach out periodically to remind the students that the librarian is available.

Therefore, another major challenge is for the librarian to remain committed to participating in Blackboard on a regular basis. A third challenge occurs whenever there is turnover in the responsibility for working with the Blackboard courses. The new librarian must become knowledgeable about using Blackboard and make a commitment to continue reaching out to students enrolled. The degree of involvement and "personal attention" will change based upon individual differences. It may be difficult to achieve consistency of service to the students.

SUGGESTIONS FOR THE NOVICE LIBRARIAN PRESENCE IN AN ONLINE COURSE

Until July 2003 when the author's involvement with Nursing ended, students were contacted each semester and asked for their reactions to the use of Blackboard as a mechanism for seeking library assistance. Because response to the idea of a librarian in the course was universally applauded by the students, it was clear that they appreciated a personalized assistance. Mechanisms used within the online course software should include a variety of attempts to "touch" the students to determine their opinions and perceived needs for librarian assistance. To begin the "contact" the librarian should post information about herself in the staff information segment of Blackboard including a photo, brief information about the role of the librarian in the course, and office address, hours of availability, e-mail address, telephone number, and chat information.

The ability both to post announcements in the online course and to contact the entire class with one e-mail are ideal for making an overture of introduction and help. At the beginning of the course, an announcement that informs the students of the availability of librarian assistance to the students and an e-mail to each of them helps break the ice. Students sometimes appear to be reluctant to ask for help from a "stranger" or to "bother" a librarian. Not unlike the students who apologize at the Reference Desk before beginning their request for help, distance learners may feel that asking for help is either an imposition or a sign of ignorance. Offering the help early and periodically within the online course during a semester are ways to help students get beyond this hesitancy to solicit assistance.

Although not every response from 1999 through 2003 was archived, a sample of the responses from students in online Nursing and Criminal Justice courses demonstrates that students will reply when the librarian reaches out to them. The question that was posted to them in a friendly e-mail included the question: "What do you need from a librarian in your online course?" Examples of the responses received follow.

"I believe you posted instructions somewhere earlier in the semester about how I can access research articles. Will you please direct me to the information again?"

"I want to emphasize how important it is for the librarian to help us locate information from home or a work location. This can be very daunting."

"I'm new to the online world of classes so I'm not yet sure of exactly what I do need. I had begun my research without utilizing all the available resources you gathered for us. This will really help."

"Most people are doing their research from home with their computers so to have someone at your fingertips to help is very useful."

"I've found this very helpful. You have helped me by suggesting where I should look for information, telling me what topics to look for, etc. I hope you get paid for the extra work!"

With a frequent "touch" to online students via an e-mail or a course announcement, the librarian begins to receive unsolicited requests for assistance. A few examples of real requests for research help illustrate how students interact with the librarian in an online course. These were e-mails received through the Blackboard e-mail access in a Nursing course:

"I am writing a literature review on high risk issues for pregnancy and delivery. I have found a few articles but I need more. If you have any suggestions that may help me with my research it would be greatly appreciated."

"I was wondering if you could help me find some research studies. I need some that pertain to the intensive care unit for adult patients. I keep finding general articles, but no research studies. Thanks for your help."

"I have been searching for information on text anxiety among nursing students. I have not found enough. If you could assist me in any way it would be greatly appreciated. Thanks so much for your time and effort!"

The above samples of e-mail communications from students in online courses who knew to ask for aid from a specific librarian who was included in the course as an instructor indicate that students will reach out to the librarian who reaches out to them. The simple fact that a librarian has the opportunity to let students know about new resources available, offer help to students individually, and be viewed as a personal resource to students may be a method to continue to demonstrate the value of the librarian to students who are tending toward remote use of the library's resources.

As face-to-face interactions with students in the library decline because they can retrieve many full-text resources remotely from the library (reference transactions are down 29% since 1991, ARL, 2003), it is imperative that librarians find new methods for teaching and assisting students with their informational needs. Online course software such as Blackboard and WebCT provide one new method. Working with students directly in the classroom, albeit online, provides this sort of method for interaction and instruction. By placing library instruction content directly into the course, perhaps in a special library "button," providing links to library resources and tutorials, and communicating directly with students via e-mail and course announcements, a whole new "teachable moment" occurs for information literacy. Within an online course, the materials and assistance provided are relevant to what is being studied. This can eliminate the need for unrelated library assignments in "one-shot" instruction sessions and replace them with meaningful research assignments created collaboratively with course instructors.

WHAT NEXT?

Librarians have experimented with online course software applications in a variety of subject areas. In most instances, the efforts have targeted students in particular majors or programs. At Central Missouri State, the next experiment is with a History professor who is translating a general education course in History to an online course. She has asked for librarian assistance, and the subject liaison to the Department of History, along with the distance education librarian and two instructional services librarians, make up a team that is working on a new project. The course is in United States History since 1865 and will be an option for undergraduate students who are attempting to complete a degree from a distance.

Tutorials on using the online catalog and a number of general and subject-related databases will be linked from within the online course. A research assignment will be collaboratively developed by the course instructor and the History liaison from the library that will use the tutorials and other instructional materials that the librarian creates. The librarian who is the History liaison will be an ongoing presence in the course, offering assistance to the students as they complete the research assignment. The goal of the librarian will be to interact with the students, offering instruction and guidance for completing the research assignment. There will be an opportunity for the two instructors to use the same research assignment in another face-to-face section of the United States History course and assess the results of the general education History course in Blackboard.

A professor of English and the library liaison for that discipline are collaborating on a similar experiment with a general education course in English Composition. The library liaison will also team with the distance education librarian and the two instructional services librarians to develop appropriate library content for the online course. The English professor assigns a variety of writing topics that require the students to do research as well as write. Because of this joint effort, the library liaison will have advance notice of the topics from which students may choose. He can plan his online assistance or library instruction and target library resources that are related to the research topics. While the best use of online course software to teach information literacy may not yet be determined, these and other experimental projects across the country will add to the body of knowledge on the topic.

REFERENCES

Association of College and Research Libraries (2000). Guidelines for Distance Learning Library Services. [Online] Accessed July 12, 2004 at http://www.ala.org/ala/acrl/acrlstandards/guidelinesdistancelearning.htm.

Association of Research Libraries (2003). *Service trends in ARL libraries 1991-2003.* Retrieved July 12, 2004, from http://www.arl.org/stats/arlstat/graphs/2003/graph1_03.xls.

Buehler, M., Dopp, E., & Hughes, K. A. (2001). It takes a library to support distance learners [at Rochester Institute of Technology]. *Internet Reference Services Quarterly, 5* (3), 5-24.

Course management software: Where is the Library? (2001). *Online Libraries and Microcomputers, 19* (10), 1-2.

Cox, C. N. (2002). Becoming part of the course: Using Blackboard to extend one-shot library instruction. *College & Research Libraries News, 63* (1), 11-13, 39.

Dinwiddie, M. M., & Lillard, L. L. (2001). Distance education library services: An opportunity for personalized customer service. In *17th Annual Conference on Distance Teaching & Learning Conference Proceedings* (pp. 127-132). Madison, WI: University of Wisconsin System.

Dinwiddie, M., & Lillard, L. L. (2002). At the crossroads: Library and classroom. In P. B. Mahoney (Ed.), *The Tenth Off-Campus Library Services Conference Proceedings* (pp. 199-212). Mount Pleasant, MI: Central Michigan.

Getty, N. K., Burd, B., Burns, S. K., & Piele, L. (2000). Using courseware to deliver library instruction via the Web: Four examples. *Reference Services Review, 28* (4), 349-359.

Grover, R., & Hale, M. L. (1988, January). The role of the librarian in faculty research. *College & Research Libraries, 49,* 9-15.

Keating, J. J., III & Hafner, A. W. (2002). Perspectives on supporting individual library patrons with information technologies: Emerging one-to-one library services on the college or university campus. *The Journal of Academic Librarianship, 28* (6), 426-429.

Lenholt, R., Costello, B., & Stryker, J. (2003). Utilizing Blackboard to provide library instruction: Uploading MS Word handouts with links to specific resources. *Reference Services Review, 31* (3), 211-218.

Roberts, G. (2003). The yin and yang of integrating TILT with Blackboard. *Computers in Libraries, 23* (8), 10-12, 54-56.

Rodman, R. L. (2001). The S.A.G.E. project: A model for library support of distance education [at Ohio State University]. *Internet Reference Services Quarterly, 6* (2), 35-45.

Sheppard, B. (2001). *The 21st century learner.* Washington, D.C.: Institute of Museum and Library Services.

Open Source Software to Support Distance Learning Library Services

H. Frank Cervone

SUMMARY. Interest in the open source software model as a means of developing software for the library community has developed considerably in the last few years. Fortunately, much of the software that has been developed for libraries can be used to provide extended library services to distance learning students. This article provides an overview of both the open source software movement and how that movement relates to providing library services. In addition to describing some software packages that related to specific areas of service for distance learning students, the article includes some guidelines for distance learning librarians to consider when making a choice to use open source software packages. *[Article copies available for a fee from The Haworth Document Delivery Service: 1-800-HAWORTH. E-mail address: <docdelivery@haworthpress.com> Website: <http://www.HaworthPress.com> © 2004 by The Haworth Press, Inc. All rights reserved.]*

KEYWORDS. Open source software, open source library applications, library reference service software, library software applications, distance learning library application software

H. Frank Cervone (f-cervone@northwestern.edu) is Assistant University Librarian for Information Technology, University Library, 1970 Campus Drive, Northwestern University, Evanston, IL 60208.

[Haworth co-indexing entry note]: "Open Source Software to Support Distance Learning Library Services." Cervone, H. Frank. Co-published simultaneously in *Internet Reference Services Quarterly* (The Haworth Information Press, an imprint of The Haworth Press, Inc.) Vol. 9, No. 3/4, 2004, pp. 147-158; and: *Internet Reference Support for Distance Learners* (ed: William Miller, and Rita M. Pellen) The Haworth Information Press, an imprint of The Haworth Press, Inc., 2004, pp. 147-158. Single or multiple copies of this article are available for a fee from The Haworth Document Delivery Service [1-800-HAWORTH, 9:00 a.m. - 5:00 p.m. (EST). E-mail address: docdelivery@haworthpress.com].

Digital Object Identifier: 10.1300/J136v09n03_11

INTRODUCTION

Interest in open source software (OSS) as a means for providing enhanced library services at a lower cost has been growing rapidly in the last several years. Throughout higher education, the use of open source software for many functions has exploded–from operating systems (Linux, http://www.linux.org) to office productivity suites (OpenOffice, http://www.openoffice.org) to course management systems (LogiCampus, http://www.logicampus.com/) to library management systems (Koha, http://www.koha.org).

However, how does this model of software development and distribution affect libraries? What is open source software? Is it a valid model for creating software or just the latest trendy thing? How can it be used to provide enhanced services to distance learning students? There are a lot of questions and many different answers.

OPEN SOURCE SOFTWARE–
A QUICK OVERVIEW OF ITS PRINCIPLES

The current understanding of the open source movement traces its beginning back to the early days of the Internet (Raymond, 1999); however, the concept of free and open software has been around since the first generation of commercial computers developed in the 1950s (Glass, 2004).

Open source software (as it is understood today) is a model for software development and distribution; however, it differs significantly from other models, such as shareware, freeware, public-domain software, and the "free" readers or viewers for proprietary software (such as the Acrobat Reader) because of the way the application is developed and provided (Krishnamurthy, 2003). Open source applications are typically developed by a community of people rather than just a single entity. Additionally, as opposed to simply getting the executable version of a program (which is what most people are most interested in), open source software also makes it possible to get the text files containing the programming language statements that perform the various operations within the program–the source code as it were.

For many organizations, having the source code for an application is not an immediately pressing concern. However, it is the availability of the source code that forms the critical component of the open source software movement. If one has the source code for a program, it is possible to inspect the program code to review it and modify it to suit local needs. In addition, it also allows the application to be incorporated into other programs to perform new and customized functions. This is not possible with closed source programs, which is the model used by commercial software vendors.

In actual practice, defining open source software is more complex than the definition above. Over the years, open source software has come to mean software that conforms to 10 general philosophical principles. The first principle is that the software should be freely distributable, meaning that the software license cannot restrict anyone from selling or giving away the software as part of a larger system or aggregation of programs nor can there be any royalties or fees for such sale.

Open source software, in addition to including the source code, must provide for both the distribution of the source code as well as the compiled form of the program. Furthermore, derived works, modifications, and derivatives should be distributed under the same terms as the original software license; however, the distributor should maintain the integrity of the original source code. Provision is made to restrict source code from being distributed in a modified form but only if the program can be modified at compilations through the use of patch files. The reason for this is that it allows the consumer to know who made changes to the source code without impinging on the rights of the original software creator.

From these principles it follows that the software must provide for the distribution of the license along with the software. This means that the rights attached to the program must apply to everyone the program is distributed to, without their having to execute additional licenses.

Along more philosophical lines, open source software creators must not discriminate against any person or group of persons in their use of the software and they cannot restrict anyone from making use of the software in a specific field or endeavor.

Additionally, open source applications should not depend on the application being part of a particular software distribution package, such as an operating system or office application suite; however, this does not mean that one program cannot depend on another program to enable functionality. From this, it follows that an open source software package cannot place restrictions on other software that is distributed along with the licensed software. That is, one piece of software cannot prevent another piece of software from being used. Finally, open source applications should be technology-neutral, meaning that no provision of the license may be predicated on any individual technology or style of interface.

Note that nowhere do these principles mention that open source software is "free of charge" although most people associate open source software with "free." It is in this point that most of the confusion about open source begins.

OPEN SOURCE SOFTWARE LICENSING

This idea that software should be "free" has caused the most controversy in the open source software community. Often this is incorrectly interpreted to mean that it is unethical to charge for software or that all open source software must be offered without any type of charge. This stems primarily from misunderstandings related to comments made by Richard Stallman, founder of the GNU project (which is a "free" UNIX-like operating system and its associated utilities).

Understandably, the philosophical debates that have ensued regarding the meaning of "free" have generated significant disagreement and as a result, there are many different takes on the issue of licensing and what is permissible and what is not in the open source model.

When implementing an open source package, it is important to note which particular license the program is being distributed under since different licenses bestow different rights to the user and imply different potential uses of the software (Petreley, 2004).

The GNU Public License (GPL) is the most popular and well-known license. It holds closely to the principles outlined above and therefore enforces the concept of "free" fully. Closely related to the GPL is the BSD style license, which was developed for the Berkeley Systems Distribution, an early open-source variant of the UNIX operating system. The main difference between the GPL and the BSD license is that source code modifications under the BSD license can be kept private and do not have to be redistributed as part of the package.

The MIT (Massachusetts Institute of Technology) license is, perhaps, the most liberal since it requires only that the copyright notice be included in any software that is distributed. It applies no other restrictions on the user. At the opposite extreme of the open source continuum is the Apple Public Source License. Many people do not consider the approach Apple takes to be an open source license at all. This is due to the restrictive clauses in the license that require that all changes to the source code to be given to Apple, that all modifications of the source code be disclosed to Apple before release of the code, and that the license can be revoked or changed by Apple at any time. Indeed, these restrictions do fly directly in the face of any articulated open source philosophy.

WHY USE OPEN SOURCE SOFTWARE
TO PROVIDE DISTANCE LIBRARY SERVICES?

The reasons for using open source software are not strictly limited to issues in providing distance library services. They are really issues that affect the library as a whole. It is no surprise then that there has been a recent surge of interest in open source software given the recent economically challenging times. Although the open source software movement has been around for over 20 years, the use of this software has gained significant momentum in the last few years (Tennant, 2003). Much of this adoption rate, in both the commercial sector and in libraries, has been based on economics.

A frequently discussed benefit of open source software is its lower cost of ownership, which is because developers typically do not charge a licensing fee for OSS. This is in contrast to proprietary software, which usually has a significant licensing fee. The Linux operating system, the Apache Web server, and the PERL and PHP programming languages are all well-known examples of open source software that is available without a licensing cost.

However, this single-minded reliance on initial cost of ownership as a determining factor may be misguided. Firstly, not all open source software is free (Warger, 2002). Secondly, those applications that are free are often analogous to a "free" kitten. While you pay nothing upfront, you certainly do have expenses over the course of the cat's life. The same is true with OSS applications.

Although OSS allows some organizations to save money, open source software may cost other organizations more in the long term. This is because all software needs to be supported on an on-going basis. Open source software is no different. In some cases, the support costs for open source software may be more than the costs for equivalent commercial software. This is mainly due to the costs of installing and maintaining open source software, which generally requires at least as much, if not more, technological sophistication than that required for commercial software.

So, the criteria for open source software adoption in distance libraries services should not be based solely on a simplistic economic model, but rather on its overall integration with the existing environment of services and resources the library can provide.

Some of the benefits that open source software unquestionably offer organizations are cross-platform simplicity and an easing of licensing restrictions. Cross-platform simplicity means that the software is not dependent on a specific hardware or operating system platform in order to function. Therefore, the software could be run on a Linux or Windows-based server depending on local practice. Eased licensing restrictions are a major boon, because people can have copies of programs on their machines at home, at work, and on the road and are not penalized by having to purchase more licenses.

A concern voiced by some library administrators is that the quality of open source software and the availability of support will not be as high as that available with commercial software (Overly, 2004). The answer to this issue is complex. While open source software typically does not come from a vendor that can support the software, open source software does offer a wide range of quality and support options. User communities can provide extremely high levels of support–witness the user communities that support Apache and Linux. Additionally, several companies have emerged that provide traditional support and maintenance services for open source software, similar in quality and scope to that of higher-end commercial software.

Nonetheless, the argument is not completely specious either. There is a wide array of open source software projects that are poorly supported or not supported at all. Support for open source software depends on many variables, the most important of which are the level of commitment to the project of the developer and the adoption rate of the software. In general, software that is used by a small niche market is not as well supported as software that enjoys wider use because the development community around the software is either small or non-existent. Before committing to any particular software package, it is important to do fieldwork to ensure that there is a robust user community that will be able to support the software should the original developer(s) lose interest.

THE PHILOSOPHICAL AND PRAGMATIC DIMENSIONS
OF OPEN SOURCE SOFTWARE

Not surprisingly, the open source software movement is predicated on a strong philosophical base. Many have claimed that there is a natural fit between the principles of open source software and the "core values" of librarianship. While there is some justification in this argument, nonetheless there are tradeoffs between a philosophically pure stance on an issue, what actually occurs, and how we perform the actual mission we claim to serve.

One of the major "common good" benefits of open source software is that the lower initial cost of most open source software packages can significantly help bridge the digital divide. This is because libraries in less-developed parts of the world often have technical personnel resources, but they do not have extensive funding for software purchases and maintenance. Because of its economic model, OSS allows the libraries to support services in ways not possible if they were forced to rely on commercial software.

This same case can be made in the "developed world" as well. In both cases, if libraries were forced to rely solely on commercial software, it would not be possible for them to do what they do because either they could not afford it or, in many cases, the functionality simply does not exist in the commercial market.

However, some of the philosophical debates and stances in the open source community serve to divide rather than unite. As Glass (2003) has observed, the people who love open source, love it with a religious fervor while the people who do not sometimes hate it with an equal fervor. Strong stances that hold that no application should ever be sold, that one license scheme is morally superior to others, and that intellectual property as it relates to programming is immoral have been used in draconian fashion to quash debate or enforce a particular world view on software developers and implementers. Unfortunately, these arguments have often slowed the adoption of open source software rather than helped it.

Nonetheless, these debates should not impede libraries from adopting open source software as a way of providing enhanced services to distance learning students. The stridency and extreme stances of a vocal minority of advocates is being moderated as more people get involved in the open source movement and a larger and more diverse user base develops. Since very few library-specific open source software packages are entangled in these divisive philosophical debates, this concern is unlikely to be a major issue in most libraries.

OPEN SOURCE SOFTWARE TO SUPPORT DISTANCE LEARNING LIBRARY SERVICES

There are several types of open source software operating systems, programming languages, utilities, and application programs. Many sources of information on these topics are available; therefore, the focus of this article will be directed to some of the more interesting and commonly used open source application software that can be used to provide enhanced services to distance learning students.

ASKAL (Ask a Librarian) is a system for managing e-mail reference. Developed at the University of Nebraska-Omaha (http://apocalypse. unomaha.edu/ask/) the program includes a simple workflow model that allows e-mail inquiries to be answered quickly and efficiently, as well as providing management reports (both qualitative and quantitative) that measure effectiveness and allow patrons to submit comments about the service received. ASKAL requires the PHP programming language and MySQL for database management.

RAKIM is a lightweight, real time, Web-based reference chat service. Developed at Miami University of Ohio (http://styro.lib.muohio.edu/ rakim/install.html), the interface is very similar to a standard chat room but with useful added features for the online reference environment. The system provides an unlimited number of librarians/operators, each with his or her own login account; a shared queue of patrons that all logged-in librarians can monitor and take calls from; the ability to refer patrons to specific librarians; limited "page-push" by cutting and pasting a URL that is displayed to the patron, audible alerts, shared and personal bookmarks, and individual customization. RAKIM requires the PHP programming language and MySQL or PostgresQL for database management.

RDM (Reference Desk Manager) is an information service management system. Developed at Oregon State University (http://www.onid. orst.edu/~reeset/RDM/), the product combines several functions into a common interface, thereby providing a portal for information service tasks. Major features of RDM include an e-mail Weblog with searching features, an electronic card file, a common links area, and Web-based administration of the system. RDM requires the PHP programming language and MySQL for database management.

Course/control is a robust, customizable system to manage course reserve materials. Developed at Emory University (http://coursecontrol. sourceforge.net/), *Course/control* is more robust than some of the other open source course management systems and provides unique features including the ability to "skin" the interface so independent branches or schools within a library system can maintain a distinct look and feel. The system also allows materials to be tracked historically, so all the items put on reserve for a class by an instructor can be reactivated into their reserve list when the course is taught again. In addition, it provides the ability for instructors to add, delete, annotate, reorder, re-catalog, and set a later activation date for the reserve items in a class, thereby relieving the library staff from having to perform some of the maintenance of course materials.

In addition, an optional public (student) interface, called *Reserves Direct*, provides students with the ability to define a customized current course list. The student can then view the reserve items in the order the instructor has set with the ability to hide items that have already been viewed. *Course/control* requires the PHP programming language and PostgresQL for database management.

Prospero was developed at Ohio State University (http://bones.med. ohio-state.edu/prospero/) and is a document delivery management system that consists of two modules. The staff module is used to scan, send, and receive documents. It can work in conjunction with Ariel® (from Infotrieve) or in place of it. It also converts Prospero/Ariel® files, which are TIFF images, into PDF files that are used by the user-interface module to provide patrons with a controlled Web-based method for retrieving their documents. Documents can be defined as being viewable for a certain number of days or certain number of views in order to conform to copyright restrictions. In addition, patrons are notified automatically via e-mail when their documents are available for viewing. Prospero requires the c, c++, and PERL programming languages.

MOSST (Modular Online Software for Self-paced Tutorials), developed at Simon Fraser University (http://www.lib.sfu.ca/MOSST/), is a lightweight instructional design tool that allows libraries to create complete Web-based tutorials. Features of MOSST include tools to add automatically generated footers, headers, and navigational links (such as "next" and "previous") to a set of HTML pages; to add JavaScript popup windows to HTML pages so users can interact with a remote Web site and refer to the tutorial designer's instructions at the same time; to create multiple choice, self-checking quizzes; and to record users' scores on the quizzes. MOSST requires the PERL programming language.

ResearchGuide, developed at the University of Michigan (http://researchguide.sourceforge.net/index.html), is a content-management-like tool for librarians to help in the creation of subject guides and specialist contact pages. Within subject guides, custom categories such as Reference Works, Indexes to Articles, and Web Resources can be created to categorize an unlimited number of resources, both print and electronic. Once the information has been entered, users may access the guide as a standard Web page. In addition, the system can be used to create specialist contact pages that include contact information for bibliographers as well as a photo (if the person wishes) and information on responsibilities and educational background. ResearchGuide is written in the PHP programming language and uses MySQL for database management.

Somewhat more complex, *LibData* (developed at the University of Minnesota, http://libdata.sourceforge.net/) is another content-management tool that provides an authoring environment but individual components are used for specific functionality within the software. Because of this modularity, not all of the components need to be enabled or used. The components of *LibData* include the *Research QuickStart* module for subject directories, *CourseLib* for course-related pages, and a general-purpose Web pages tool named *PageScribe*.

The *Scout Portal Toolkit* (SPT) allows groups or organizations that have a collection of knowledge or resources they want to share via the World Wide Web to put that collection online without making a big investment in technical resources or expertise. It allows for the creation of subject directory with Web forms, supports multiple contributors, allows visitors to browse and search directories, rate resources, and recommend resources as well as providing an alert service and the ability to export data as RSS, OAI, or tab delimited files. Developed by the Scout Project (http://scout.wisc.edu/research/SPT/), SPT requires the PHP programming language and MySQL for database management.

EPrints is used for creating online archives of primarily textual material, although other material types are supported. The software was designed to be used by researchers and their institutions to maximize the access to, and therefore the impact of, their research output. The software is OAI (Open Archives Initiative) compliant. Specific features of the software include the ability to store documents in any (and multiple) formats and to use any metadata schema. Part of the Open Citation Project, a DLI2 International Digital Libraries Project funded by the Joint Information Systems Committee (JISC) of the Higher Education Funding Councils, in collaboration with the National Science Foundation (http://software.eprints.org/), EPrints requires the PERL programming language and MySQL for database management.

DECIDING TO IMPLEMENT OPEN SOURCE SOFTWARE

Open source software can provide a great opportunity for a library to experiment with new services at a lower initial cost of entry compared to commercial software. In many cases, open source software provides the only option for a library service (Chudnov, 1999). However, just because something is open source, it is not inherently good.

In order to make a wise choice, several guidelines can be used as a starting point in the evaluation of an open source software package. All of these guidelines follow from a single principle–thoroughly investigate the software before implementing.

Some questions to ask when evaluating open source applications are:

- What are the programming language requirements? Are there people on staff who can program in the language the software is written in? If not, does the library have ready access to people who can? If not, are there other packages that can be supported in the current environment?
- What is the operating environment? Is the software supported on existing hardware or will new hardware be required? Does it run on the operating systems currently in use? Is there a large, active user base?
- How is maintenance handled? Who is currently supporting it? Is there a list serve, newsgroup, or blog that can be used for support? Is there a commercial entity that could provide support? Is there a community of peers providing input on enhancements and modifications? What sort of functional and integrated testing is performed by the user community?
- Does the software have the necessary functionality? Is the product mature? That is, is it in a greater than 1.0 release? Will it require modification? If so, does the library have access to the expertise to perform required modifications? How will local modifications be folded back into the base product so the same modifications do not have to be recreated for each new release?

Open source software has a lot to offer libraries and offers an unparalleled opportunity to experiment with "proof of concept" technologies and services. It also provides a way of equalizing some of the issues of access to library services (Lebowitz, 1997) that distance students encounter. Using the guidelines above, open source software can significantly extend the range of services a library can offer to its distance-learning students, enabling a level of functionality that is not possible using only commercial software.

REFERENCES

Chudnov, D. (1999). Open source software: The future of library systems? *Library Journal, 124*(13), pp. 40-43.

Glass, R. L. (2003). A sociopolitical look at open source. *Communications of the ACM, 46*(11), pp. 21-23.

Glass, R. L. (2004). A look at the economics of open source. *Communications of the ACM, 47*(2), pp. 25-27.

Krishnamurthy, S. (2003). A managerial overview of open source software. *Business Horizons 46*(5), pp. 47-56.

Lebowitz, G. (1997). Library services to distant students: An equity issue. *The Journal of Academic Librarianship.* July 1997, pp. 303-308.

Overly, M. (2004). Open source's Pandora's box. *Optimize,* January 2004, pp. 39-45.

Petreley, N. (2004). Why free beer trumps free speech. *Computerworld, 38*(10), p. 39.

Raymond, E. S. (1999). *The cathedral and the bazaar.* Sebastapol, CA: O'Reilly and Associates.

Tennant, R. (2003). Open source goes mainstream. *Library Journal.* August, 2003, p. 30.

Warger, T. (2002). The open-source movement. *Educause Quarterly, 3/2002,* pp. 18-20.

Integrating Library Reference Services in an Online Information Literacy Course: The Internet Navigator as a Model

Amy Brunvand

SUMMARY. The Internet Navigator, an online information literacy course developed by a team of academic librarians in Utah, offers a model for teaching independent research skills to remote students. The course uses an online textbook that doubles as a self-paced tutorial, and a set of assignments that take students step-by-step through the research process. Assignments are submitted by e-mail and evaluated by reference librarian/instructors. Questions on the assignments follow the pattern of a reference interview helping instructors guide students to use useful research strategies and information sources. Other methods of integrating reference services with online learning are discussed. *[Article copies available for a fee from The Haworth Document Delivery Service: 1-800-HAWORTH. E-mail address: <docdelivery@haworthpress.com> Website: <http://www.HaworthPress.com> © 2004 by The Haworth Press, Inc. All rights reserved.]*

KEYWORDS. Reference services (libraries), online courses, online instruction, information literacy, distance education, college students, electronic mail systems in education, library orientation for college students

---

Amy Brunvand (amy.brunvand@library.utah.edu) is Documents Librarian, University of Utah, J. Willard Marriott Library, 295 South 1500 East, Salt Lake City, UT 84112-0860.

[Haworth co-indexing entry note]: "Integrating Library Reference Services in an Online Information Literacy Course: The Internet Navigator as a Model." Brunvand, Amy. Co-published simultaneously in *Internet Reference Services Quarterly* (The Haworth Information Press, an imprint of The Haworth Press, Inc.) Vol. 9, No. 3/4, 2004, pp. 159-177; and: *Internet Reference Support for Distance Learners* (ed: William Miller, and Rita M. Pellen) The Haworth Information Press, an imprint of The Haworth Press, Inc., 2004, pp. 159-177. Single or multiple copies of this article are available for a fee from The Haworth Document Delivery Service [1-800-HAWORTH, 9:00 a.m. - 5:00 p.m. (EST). E-mail address: docdelivery@haworthpress.com].

Digital Object Identifier: 10.1300/J136v09n03_12

INTRODUCTION

For librarians, one major dilemma in online and distance education is how to engage students in independent, self-directed research without creating a sense of frustration if they encounter barriers without immediate access to help. Gandhi (2003) presents a review of the research on the relationships between libraries and distance education programs that outlines some of the difficulties distance education students encounter when they try to do independent, self-directed library research. The review raises some specific questions about online library instruction: How can librarians offer library instruction to students whom the librarian may never see? How can librarians integrate research skills with online learning? How can librarians evaluate whether students are actually learning research concepts?

The experience of developing and teaching the "Internet Navigator," an online information literacy course for undergraduate students, has provided some practical answers to these questions. The in-person library reference desk and the reference interview are time-tested models for helping to guide researchers through the information-seeking process and for helping novice researchers cut through confusion. A number of library projects have shown how to translate reference services into an online setting and have examined effective methods of offering online reference help. The Internet Navigator course integrates the principles of reference help into an online learning environment in order to provide a learner-centered guided research experience that is directed by the student. In order to help students through what may be a confusing process, interactive feedback is given by human reference librarians who evaluate and offer comments on student research. The methods used by the Internet Navigator class offer examples for how using the model of library reference services can enable undergraduate students in any class to engage in independent, self-directed research.

THE INTERSECTION
OF REFERENCE AND INSTRUCTION

The difference between instruction and reference can already be a bit fuzzy. Translated into the context of an online literacy course the distinction is even less clear. In librarian parlance, "instruction" usually implies a one-to-many relationship between teacher and students using a lesson plan designed to teach generalized, abstracted principles of information research that students can apply to any research question. "Reference" usually implies that a librarian is giving one-to-one help with a specific research problem. Contrary to the common assumption that well-trained users need less reference help, library instruction has actually been shown to increase the use of reference services as students become more sophisticated library users who recognize their own limits and the advantages of asking an expert for help (Saunders, 2003). Likewise, the effectiveness of reference services can be enhanced when a librarian takes a teaching approach to answering questions, explaining choices and guiding the student through the decision process by asking leading questions rather than supplying answers (Elmborg, 2002). In a reference interaction, the teachable moment may be lost if the librarian takes control of the keyboard and fails to explain the process behind the advice.

An article on Web-based pedagogy for library instruction by Dewald (1999) discusses necessary components of online learning including sequencing of component skills, learner-centered applied knowledge, and interactivity. However, when library instruction is translated into an online environment the term "interactive" often implies interaction with a computer program rather than interaction with a human being. There is a tendency for librarians to imagine ourselves in a passive role writing user guides and resource lists that are put up as Web pages or hyperlinked resource lists in hopes that students will use them self-sufficiently without needing to ask for help. Most tutorials described in the library literature are designed to be self-scoring as well as self-paced and provide interactivity through the use of technologies such as radio-button quizzes or CGI scripts.

Daunted by the complexities of teaching research skills at a distance, librarians sometimes just give up and substitute pre-selected materials for a direct research experience, as did the authors of a recent article on "Rethinking Online Instruction" (Ladner, Beagle, Steele & Steele, 2004) who decided that it would cause too much confusion to give database links to online undergraduate students in a health sciences class without also giving them detailed search training. These researchers concluded: "Rather than try to teach the intricacies of online searching as part of the course, it was felt that providing 'stored searches' on topics corresponding to the chapters of the online text would bring the students directly into the medical database, and allow them to see professional, relevant articles on course-related topics."

These authors reported success with this strategy since the students felt that the selected material supported their learning. However, this example also illustrates two pitfalls of information literacy instruction: first, librarians taking over the keyboard and second, allowing the subject matter of the class to distract from a focus on learning the research process.

In fact, earlier in the same article these authors had described a strategy that could have made it more practical for students to work directly in appropriate research databases. Known as the "classroom flip," this technique for adapting classroom instruction to computer-aided instruction involves moving lecture material out of the classroom so that background reading may be done independently and moving homework into the classroom where students can get one-on-one help as they engage in practical applications of what they have read. The idea of offering one-on-one instruction for a practical application is not new to librarians since it accurately describes the reference model of library teaching. Of course, there is no particular need to limit reference work to in-person reference desk service or in-class help since ample research shows that e-mail and live chat are effective ways of moving reference services into the online environment. Once you flip the classroom and recognize that library reference services may be framed as one-to-one instruction, the solution to the problem of confused remote students becomes much simpler since the situation is not much different than it is within the walls of a physical library building where students work on research independently but with the constant offer of support from a reference desk should they require it. Thus, an online course with a research component needs to have some built-in methods either to encourage students to ask for research help while they are working on research tasks, or better yet, methods to provide reference help whether the students ask or not. Instead of teaching research theory and hoping students can abstract from it to complete their assignments, librarians can intervene with reference advice at the point of need.

The ideas discussed above are being used in the Internet Navigator, an online information literacy course that was developed by a committee of the Utah Academic Library Consortium. This course, which may be taken entirely online (though access to a physical library is helpful for most students) guides undergraduate students through an independent, student-defined research experience of selecting a topic, exploring research tools, writing accurate citations, and selecting the best, on-topic sources. The course is based on the simple technologies of Web pages and e-mail, and teaching takes the form of reference advice, guidance, and leading questions offered by librarian/instructors who communicate mainly by e-mail. An examination of the course shows several different ways that reference services have been built into the structure of the course. The example of the Internet Navigator shows that it is practical for online and remote undergraduate students to engage in independent, self-directed research, and the ideas presented could be easily adapted to help integrate research in any subject-specific online class as well.

A BRIEF HISTORY OF THE INTERNET NAVIGATOR

The Internet Navigator is a Web-delivered information literacy course that teaches basic research techniques using libraries and the Internet that will help students succeed in college and in their future careers. The course is intended for first-year college and university students, high school students making the transition to higher education, or returning students who need to update their research skills. The course content is based on the ACRL Information Literacy Standards, and the course was developed by a team of librarians from academic libraries in Utah associated with the Utah Academic Library Consortium (UALC). The prepared course consists of an online text, automatically scored quizzes, and assignments which are open-ended enough to be adaptable to the preferences and needs of the instructors at any institution where the course is used. The course may be taught entirely online without ever meeting in a classroom, and students can also complete the coursework entirely online, though most find that access to a physical library is helpful. Communication between instructors and students is usually by e-mail, though students are asked to provide a phone number and occasionally a student makes an appointment to meet with the instructor in person. Since development of the course was a UALC project, the course content includes links to libraries in Utah, but it does not focus on the resources of any specific library, and the prepared course is currently being used successfully by institutions outside of Utah.

Lombardo (1998) gives a history of the original development and intent of the Internet Navigator course, which was first taught in winter of 1996. The original version focused on the then brand-new technology of the Internet and taught such information as e-mail netiquette, how to FTP documents, and how to subscribe and unsubscribe to a Listserv. The section on information search involved using primitive search engines such as Gopher and Archie. The dual purpose of developing the course was to help librarians gain knowledge of developing information technologies as well as to provide a tool that librarians could use for instruction classes.

As the Web developed it changed in ways that made it more integral to the research process. First, the Web became far more user friendly so that users faced fewer technical difficulties. It also moved from being primarily a tool of researchers and universities and became far more commercial. Research by Rashtchy and Avilo (2003) showed that the three largest market segments on the Web are E-commerce, advertising, and the search function. The rise of search was particularly relevant to librarians for several reasons: the commercial importance of search meant that bells and whistles as well as genuine improvements in Internet search engines outstripped what library catalogs were able to offer, making the Web seem superficially more attractive than other research options. Easy-to-use search engines made the Web a more useful research tool and even as library visits rose (perhaps in response to a "post-Internet bounce" of researchers seeking referenced sources that weren't available open-access on the Web), in-house library reference desk statistics began to plummet as research moved from paper sources held in a library building to the computer screen (Albenese, 2003). The new user friendly Web also meant that many database vendors transitioned to Web-based interfaces so that many library services could now be viewed and used via Web browser software. The result was that library subscriptions and databases looked similar to any other Web pages, obscuring the differences between library offerings and the open-access Web. All of these changes meant that the Internet Navigator course was due for a rewrite.

In 1999 the Utah Academic Library Consortium Information for Life Task Force formed with a mission to revise the older technology-oriented version of the Internet Navigator course into an information literacy course that emphasized information search features and the use of the Web for research. The revised course was envisioned as a component of Consortium support for distance learning (Brunvand et al. 2001), and the contents and use of the new revision are described by Hanson (2001).

Currently, the Internet Navigator course is offered for one credit by a number of colleges and universities. It is also used for course-integrated instruction or other independent study. It is being most heavily used at Weber State University where it fulfills an undergraduate information literacy requirement, and some instructors there handle classes of more than one hundred students. Heavy use among Nursing students at the University of Utah prompted librarians there to write a parallel "health track" that substitutes health-oriented examples and hyperlinks for the generic examples used by the original course.

THE INTERNET NAVIGATOR AS A MODEL

The Internet Navigator is specifically designed to teach independent research skills at a basic level regardless of the subject matter students are researching and regardless of the size or quality of the physical library resources they can access. Despite the fact that the course can be entirely Web-based, the title "Internet Navigator" is not meant to imply that students are limiting their research only to sources available on the open-access Web. In fact, the lesson plan takes advantage of the fact that library catalogs, databases, and guides are searchable on Web pages and library resources are presented as a particularly valuable Internet resource. Students are required to try different ways of using the Internet for research by using search engines, library catalogs, and article databases in order to understand how the Internet fits into a larger information system that includes the open-access Web, libraries, and other published information.

The class content first introduces Web browser software and the structure of the Internet in order to help students understand a few basics about how information gets published on the Web and how it is accessed. By understanding the limits of Internet search engines, students are encouraged to use the contents of libraries, databases, books, newspapers, magazines, and other sources from the so called "deep Web" that are not found by using a general Internet search engine.

The prepared Internet Navigator course includes an online textbook with four modules that break the research process down into a sequence of four well-defined components:

* Module 1–Introduction and Internet Communication
* Module 2–Beginning Your Research
* Module 3–Information Navigator
* Module 4–Introduction to Web Publishing

Each module features an automatically scored quiz that relates directly to assigned reading in the online textbook and an assignment that is submitted using a form and scored by a librarian/instructor. The assignments do not specify particular topics or sources a student will use. Rather, they guide students to choose topics that are of personal interest or that they have been asked to work on for another class. Thus, each student works independently, but at specific points in the research process when the assignment is submitted, the instructor is able to evaluate the student's work and give feedback and recommendations on the quality of the research produced so far. If the student is on the wrong track the instructor has the option of asking the student to try again and re-submit an assignment, perhaps using different sources or different search strategies to produce more relevant on-topic results.

Using flexible assignments with structured library-reference style feedback makes the Internet Navigator online course adaptable to different levels of research skills and to various research topics, and so it serves as a model of how to use Web-based library instruction to involve undergraduate students in self-directed, independent research regardless of whether they are studying in a classroom or distance education setting. Using the classroom flip on a library instruction session means that instead of hearing an instruction lecture from a librarian and then doing research with guidance from a non-librarian instructor the student reads the lecture and then engages in a guided independent research experience with point-of-need help from a reference librarian.

The prepared Internet Navigator class also serves as a model because the simplicity of the design means that the ideas can be easily imitated without requiring a high level of technical expertise. The lesson plan is based on the simple technologies of published Web pages and e-mail. Though much research has been devoted to methods of simulating classroom interaction in online classes, a study of Web-assisted teaching strategies by Frey, Faul and Yankelov (2003) suggests that simpler Web-based course design is equally effective. The study identified the core strategies that students find most useful in online teaching, and the top six were as follows:

1. Posting of grades online
2. Posting of detailed assignment instructions online
3. Online feedback regarding assignments
4. E-mail communication with the instructor
5. Posting of lecture notes online
6. Posting of syllabus online

Of these favored strategies, the only one lacking in the prepared Internet Navigator course is an online grade book. In order to remedy this omission, some instructors have used the course materials embedded in online course authoring software such as WebCT, which allows them to add accessories such as online grade books, discussion lists, or course calendars. Though the prepared course comes with a basic syllabus, as with any textbook, individual instructors will usually give students a second syllabus specific to their own section of the class that includes information such as instructor contact numbers, due dates for assignments and quizzes, tips on completing assignments, and hypertext links to sources in the particular library students are most likely to use.

In the Internet Navigator class, the relationship between teacher and student more closely resembles the one-on-one reference desk teaching relationship than the one-to-many teaching relationship in a typical library instruction classroom setting. The online textbook is similar to a self-guided tutorial which the instructor may choose to supplement with group e-mails. Generic, abstracted advice on how to approach a research question is given in the assigned reading and reinforced by automatically scored multiple choice quizzes that are drawn directly from the reading. The corresponding assignments consist of questions that follow the general form of a reference interview. Answers to questions inform the instructor of the student's existing level of research skills, the chosen research topic, and the planned research strategy. The assignments also include self-evaluation questions that ask the student to reflect on the research process, evaluate the sources that have been found, and consider the next steps.

INTEGRATING REFERENCE SERVICES INTO ONLINE TEACHING

The Internet Navigator course integrates reference services into online teaching using a variety of methods listed and discussed in greater detail below. Each of these examples suggests a point during a student research project where it is appropriate for a librarian/instructor to interject feedback, advice, or help. Using a combination of these ideas should make it possible for librarians to coordinate with other instructors in order to offer one-on-one research help in an online learning environment. In course integrated classroom instruction, these ideas could help encourage student research while avoiding the drawback of using up class time. These methods help solve two of the major difficulties of online information literacy instruction: teaching information literacy skills to students whom the instructor may never see, and determining if students are actually understanding the research concepts presented.

Seven Ways to Integrate Reference Services into Online Teaching

1. Assignments follow the pattern of a reference interview.
2. Assignments evaluated by librarians who are experts at offering reference help.
3. Reference services are described in assigned reading.
4. A reference tool (for background information) is required on the student bibliography.
5. Assignments involve students in a real-life information-seeking process.
6. Instructor directs students to library reference services.
7. Help icon on each page links students to reference help.

1. Assignments Follow the Pattern of a Reference Interview

Perhaps the most important principle for designing online assignments is to make sure that questions prompt the student to provide enough information of the right kind. This is important not only to help the instructor evaluate and score the assignment but also to help an instructor offer helpful feedback and research suggestions. The method of questioning that will most effectively gather this type of information is the reference interview, a technique that has long been used in-person at library reference desks, and more recently in e-mail and live chat reference services. Best practices for a reference interview are described in great detail by Ross, Nilsen and Dewadney (2002) who also provide a succinct definition:

> The term *reference interview* suggests to most librarians a short face-to-face interview conducted for the purpose of finding out what the user really wants to know so that the staff member can match the user's question to the library's store of information. It is generally agreed that users' initial questions are often unclear or incomplete. The purpose of the interview is to elicit from the user sufficient information about the real need to enable the librarian to understand it enough to begin searching. The user's initial question often needs to be clarified, narrowed down, made more detailed, and contextualized.

When reference interviews are conducted by e-mail, Ables (1996) showed that it is most helpful to use a form in order to prompt helpful information and avoid the frustration of drawn-out asynchronous e-mail conversations. The recommended form should include personal data, subject details, and a description of desired search results including external and internal constraints on the kind of data the researcher desires. A well-constructed reference interview can also help student researchers clarify for themselves what kind of information will best answer their questions. Elmborg (2002) suggests ways of turning the reference interview into a form of teaching by using different forms of questions termed "opening questions," "following questions," "basic structure questions," "process questions," and "loss of control questions" (questions that help shake up a complacent researcher). Since an online reference interview does not contain non-verbal clues such as facial expression, body language, gestures, or tone of voice, it is also important to ask students self-reflective questions that can provide the librarian/instructor with additional information about what the student really wants. A particular advantage of online reference is that researchers may be more candid about choosing topics that might be embarrassing to discuss in person or in front of a class.

Some examples will show how different kinds of reference interview questions are used on assignments. The Module 1 assignment asks students for a self-evaluation of pre-existing skills (revealing that a surprisingly large number of students have never used either a library catalog or article database. Carol Hanson at Weber State University is currently using data gathered from this question to conduct research on the research skills of students entering college). The assignment also includes an opening question that is especially useful to the instructor:

> *Describe a situation where you felt you had difficulty in finding the information you needed. What was the situation? Why were you frustrated? What were the barriers? What could have helped?*

This question provides an opportunity for the instructor to suggest ways a student could have solved the problem, often a hint that asking for help at the reference desk could have helped avoid frustration.

The student follows with the Module 2 assignment proposing a research topic and answering basic reference interview style questions about what type of information is needed, as well as process questions that propose a research strategy. Again, the assignment includes a question that provides the instructor with enough information to guide the student:

> Why is this research topic important to you? Why do you want to learn more about this topic? Think critically about this and provide a detailed answer. Please write 4-8 sentences.

This question is of key importance because the topics that students propose are very often ill-formed or overly vague. However, a student's response to the question of why the topic is interesting and important usually gives enough additional information for the librarian/instructor to suggest helpful ways the student can improve the topic and find better keywords. The information from this question provides an opportunity for instructors to offer students a second chance to write a more focused topic statement with more descriptive keywords. Once the topic has been refined to a researchable form, the instructor can offer actual reference suggestions for finding sources. As at a reference desk, these suggestions may include useful synonyms or keywords, possible search statements, subject-specific databases, or even a suggestion for the student to consult library reference services.

On the Module 3 assignment, students present the results of their research: a bibliography of six good, on-topic information sources. The assignment requires one reference tool, one book, two articles, and two Web sites. Students are asked to write citations in proper MLA or APA style, to evaluate the sources, and describe why they were chosen. Again, the assignment gives the instructor an opportunity to evaluate the student's research and offer feedback and suggestions. If the selected sources are off-topic or obviously poor choices for college-level research, the instructor can make specific suggestions to improve the quality of information and ask the student to try again.

Module 4 asks the students to turn in their work in the form of a basic Web page, but the conclusion to the reference interview is also contained in the specific questions asked on the assignment. Students are asked to pick the two best sources they found (often, though not always, scholarly articles or library sources rather than Web pages) and to explain why they are the best. Students are also asked to self-evaluate what they learned about their topic by doing research and what they learned about research in the class, thus answering the online equivalent of the question "Did you find what you need?"

2. Assignments Are Evaluated by Librarians Who Are Experts at Offering Reference Help

Having instructor/librarians evaluate assignments is another important way that reference services are integrated into the class. The assignments break down the research process into a series of steps, and at each step in the process the instructor is able to evaluate and give feedback on the student's research. One advantage to having librarians evaluate the work is that librarians habitually abstract the research process from the particular subject of research and they are less likely than non-librarian instructors to be distracted by the content of the student's topic. Another advantage is that librarian/instructors know what resources are available either through the library or on the Web and can offer reference help by suggesting specific databases, research tools, and Web sites that seem most useful for the proposed topics. Without taking over the keyboard, a librarian/instructor can guide students to try helpful sources or strategies, and ask them to try again if the first strategy fails to produce good results.

Some of the librarian/instructors who are currently teaching the course have over one hundred students enrolled in their sections and so it has been necessary to develop ways to give efficient feedback to large numbers of students. The use of forms for the assignments helps assure that answers arrive in the proper e-mail box in the same order and in a standard format. One way to grade papers efficiently is to develop a scoring rubric. In order to offer personal comments on each student's work, it is paradoxically useful for instructors to develop a set of pre-written responses. Undergraduate students typically make the same kinds of errors in their research (such as picking a topic that is too broad, picking sources that appear first on a list, using sources that are off-topic or clearly unreliable, writing incomplete citations and so on). In order to offer feedback on assignments, instructors can write out a series of responses and then cut and paste the appropriate comments into a response e-mail. It is easy to type a few additional lines if a particular student needs more specific or unique advice.

Another benefit of having reference librarian/instructors is that the task of grading assignments is quite similar to the task of answering other e-mail reference questions. In periods where traffic at the physical or live chat reference desk is slow, it is easy to multi-task while evaluating online research assignments.

3. Reference Services Are Described in Assigned Reading

The assigned reading in Module 2 describes the library as a service organization, including reserve, interlibrary loans, and reference services officered in person, by e-mail, by telephone, or by live-chat. A tip explains the best way to ask a question, and several suggested exercises at the end of the reading direct students to look on the homepage of the library they most often use in order to locate links to reference services. Merely mentioning reference services in the text is probably not an efficient way to get students to ask a reference question, but on the other hand it may not be entirely useless. A study by Hutcherson (2004) found that the term "Reference Services" is the single most commonly understood library term and the meaning was recognized by 94.6% of subjects in the study. A description of reference services in the text at least helps remind students that such services exist.

4. A Reference Tool (for Background Information) Is Required on the Student Bibliography

While Hutcherson (2004) found that most students understood the term "reference services," he also found that by contrast only 75% knew what "reference books" were. In the Internet Navigator text, the term "reference tools" is used to imply that background sources may include Internet and online sources as well as print materials, and that term is likely understood by even fewer students. Despite the fact that finding background information is an important step in the research process, many students neglect to do it since non-librarian instructors often forbid students to include encyclopedias in their research papers in hopes of getting students to use more scholarly sources. Nonetheless, libraries typically devote large amounts of money, space, and staff time to developing and supporting reference collections. The purpose of requiring a reference tool is to help students understand that an important step in the research process is to gather enough background information to generate descriptive keywords and understand the context of the question. Including this requirement also allows the instructor to comment on the difference between broad background information and targeted information that more specifically addresses a research topic.

5. Assignments Involve Students in a Real-Life Information-Seeking Process

Instead of trying to model an idealized research process, the open-ended research assignments in the Internet Navigator aim to involve students in real-life information seeking, albeit with guidance from an instructor. In an online classroom there is a practical reason to get personal answers from each student rather than fishing for canned answers, trying to model a strictly controlled research environment, or limiting sources to those that are already known to provide an answer. Even though open-ended assignments may be slightly harder to score and evaluate, the remote instructor needs to avoid setting up a situation in which students can just copy the answers from each other without doing the coursework. Another benefit is that open-ended questions involve students in all the messiness and ambiguity of real-life research. Instead of specifically designing an assignment that can be done entirely with electronic resources, the student may encounter references to great sounding sources that aren't open-access or full-text on the Web. In this case, the instructor may get a chance to lead the student to other library services such as interlibrary loans or document delivery services.

Even in a physical library building, researchers are more or less left on their own to locate and evaluate information, but a reference desk staffed by an expert is close at hand when point-of-need help is required. Not only can an online course mimic this arrangement; in the context of online information literacy instruction having a remote instructor may even be something of an advantage. Life-long information literacy skills require that students know where to go for help after they complete their classes. An Internet Navigator instructor who reaches the limits of help that is possible to give by e-mail can suggest that students seek additional help using the reference services offered by a library.

One possible difficulty is that reference librarians sometimes view distance education students as a burden if students are frequently referred to a library that is not connected with their academic program, and many Internet Navigator students report using public library resources rather than those of an academic library. The counter argument is that it is a beneficial learning experience for students to practice using the resources of the library most familiar and available. If the available resources happen to prove inadequate, it is yet another opportunity for the instructor/librarian to help solve the problem in a realistic way by offering a referral to more scholarly sources or the reference services of an academic library. If students use actual library Web pages and actual library reference services, they are more likely to be able to reconstruct the research process on their own for future projects when they will be without the guidance of the librarian/instructor.

6. Instructor Directs Students to Library Reference Services

One way instructors can encourage students to try library reference services is by including an electronic link to library reference either in e-mail communications or on online course pages created by the instructor. Links to reference services may be included on the instructor's online syllabus or on a course page created with course-authoring software. E-mail may include links to reference in responses to student assignments, in group e-mails that offer tips on how to complete assignments, or links may be included as a standard component of the signature line of the instructor's e-mail.

7. Help Icon on Each Page Links Students to Reference Help

Each page of the Internet Navigator course includes an icon shaped like a question mark that allows students to ask for help at any point during their reading without needing to look up the instructor's e-mail address or having to search though the course material for other links to help. This is a simple way to make sure that reference help is constantly offered.

STUDENT SELF-EVALUATION OF LEARNING

In the end, the most important outcome of any information literacy course is for the student to feel more confident about being able to locate needed information. The most common way to close a face-to-face reference interview is for the librarian to ask a question that invites follow-up such as "Did you find what you need?" or "Please come back if you don't find what you need." In the Internet Navigator class, those questions would be likely to prompt an uninformative yes or no response that would not be helpful for evaluating student learning, so students are asked to give more details. In the Module 4 assignment, two questions ask students to self-evaluate their course experience. One question asks student to evaluate whether they consider that their research was successful in relation to their chosen topics:

> *After completing the research process, what new things have you learned about your topic? Please write 4 or more sentences.*

Another key question asks students to evaluate what they learned in the abstract about the research process by doing the assigned coursework:

> *How will these research skills be useful to you for future classes and for your everyday life? Discuss new resources you have learned about that will be useful to you. Provide specific examples. How can what you learned in this course enhance your lifelong learning? Please write 4 or more sentences.*

A summary of student self-reports was taken from 71 students enrolled in one section of 2002-2003 classes in answer to the question above. These answers suggest which lessons the students found most valuable in their online information literacy class (most students mentioned more than one useful skill). The results don't mean that only 2 out of 71 students used reference services. It means that 2 out of 71 were excited enough to learn about reference that they mentioned it. By far the most common comment on the class was that it had expanded the students' understanding of research beyond generic Internet search engines, a skill that students felt would be helpful in other college classes. Frequent mention of specific library resources and services shows that students had learned to incorporate library resources in their Web-based research strategies:

- 32 Variety of research tools
- 29 Helpful in other classes
- 22 Evaluation, scholarly vs. popular
- 20 Save time, efficient searching
- 15 Constructing a search statement
- 10 Became more familiar with library
- 9 More confidence with Internet
- 8 Choosing and narrowing a topic
- 5 Write proper citations
- 5 Make a Web page
- 3 Online class experience
- 2 Interlibrary loan
- 2 Library reference
- 2 Organized research process

CONCLUSION

The example of the Internet Navigator course shows that effective online library instruction can be accomplished without the need for technological bells and whistles. Online reference services that are already provided by many libraries are a useful guideline for how best to help and direct remote students, and time-tested reference interview techniques provide a helpful model to use when designing online materials for library instruction. The technique of using forms to gather information for e-mail reference is equally useful when translated into assignments for an online classroom. Rather than relying on self-scoring quizzes or self-checking tutorials, students benefit by getting feedback from a human librarian. Though e-mail reference can be time consuming, the use of grading rubrics and prepared cut-and-paste comments can allow librarian/instructors to teach large numbers of students while still offering specific comments and suggestions to help guide student research. Specific examples from the Internet Navigator class show ways that reference services can be used in conjunction with any online library instruction, whether it is a separate information literacy class or course integrated library instruction.

REFERENCES

Abels, E. G. (1996). The e-mail reference interview. *RQ*, 35(3), 345-58.

Albanese, A. R. (2003). Deserted no more. *Library Journal*, 128(7), 34-36.

Brunvand, A., Lee, D. R, McCloskey, K. M., Hanson, C., Kochan, C. A., & Morrison, R. (2001). Consortium solutions to distance education problems: Utah academic libraries answer the challenges. *Journal of Library Administration*, 31(3/4), 75-92.

Dewald, N. H. (1999). Web-based library instruction: What is good pedagogy? *Information Technology and Libraries*, 18(1), 26-31.

Elmborg, J. K. (2002). Teaching at the desk: Toward a reference pedagogy. *portal: Libraries and the Academy*, 2(3), 455-464.

Frey, A., Faul, A., & Yankelov, P. (2003). Student perception of Web-assisted teaching strategies. *Journal of Social Work Education*, 39(3), 443-457.

Gandhi, S. (2003). Academic librarians and distance education. *Reference & User Services Quarterly*, 43(2), 138-154.

Hansen, C. (2001). The Internet Navigator: An online Internet course for distance learners. *Library Trends*, 50(1), 58-72.

Hutcherson, N. B. (2004). Library jargon: Student recognition of terms and concepts commonly used by librarians in the classroom. *College & Research Libraries*, 65(4), 349-354.

Ladner, B., Beagle, D., Steele, J. R. & Steele, L. (2004). Rethinking online instruction from content transmission to cognitive immersion. *Reference & User Services Quarterly*, 43(4), 337-345.

Lombardo, N. (1998). The Internet Navigator: Collaborative development and delivery of an electronic college course. *PNLA Quarterly*, 63(1), 12-14.

Rashtchy, S. & Avilo, J. M. (2003). The golden search: Dynamics of the online search market and the scope of opportunity. U.S. Bancorp Piper Jaffray, Equity Research.

Ross, C. S., Nilsen, K., & Dewdney, P. (2002). Conducting the reference interview: A how-to-do-it manual for librarians. New York, London: Neal-Schuman Publishers.

Saunders, E. S. (2003). The effect of bibliographic instruction on the demand for reference services. *portal: Libraries and the Academy*, 3(1), 35-39.

UALC Information for Life Taskforce. (2001). Internet Navigator, <http://www-navigator.utah.edu/>.

Copyright
and the Delivery of Library Services
to Distance Learners

Irmin Allner

SUMMARY. Library service for distance education necessitates knowledge of important new regulations that were enforced by recent amendments to copyright law. This article begins with an overview of the copyright law of 1976 related to nonprofit educational institutions. Then the Digital Millennium Copyright Act (DMCA) of 1998 and the Technology, Education and Copyright Harmonization Act (TEACH Act) of 2002 are discussed. These acts, which amended the Copyright Act of 1976, require more rigorous measures by nonprofit educational institutions to ensure compliance. The article concludes with how to avoid copyright infringement and the necessity to educate library personnel about copyright law. *[Article copies available for a fee from The Haworth Document Delivery Service: 1-800-HAWORTH. E-mail address: <docdelivery@haworthpress.com> Website: <http://www.HaworthPress.com> © 2004 by The Haworth Press, Inc. All rights reserved.]*

Irmin Allner (kfiba00@tamuk.edu) is Head of Reference and Instructional Services, James C. Jernigan Library, Texas A&M University-Kingsville, MSC 197, Kingsville, TX 78363-8202.

[Haworth co-indexing entry note]: "Copyright and the Delivery of Library Services to Distance Learners." Allner, Irmin. Co-published simultaneously in *Internet Reference Services Quarterly* (The Haworth Information Press, an imprint of The Haworth Press, Inc.) Vol. 9, No. 3/4, 2004, pp. 179-192; and: *Internet Reference Support for Distance Learners* (ed: William Miller, and Rita M. Pellen) The Haworth Information Press, an imprint of The Haworth Press, Inc., 2004, pp. 179-192. Single or multiple copies of this article are available for a fee from The Haworth Document Delivery Service [1-800-HAWORTH, 9:00 a.m. - 5:00 p.m. (EST). E-mail address: docdelivery@haworthpress.com].

Available online at http://www.haworthpress.com/web/IRSQ
© 2004 by The Haworth Press, Inc. All rights reserved.
Digital Object Identifier: 10.1300/J136v09n03_13

KEYWORDS. Copyright law, distance education, library services, Digital Millennium Copyright Act (DMCA) of 1998, Technology, Education and Harmonization Act (TEACH Act) of 2002, Copyright Law of 1976, Fair Use Doctrine

INTRODUCTION

A significant development in education during the past quarter century has been the development of distance education. Technological innovations have changed how we conduct research and engage in teaching and learning. In distance education we do not have the traditional teaching model of face-to-face interaction. Those who learn and those who teach are usually in different locations. The recent development of new computer-based communication technologies is a primary factor in the increase of distance education. Modes of distance education include interactive video-conferencing, online discussions, asynchronous instruction accessed at the convenience of students, and tutorials. Furthermore, students have instant access to information posted on the educational institution's Web site and a multitude of other information available on the Internet. Digital learning applications used in distance education depend on the transmission of instructional materials via the Internet. However, the transmission via the Internet raises the difficult question of how to adequately protect copyrighted materials in a networked environment which provides instantaneous world-wide access.

Academic libraries play a crucial role in providing adequate support for distance education. Students enrolled in distance education courses need access to library resources and services so that they can succeed in their studies. These services include timely delivery of books and journal articles through interlibrary loan, reciprocal borrowing agreements with libraries in close proximity to distance education students, e-reserves, help with research projects through library instruction via video-conferencing, interactive Web-based tutorials, e-mail reference, live virtual reference, access to electronic databases that the library subscribes to, and instructional materials made available online by instructors and library personnel. However, copyright issues may limit a library's ability to provide support. It is important to know about recent changes in copyright law in a networked environment, not only for instructors of distance education but also for librarians, in order to avoid violations of the law.

COPYRIGHT AND FAIR USE DOCTRINE

As background, it is important to be aware of significant features of copyright, the copyright statute of 1976, and the Fair Use Doctrine. Copyright is the exclusive right of an author or other creator to make copies, license, and otherwise exploit a literary, musical, or artistic work, whether printed, audio, video, etc. When a work has been copyrighted, permission from the copyright holder must be obtained in order to reproduce the work. If a work is reproduced without permission, the holder of the copyright may sue for damages. Presently, U.S. copyright grants exclusive rights to a work in the United States for the life of the author plus 70 years after the author's death.[1]

The copyright statute of 1976 refers to copyrighted works as "original works of authorship fixed in any tangible medium of expression, now known or later developed, from which they can be perceived, reproduced, or otherwise communicated, either directly or with the aid of a machine or device" (17 U.S.C. Sec. 102[a]). Works protected under the Copyright Act of 1976 include: (1) literary works, (2) musical works, including any accompanying words, (3) dramatic works, including any accompanying music, (4) pantomimes and choreographic works, (5) pictorial, graphic, and sculptural works, (6) motion pictures and other audiovisual works, (7) sound recordings, and (8) architectural works.

Copyright protects the expression of an idea, not the idea itself. Also a copyrighted work needs to meet three requirements: (a) originality, (b) creativity, and (c) fixation. Originality means that the work needs to be an independent creation; the work should not be copied from another. Creativity is considered a separate element but is closely interrelated to originality. Fixation refers to the work being "sufficiently permanent or stable to permit it to be perceived, reproduced, or otherwise communicated for a period of more than transitory duration" (17 U.S.C. Sec. 101).

An important limitation imposed on the exclusive rights granted to copyright owners is the Fair Use Doctrine (17 U.S.C. Sec. 107). The Fair Use Doctrine is a legal principle that provides certain limitations on the exclusive rights of copyright holders. As defined in *Black's Law Dictionary*,

> Fair Use is a reasonable and limited use of copyrighted work without the author's permission, such as quoting from a book in a book review or using parts of it in a parody. Fair use is a defense to an in-

fringement claim, depending on the following statutory factors: (1) the purpose and character of the use, (2) the nature of the copyrighted work, (3) the amount of the work used, and (4) the economic impact of the use.[2]

Determining whether the use of specific materials falls under the Fair Use Doctrine is not easy. The four factors (i.e., purpose, nature, amount, and effect) need to "be considered in each instance, based on the particular facts of a given case."[3]

A common practice in schools and universities has been to follow the *Agreement on Guidelines for Classroom Copying in Not-For-Profit Educational Institutions with Respect to Books and Periodicals*, which was reached in 1976 between various interest groups. As pointed out by Lan and Dagley, "The agreement does not constitute statutory or regulatory language; it is merely an agreement made by parties that include some groups that are most likely to bring a copyright action. The agreement provides a 'safe harbor' for classroom teachers on where fair use applies."[4] The agreement allows teachers to make single copies for research and instructional purposes of the following: (a) a chapter from a book, (b) an article from a periodical or newspaper, (c) a short story, (d) a short essay or poem, (e) a chart, graph, diagram, drawing, cartoon, or picture from a book, periodical, or newspaper. Multiple copies for classroom use are allowed. Teachers may make one copy for each student, if the copying meets the test for brevity and spontaneity and a notice of copyright is included on each copy.

COPYRIGHT AND DISTANCE EDUCATION

Digital Millennium Copyright Act (DMCA)

Obviously, the aforementioned guidelines do not apply to distance education. In the early 1990s "with the emergence of digital technology and its growing use in education," it became increasingly clear "that an update to copyright legislation was needed. After several years of discussion, study, public hearings, and repeated attempts at legislation, the Digital Millennium Copyright Act (DMCA) was signed into law on October 28, 1998."[5]

The DMCA, as described by Lutzker, "is a very complex Act, which generated controversy and left unfinished business in its wake."[6] Important new rules of the DMCA, as outlined by Lutzker,[7] are:

1. *Prohibition of the circumvention of Technological Protection Measures (TPMs):* The use of equipment or services that circumvents technology limiting access to copyrighted works is prohibited. Libraries and non-profit educational institutions are allowed on a limited basis to circumvent a TPM in order to review a work for possible licensing.
2. *Copyright Management Information:* Alteration of information embedded in digital works, such as ownership, authorship, and licensing is prohibited.
3. *Change in Library Archival Preservation Rules:* Up to three (3) copies may be made: one for archival purposes, one as a master, and one as a use copy from which other allowable copies may be made.
4. *Online Service Provider (OSP) Limitation on Liability:* Online Service Providers who transmit and store, as well as provide hyperlinks and software to facilitate online access are not held liable for copyright infringement, provided that they are unaware of copyright infringement and they take the necessary measures to disable access upon discovery of wrongful online access.

Libraries and educational institutions fall under the category of Online Service Provider and need to abide by OSP copyright rules. The reasons for this are explained very well by Lutzker as follows:

Traditionally, common carriers have been exempt from liability for copyright infringement because they merely provide the facilities that link sender and receiver and have no control over the actual content of the transmission. Many libraries and educational institutions feel this describes their functions for patrons, students and faculty in connection with the Internet. However, in their capacity as OSPs, libraries and educational institutions do more. Technically, they provide software to link users to sites, they store information on their server and they facilitate recordings and displays by subscribers. Each of these activities is a function recognized in copyright law as an exclusive right of copyright owners. Copyright law holds that helping someone else to violate copyright rights is an infringement, so-called "vicarious" or "contributory" infringement. Thus, when certain commercial OSPs were accused of violating copyright law, some courts held them liable for copyright infringement. The fact that an institution is "not for profit" does not eliminate exposure to the copyright infringement claim.[8]

What this means is that libraries and educational institutions need to understand the rules and institute proper procedures to ensure compliance.

Distance Education

In the DMCA, important issues related to distance education using digital networks remained unresolved. However, the Copyright Office was commissioned to study key issues and to report back to Congress. Key issues to be studied included "the need for an exemption from exclusive rights of copyright owners for distance education through digital networks," "categories of works to be included in any exemption," "limitations on the portions of works that may be used under any distance education exemption," "the parties who should be entitled to the benefits of any exemption," "the parties who should be eligible to receive distance education materials under the exemption," and "technological measures to safeguard against unauthorized access."[9]

Technology, Education and Copyright Harmonization Act (TEACH Act)

The aforementioned key issues related to distance education were addressed several years later. On November 2, 2002, the "Technology, Education and Copyright Harmonization Act" (TEACH Act) was signed into law by President Bush. As summed up by Crews, "TEACH redefines the terms and conditions on which accredited, nonprofit educational institutions throughout the U.S. may use copyright protected materials in distance education–including on websites and by other digital means–without permission from the copyright owner and without payment of royalties."[10] This new law is an improvement over the previous version of Section 110 (2) of the Copyright Law; however, its rigorous requirements necessitate adequate measures by non-profit educational institutions in order to avoid violations leading to law suits. As explained by Crews, "both the meaning of fair use and the details of the specific statute [Section 110 (2)] become much more rigorous when the materials are uploaded to websites, transmitted anywhere in the world, and are easily downloaded, altered, or further transmitted by students and other users–all posing possible threats to the interests of copyright owners."[11]

The TEACH Act is not written in plain English. As Crews says, "the statutory language itself is often convoluted and does not necessarily flow gracefully."[12] The following is a summary of the major benefits as well as statutory requirements of the TEACH Act as outlined by Crews:

Benefits

- Expanded range of allowed works. "The display and performance of nearly all types of works" is allowed.
- Expansion of receiving locations. The transmission of educational content is no longer limited to classrooms and other locations. "Educational institutions may now reach students through distance education at any location."
- Storage of transmitted content. Storage of transmitted content, even if it includes copyright content owned by others, is allowed. Also the law "allows retention of the content and student access for a brief period of time."
- Digitizing of analog works. Digitization of some analog works is allowed. However, the material converted into digital format needs to be within the materials and scope limitations specified under the new law.

Requirements

1. The educational institution must implement copyright policies and issue informational materials that explain and promote compliance with copyright law. These materials must be provided to faculty, students, and relevant staff members.
2. Materials distributed to students must have a notice about copyright.
3. The transmission of content must be made only for students officially enrolled in the course for which the transmission is made.
4. There must be technological controls on storage and dissemination. Technical measures must be applied to prevent "retention of the work in accessible form by recipients of the transmission . . . for no longer than the class session" and also prevent recipients of the content from engaging in "unauthorized further dissemination of the work in accessible form." The term "class session" is ambiguous in the context of distance education and most likely means that students should be unable to access a transmission after a specified time.

While the TEACH Act allows an expanded range of works, it does not include uses of textbooks and other materials that should be purchased by students. An instructor should not scan and upload "chapters from a textbook in lieu of having the students purchase that material for their own use." However, "occasional, brief handouts–perhaps including entire short works–may be permitted in distance education, while reserves and other outside reading may not be proper materials to scan and display under the auspices of the new law."[13]

CRITIQUE OF CURRENT LEGISLATION

While the new legislation has brought the copyright law more up-to-date for distance education, it is not perfect. Both Crews and Lipinski point out its limitations. Crews expresses his reservations as follows:

> Some news announcements anticipating the TEACH Act have suggested that the use of materials in distance education will be on a par with the broad rights of performance and display allowed in the face-to-face classroom. This characterization of the law neglects the many differences between the relevant statutes. In the traditional classroom, the Copyright Act long has allowed instructors to "perform" or "display" copyrighted works with few restrictions (Section 110(1)). By contrast, both the previous and the new versions of the statute applicable to distance education are replete with conditions, limits, and restrictions. Make no mistake: While the TEACH Act is a major improvement over the previous version of Section 110(2), the law still imposes numerous requirements for distance education that reach far beyond the modest limits in the traditional classroom.[14]

Lipinski goes into more detail as to why the new law fails to provide equivalent rights to distance education given under the Fair Use Doctrine for use of materials in face-to-face instruction. Lipinski argues: "There is an ascendancy of digital ownership rights that threatens to undermine the concept of technological neutrality, which in essence guarantees that ownership as well as 'use' rights apply equally to analog and digital environments." The result is a diminution of "access and use rights of individuals, institutions, and other users of copyrighted material, and the incentive of copyright owners to present works to the public in digital formats alone."[15] Rulings discussed by him that exemplify the ascendancy of digital ownership rights are restrictions imposed on digital copies of archival materials, anticircumvention and antitrafficking rules of Section 1201, and increased compliance requirements and exclusions in online (digital) education.

In the DMCA, the amendment to Section 108 of the copyright law allows qualifying libraries and archives "to make up to three digital copies of works in its collection, for preservation and security of unpublished works . . . and for replacement purposes for items damaged, deteriorating, lost, or stolen, or when in an obsolete format."[16] However, the digitized materials must not be "distributed or available to the public outside the premises of the library or archive." Lipinski justifiably asks: "Why must [only] in-house library and archive patrons be granted" access, "while remote users, the sort of patron for whom a digital version of the collection would be the most logical format, be denied that ability?"[17] Lipinski elaborates on this point further. What were the reasons for the imposition of these restrictions on libraries and archives in the digital environment? They are clearly spelled out in the Senate DMCA Report:

> Although online interactive digital networks have since given birth to online digital "libraries" and "archives" that exist only in the virtual (rather than physical) sense on Web sites, bulletin boards and home pages across the Internet, it is not the committee's intent that section 108 as revised apply to such collections of information . . . The extension of the application of Section 108 to all such sites is tantamount to creating an exception to the exclusive rights of copyright holders that would permit any person who has an online Website, bulletin boards, or home page to freely reproduce and distribute copyrighted works. Such an exemption would swallow the general rule and severely impair the copyright owner's right and ability to commercially exploit their copyrighted works. (S.Rpt. 105-109, 105th Cong., 2d Session 62 (1998))[18]

The anticircumvention and antitrafficking rules of Section 1201, enacted as part of the DMCA, are another example of increased copyright ownership rights in the digital environment. This section specifies that "distributing or sharing" as well as "creating and marketing a technology that circumvents a use control" is a legal offense. Furthermore, this section mandates that "circumventing copyright access controls is a separate offense, in addition to copyright infringement."[19]

Finally, amendments to the copyright law established increased compliance requirements and exclusions in online (digital) education. The Technology, Education and Copyright Harmonization (TEACH) Act of 2002 amended 17 U.S.C. Section 110(2), i.e., the section "which governs transmission of copyrighted materials . . . in distance education." The revised law requires "extensive compliance and monitoring provisions, such as expanded use of warning notices, regulation of student access to secure site material and the use of technological measures that prevent retention or downstream distribution by students, and the establishment and dissemination of an institutional compliance policy."[20] It is wrong to assume that the TEACH Act provides expanded rights for online course content delivery. On the contrary, as Lipinski points out, the "previous law governing performance and display rights of educators in live, face-to-face teaching scenarios offered a greater bundle of rights to teachers under Section 110(1) than instructors in 'broadcast' settings under section 110(2)."[21] Furthermore, "there are increased compliance requirements that the institution must now undertake." The institution is required

> to take an active role in promoting copyright compliance. Under TEACH section 110(2)(D)(i) the transmitting body or institution must institute copyright policies, provide informational materials to faculty, staff, and students about copyright law in the hopes of promoting compliance, and provide notice to students that course material may be subject to copyright protection. Institutions can no longer turn a blind eye to the extensive uploading, downloading, and printing of course materials that occurs by educators and students in the course of a distance class scenario; uploading, downloading, and printing that administrators know occurs and which at least in some instances is beyond the limits of the copyright law, and arguably beyond the reach of TEACH.[22]

DISTANCE EDUCATION AND LIBRARY SERVICES

The impact of the new copyright rules on library services in general and library services for distance education in particular is undoubtedly considerable. Postings of instructional materials for remote users on the library's Web site are a common practice. However, if instructional materials are copied from another institution's Web site and adaptations are made, then they should not be posted without copyright permission. Information on the Internet is copyrighted, and free access to materials does not put them in the public domain. Linking to other Web sites is usually not seen as copyright infringement; however, in some instances it may subject one to liability "for infringement as a contributory infringer."[23] Libraries should not knowingly link to infringing sites.[24]

Linking to other Web sites is a widespread practice in libraries. As pointed out by Shkolnikov, "Linking allows librarians to extend their library collections virtually and transform conventional libraries into 'libraries without walls.'"[25] However, some linking may unknowingly be done in violation of copyright. There have been a number of legal cases, involving mostly for-profit organizations, involving accusations of unlawful linking, as for example linking to unauthorized copyrighted music or illegal software. None of these lawsuits affected libraries. However, as argued by Shkolnikov, it is important for librarians to be on the safe side and not to link to infringing materials and, if necessary, obtain permission to link to a particular site.[26]

The use of database screen captures for illustrations of online searching guides and tutorials is another instance where librarians may not consider it necessary to obtain copyright permission. Leger recommends obtaining permission from the copyright holder, which is best started by contacting the company that provides the online interface for searching a database, but may also include among others the content provider, i.e., the publisher of the database.[27]

Making the library's Web site copyright-correct may not always be given sufficient attention.[28] Also worth mentioning here is that not only content but also the page design is copyrighted. For example, the main page of a private Louisiana university had to be taken down because it closely resembled the main page of a university in Wisconsin. This action had to be taken because the Wisconsin university had instituted legal proceedings.

Aside from avoiding copyright infringement on the library's Web page, the licensing of access to online databases and electronic reserves is another important issue. The library needs to be careful not to inadvertently provide unauthorized access to online databases. If, as generally is the case, the license agreement allows access only by faculty, students, and staff affiliated with the institution, then proper authentication procedures need to be put in place. Another issue is e-reserves. Before making materials available for remote access via e-reserves, all materials need to be evaluated on a case-by-case basis, using the fair use factors (i.e., character of the use, nature of the work to be used, the amount used, and the effect of the use on the market for a value of the work). In order to comply with the stipulations under the fourth factor (the effect of use on the market), many libraries "limit e-reserves access to students within the institution or within a particular class or classes" and "terminate student access at the end of a relevant semester . . . or after the student has completed the course." Also, "as a result of the increase in licensed electronic resources, the percentage of print materials requested and digitized for e-reserves is diminishing."[29] In order to avoid copyright infringement for repeat use, some libraries prefer to use only materials in electronic format for which they paid to have access and for which the license agreement allows the use for e-reserves.

CONCLUSION

Library personnel need to be knowledgeable about copyright law in a networked environment. The TEACH Act specifically stipulates that institutions are responsible for instituting policies regarding copyright and providing faculty, students, and relevant staff members with informational materials that accurately describe and promote compliance with copyright law. The TEACH Act mandates increased compliance requirements of copyright law by nonprofit organizations. This means that "institutions will have to plan, adopt, and implement a copyright compliance program that includes copyright policies and organizational development programs that seek to inform students and staff of copyright law requirements and responsibilities."[30] Ideally, an Intellectual Property Attorney, heading the University Copyright Office, will ensure that these requirements are met and also act as consultant to the teaching faculty and librarians. Unfortunately, these ideal conditions do not exist at many institutions. The responsibility rests with librarians to keep themselves up-to-date on copyright law related to library services and to take the initiative in establishing guidelines and training.

Finally, the following excellent suggestions by Walther may be helpful:

1. Build solid and diverse relationships across academic units to assist in intellectual property discussions.
2. Develop a cross campus committee that reviews intellectual property issues and communicates guidelines.

3. Publish intellectual property policies in campus documents, on relevant parts of the campus Web site, and in other locations visible to the campus community.
4. Develop institutional expertise in intellectual property issues to foster collegiality and distribute appropriate training.
5. Use guidelines, policies, and contracts to balance the interests of intellectual property creators and the institution.[31]

NOTES

1. In fact, the rules for determining whether a work is under copyright protection is more complex and summarized as follows in "Fair Use of Copyrighted Materials":

> Any work published on or before December 31, 1922, is now in the public domain. Works published between January 1, 1923 and December 31, 1978, inclusive, are protected for a term of 95 years from the date of publication, with the proper notice. But if the work was published between 1923 and December 31, 1963, when there used to be a (non-automatic) "renewal term," the copyright owner may not have renewed the work. If he or she did not renew, the original term of protection (28 years) would now be expired and these works will be in the public domain. After 1978, the way we measure the term of protection changes. It is no longer related to a date of publication, but rather runs for 70 years from the date the author dies (called, "life of the author" plus 70 years). Further, publication is irrelevant. Works are protected whether they are published or not. Finally, those works that were created before December 31, 1978, but never published, are now protected for the life of the author plus 70 years. (Fair Use of Copyrighted Materials, p. 4-5. Available: http://www.utsystem.edu/ogc/intellectualproperty/copypol2.htm. Accessed: 5/31/2004)

2. Bryan A. Garner, Ed. *Black's Law Dictionary*. 7th ed. (St. Paul, Minn.: West Group, 1999), 617.
3. Educational Fair Use Guidelines for Distance Learning, Revised Draft, November 18, 1996, p. 1. Available: http://www.utsystem.edu/ogc/intellectualproperty/distguid.htm. Accessed: 5/31/2004.
4. Jiang Lan and Dave Dagley. "Teaching via the Internet: A Brief Review of Copyright Law and Legal Issues." *Educational Technology Review* no. 11 (1999): 27.
5. Kathe Hicks Albrecht. "The Digital Dilemma: Legislative Issues in Distance Education." *Art Documentation* 18, no. 2: 12.
6. Arnolf P. Lutzker. Primer on the Digital Millennium: What the Digital Millennium Copyright Act and the Copyright Term Extension Act Mean for the Library Community, p. 2. Available: http://www.arl.org/info/frn/copy/primer.html. Accessed: June 13, 2004.
7. Lutzker, 8, 9, 27.
8. Lutzker, 12.
9. Lutzker, 18.

10. Kenneth D. Crews. New Copyright Law for Distance Education: The Meaning and Importance of the TEACH Act, p. 2. Available: http://www.ala.org/Template. cfm?Section=Distance_Education_and_the_TEACH_Act&T. Accessed: June 13, 2004.

11. Crews, 4.

12. Crews, 3.

13. Crews, 3-12.

14. Crews, 5.

15. Thomas A. Lipinski. "The Myth of Technological Neutrality in Copyright and the Rights of Institutional Users: Recent Legal Challenges to the Information Organization as Mediator and the Impact of the DMCA, WIPO, and TEACH." *Journal of the American Society for Information Science and Technology* 54, no. 9 (2003): 824.

16. Lipinski, 827.

17. Lipinski, 827.

18. Lipinski, 827-828.

19. Lipinski, 828.

20. Lipinski, 831.

21. Lipinski, 831.

22. Lipinski, 832.

23. Mary Minow and Thomas A. Lipinski. *The Library's Legal Answer Book.* (Chicago: American Library Assoc., 2003), 106.

24. "A link to a site that is known to contain infringing material or is otherwise highly suspect, along with encouragement to patrons to download content from that site, would meet the standards of contributory infringement" (Minow and Lipinski, 109).

25. Tanya Shkolnikov. "To link or not to link: How to avoid copyright traps on the Internet." *The Journal of Academic Librarianship* 28, no. 3 (2002): 133.

26. Shkolnikov, 137.

27. Linda Leger. "Obtaining copyright permission to use screen captures in Web-based instructional materials." *Feliciter* 47, no. 5 (2001): 249.

28. An excellent more detailed discussion of copyright and the library Website, covering liability for direct, contributory, and vicarious infringement, is given in Minow and Lipinski, 103-117.

29. "ACRL Issues Statement on Fair Use and Electronic Reserves Systems," November 21, 2003, p. 1. Available: http://www.ala.org/PrinterTemplate.cfm?Template=/ ContentMangement/HTMLDisplay.cf. Accessed: July 1, 2004.

30. Thomas A. Lipinski. "Legal Reform in an Electronic Age: Analysis and Critique of the Construction and Operation of S. 487, The Technology, Education and Copyright Harmonization (TEACH) Act of 2001." *Brigham Young University Education and Law Journal* 95 (2003): 19.

31. James H. Walter. *Copyright Concerns in the Age of Distance Education.* ERIC Digest ED 446727, p. 3.

From Cameras to Camtasia:
Streaming Media Without the Stress

Christopher Cox

SUMMARY. Librarians are always looking for new and innovative ways of delivering content to their users. Camtasia Studio, a screen capture program, offers a simple, low-cost alternative to live video when it comes to creating streaming audio and video content. Following up on a 2001 article in *Computers in Libraries*, the author compares his experiences using Camtasia Studio to his original experience using live video. He determines that Camtasia offers similar functionality with less equipment and lower cost than the traditional method. *[Article copies available for a fee from The Haworth Document Delivery Service: 1-800-HAWORTH. E-mail address: <docdelivery@haworthpress.com> Website: <http://www.HaworthPress.com> © 2004 by The Haworth Press, Inc. All rights reserved.]*

KEYWORDS. Streaming media, streaming video, Camtasia, screen capture, tutorials, library instruction, information literacy, distance learning, distance education

It was a cold, winter day in Worcester. A fresh snow forced the tree limbs to kiss pavement. Unhappy with the weather, my boss chose this

---

Christopher Cox (coxcn@uwec.edu) is Assistant Director of Libraries, William D. McIntyre Library, University of Wisconsin-Eau Claire, 105 Garfield Avenue–L 3002A, Eau Claire, WI 54702-4004.

[Haworth co-indexing entry note]: "From Cameras to Camtasia: Streaming Media Without the Stress." Cox, Christopher. Co-published simultaneously in *Internet Reference Services Quarterly* (The Haworth Information Press, an imprint of The Haworth Press, Inc.) Vol. 9, No. 3/4, 2004, pp. 193-200; and: *Internet Reference Support for Distance Learners* (ed: William Miller, and Rita M. Pellen) The Haworth Information Press, an imprint of The Haworth Press, Inc., 2004, pp. 193-200. Single or multiple copies of this article are available for a fee from The Haworth Document Delivery Service [1-800-HAWORTH, 9:00 a.m. - 5:00 p.m. (EST). E-mail address: docdelivery@haworthpress.com].

Digital Object Identifier: 10.1300/J136v09n03_14

opportunity to remind me that I hadn't updated the streaming videos produced over a year ago. Policies and interfaces had changed; reappraisal was necessary. But how? Steve, my partner in crime in the creation of the videos, had left for greener pastures. I was left holding the bag, with no notion of how to re-record or re-edit the content. I needed a solution and I needed it now.

In March 2002, an article written by Stephen Pratt and myself appeared in *Computers in Libraries*. In the style of a hard-boiled detective novel, the article details how Steve and I solved the mystery of how to reach untapped populations like distance learners by using streaming media to create library resource tutorials. Not long after the article was published, Steve left WPI. I was left with a disk full of clips, videos that were aging quickly and required updating, and another mystery to solve: how would I be able to update them? The solution? Camtasia Studio, a screen capture program that allows you to record everything happening on your computer monitor, a program that is not only easy to use but also produces videos of equal quality in less time for less money. This article will detail my experiences with Camtasia Studio and offer advice on how you can create your own streaming media.

For those unfamiliar with streaming media, Mortensen describes it as "an audio/video presentation delivered across a network in such a way that it is viewed while being downloaded onto the user's computer" (37). Since the technology is often used on the Internet for movie trailers, TV program clips, and live events, users are familiar with it. To view the file, users need to have a video client like Windows Media Player installed on their PCs. When clicking a link to a streaming media file, a request is sent to the server containing the file to begin downloading the media to your desktop. Once a few seconds of media are buffered, the client plays the file while it continues to download the rest of it in the background.

There are numerous benefits to using streaming media in education. Steaming media is more engaging and interactive for students than the common, stale lecture. Studies have shown that students receiving streaming instruction in addition to traditional instruction show dramatic improvements in achievement (Reed 14). Files are viewable virtually anywhere, anyplace, thus an unlimited number of users can be reached. They can be viewed multiple times, enforcing lessons and accommodating slower learners. Finally, they are indexable, so sections can be watched and re-watched as often as desired.

Librarians and educators have made good use of video and streaming media to deliver content to their clientele. A great deal of literature exists detailing the process of creating the more common VHS format instruction video. For example, Stey and Walton of the New England Region of the National Network of Medicine (1996) detail how they created two VHS format videos to assist users in searching GRATEFUL MED and DOCLINE. When it comes to streaming media, however, the literature is a bit sparse. From an educational standpoint, there are a variety of helpful overview articles. Mortensen, Schlieve, and Young (2000) and Knee, Musgrove, and Musgrove (2000) offer clear explanations of what streaming video is and step-by-step instructions on how to create it. These articles, however, offer no practical applications of the technology.

Crowther and Wallace (2001) were one of the first to write about using streaming media for library instruction, specifically the creation of a streamable video tour of the library's main reference room for business students at the University of Tennessee. Other librarians such as Hickok (2002), Pasch and Stewart (2002) and Lee and Burrell (2004) have since published articles detailing their applications. Hickok used the technology to create a series of videos orienting students to the Cal Fullerton library. Pasch and Stewart created 55 tutorials for students in their for-credit "Information in Cyberspace" class. Lee and Burrell created short video modules on different library tools and topics for a more general audience. As time went on and the process of maintaining tutorials grew more costly, librarians and educators stumbled upon TechSmith's screen-capture program Camtasia Studio.

Camtasia Studio (http://www.techsmith.com) lets you capture full motion activity on your computer screen for later playback. The software suite includes a screen recorder (Camtasia Recorder) and a video production tool (Camtasia Producer). Audio can be recorded separately or at the same time as the screen activity. A compression tool is also provided. The software is priced at around $300. Other screen-capture products do exist, such as Macromedia's RoboDemo, but they are not as simple to use and don't often record in non-proprietary file formats like .AVIs.

The use of Camtasia Studio to create streaming media for educational purposes is recorded as early as 2001 by Ordonez in *Educause Quarterly*. A business faculty member at Southern Oregon University, Ordonez explains how he uses Camtasia to digitize and package class lectures. Faculty who teach as part of WPI's Advanced Distance Learning Network (ADLN) have been using Camtasia Studio for the last year to record lectures for delivery via Blackboard. Though commonly used by librarians as well, a search of the literature yields few results. Pasch

and Stewart (2002) explain how they moved from traditional video capture to Camtasia Studio, while Tempelman-Kluit and Ehrenberg's 2003
article in *Feliciter* describes the creation of short tutorials on library
products and services for NYU.

The steps required to create streaming media using more traditional
video methods are exactly the same with Camtasia Studio. The first step
is preproduction, which involves a needs analysis and the creation of a
script. Next comes production, the actual capturing of video content. Finally, post-production, usually the most time-consuming of the three,
involves editing the video and encoding or compressing the media for
delivery. All that's left at that point is publishing the video to a Web
server assessing the material's success.

Preproduction is probably the most important step in the process. Inadequate planning at this stage will result in wasted time and an inferior
product. There are a number of things to consider. First of all, who is
your audience? Distance learners? Students? Faculty? This will determine not only the content of your videos but also whether streaming media is the best method of delivery. What information are you trying to
convey to your audience? For the 2001 project with Steve, our audience
was ADLN students who were already familiar with technologies such
as streaming media and who rarely came to campus. Knowing this, we
created a series of five videos on topics such as accessing the proxy
server, searching the library catalog, and using interlibrary loan. To
evaluate Camtasia Studio's effectiveness, I re-created the "Using Interlibrary Loan" video. The next few pages will document what was
required, share tips and tricks I've discovered using Camtasia, and
compare the processes and final products of each method.

Once you've determined your audience and subject matter, it's time
to write the script. This step is the same whether you shoot live video or
use Camtasia Studio. The script should include all dialogue and note all
camera and screen shots. In general, base them on the presentations you
make in class every day. Cut down on library jargon since the videos
won't offer much opportunity for clarification. Be sure you read the
script aloud to see how it sounds and pass it along to your colleagues for
feedback. Include contact information in the form of the library's telephone number and e-mail address at the end of each video in case there
are any questions.

When comparing a standard video shoot to screen capture using
Camtasia, the production phase is quite different. The original video
shoot had to be scheduled weeks ahead of time. The shoot occurred in
WPI's TV Studio, a state-of-the-art facility equipped with a lighting

grid, a digital video camera with remote tilt/pan control, and a high-quality tape deck. At the time we opted not to shoot any footage on location because of the time and cost involved in setting up cameras and lights in another place. Steve and one other person were required to record the shoot and two tracks were recorded—an audio track of the script and a video track of the computer screen. Steve combined them to create the video. Mistakes had to be limited so multiple passes were recorded for each video. The studio time required to record the five five-minute videos was approximately two hours.

With Camtasia, the equipment needed to record content is significantly reduced. All that is required is a copy of Camtasia Studio (approximately $300), a computer ($3,000), and a good quality microphone ($50). In addition, I used a digital video camera ($30) for live-feed video of myself and a digital camera ($200) to take stills of locations within the library. Total cost: $3,580, vs. $36,000 alone for the TV Studio camera. You can see that Camtasia Studio offers a low-cost streaming media alternative for libraries with limited funds and staff.

Camtasia Recorder, which comes bundled in the Camtasia Studio suite, is used to capture content. The software is as simple to use as a tape recorder. Simply start Camtasia Studio, choose the content you wish to record (a region of the screen, a particular window or the entire screen) and click the record button. All screen activity will be recorded until you hit the stop button.

I found it easier to record short snippets of content and then edit them together rather than record the entire lesson at once. When doing that, I inevitably screwed up enough that I would have to start the entire recording process over again. I found that by recording short clips I was less prone to make mistakes. The shorter clips were also easier to handle when editing. Shorter clips make for easier updating as well.

Using a digital video camera, I recorded a few video snippets of myself to add later to recreate the video more accurately. These "talking head" shots probably are not necessary to user learning but in the interest of this experiment I kept them in. To avoid awkward transitions, it's best to change your background and window settings to something standard. I also hid the task bar to gain more screen space and changed the resolution to 800 × 600.

Practice your typing and moving the mouse at a certain pace prior to recording. Mouse jerking can be edited out with Camtasia, but it's a pain to do. I found it easier to record the audio with the video rather than do it afterwards. It was extremely difficult to keep the audio and video in synch when recording them separately. Also, make sure you have a nice, quiet place to record the audio so there isn't any background interference. Lastly, buy a good quality microphone headset and be sure to do a few audio tests for positioning.

Once recording is complete, it's time for editing or post-production. It took Steve two months working alone to edit the live videos. Steve used Adobe Premiere, a $550 digital video-editing software package. Steve logged the video and cut it into clips. He used Adobe Photoshop ($600) to capture screenprints and then brought them into Premiere to create transition effects such as wipes, blurs, and zooms.

Camtasia Producer includes all the editing equipment you'll need at no extra cost. I was able to duplicate Steve's work quite effectively in just about a week. Camtasia allows you to edit in storyboard or timeline view. Storyboard view is easier to use if you want to combine several video clips with transitions or with still images. Simply load each clip, drag each from the clip bin into the storyboard in the desired order, add transitions, and produce the video. Timeline view offers more advanced editing features so you can edit the clips themselves. Again, simply drag the loaded clips from the clip bin to the timeline and then drag the green arrow or play head to where you want to start viewing the video. View it until you want to make the cut and click the cut button.

Steve compressed the original videos using Adobe Premiere. Camtasia Studio has its own compression settings, though they are not as sophisticated at Adobe Premiere's. A slider bar allows you to choose faster but larger file sizes vs. slower compression but smaller file sizes for either recording or editing.

Encoding is the last step in the process, and it works the same whether you've edited live video or used Camtasia Studio. Following compression, we were left with an .AVI file, our file type of choice. Encoding the file requires an encoding application such as Windows Media Encoder, which is freely downloadable, to convert the .AVI file (or other file type) into a .WMV file. The encoder offers several predefined profiles for quality and bandwidth settings, as well as the ability to create custom profiles. Be sure you know your audience and their technology requirements. On-campus students and faculty tend to have up-to-date computers and T-1 line Internet access. They can handle larger files and higher encoding quality. Though there is a hardware requirement for WPI ADLN students, the lack of high quality Internet connections means that smaller files and lower quality encoding are warranted. The last thing you want is for viewers to get frustrated, having their computers freeze when they attempt to view the videos, or asking them to endure constant pauses or choppy video quality.

For the 2001 project, Steve chose to encode the videos at a reasonably high quality but with multiple bandwidth requirements, or variable bit rates. That way the server could detect the user's connection and compensate for lower bandwidths by dropping back the transmission rate to deliver a stream providing frames at a speed the user's connection could handle. A similar encoding scheme was used for my experiment. Hickok solved this problem by offering users two connection options: 56K modem or DLS/Cable (106).

Once the settings are in place, the files can be converted into Windows Media Viewer format (.WMV) and mounted on the server. Regardless of how the video content is captured and edited, you'll need a good quality server to deliver the videos to your users. Rather than spending $6,000 to purchase our own server, we just asked the Academic Technology Center (ATC) to host our content. The ATC has an HP ProLiant server, running at dual 3.2 Ghz with 4GB of RAM and 700GB of fiber channel storage. It has a redundant gigabit connection to our campus infrastructure. It runs Windows 2003 Server Enterprise and uses Microsoft Media Services.

While no official assessment of the two versions has been completed, the quality of the Camtasia Studio video is roughly equal to the original live video, with the computer screenshots actually crisper with Camtasia but the video feed of much lower quality. In terms of money, time and the ability to update the finished product, however, Camtasia is far superior to live video.

Future plans include revisiting all of the videos we've previously produced, determining which should be updated and if any new ones should be recorded, using Camtasia Studio to do most if not all of the work. Due to the simplicity with which one can record content, Camtasia lends itself to other applications in the library. With users' permission, librarians could record research consultations or reference encounters and send the files to the users for later review. These videos could also be used for assessment purposes.

One-shot, in-class sessions could be recorded and posted on Blackboard. Edited canned versions of sessions could be created ahead of time, something I've already explored with a WPI Management professor. Files in Blackboard can be tracked statistically so the number of users viewing the videos can be determined. Camtasia Studio could also be used to record supplemental materials or class refreshers for that semester-long information literacy course, or pre-course prep to whet students' appetites for your one-shot. Like Crowther and Hickok, video tours could be created. Finally, short videos on library topics such as searching, citation, brainstorming or plagiarism could be used by librarians and faculty alike, whether in the classroom or at the Reference desk.

All-in-all, Camtasia Studio is an easy, inexpensive tool that anyone can use to create streaming media without the stress or cost of a big-time video shoot. Camtasia's crisp screenshots and the money and time it saves make it an indispensable tool for librarians and educators alike, offering multiple opportunities to teach our users all the library has to offer.

REFERENCES

Crowther, Karmen N. T. and Alan Wallace. "Delivering Video-Streamed Library Orientation on the Web: Technology for the Educational Setting." *College & Research Libraries News* 62, no. 3 (March 2001): 280-5.

Cox, Christopher and Stephen Pratt. "The Case of the Missing Students, and How we Reached Them with Streaming Media." *Computers in Libraries* 22, no. 3 (2002): 40-5.

Hickok, John. "Web Library Tours: Using Streaming Video and Interactive Quizzes." *Reference Services Review* 30, no. 2 (2002): 99-111.

Knee, Richard, Ann Musgrove and Jake Musgrove. "Lights, Camera, Action: Streaming Video on Your Web Site." *Learning & Leading with Technology* 28, no. 1 (September 2000): 50-3.

Lee, Scott and Carolyn Burrell. "Introduction to Streaming Video for Novices." *Library Hi Tech News* 2 (2004): 20-24.

Mortensen, Mark, Paul Schlieve and Jon Young. "Delivering Instruction Via Streaming Media: A Higher Education Perspective." *TechTrends* 44, no. 2 (2000): 36-41.

Ordonez, Rene Leo E. "A Hassle-free and Inexpensive Way to 'Videotape' Class Lectures." *Educause Quarterly* (September/October 2001): 14-5.

Pasch, Grete and Quinn Stewart. "Using the Internet to Teach the Internet: An Opportunistic Approach." *The Electronic Library* 20, no. 5 (2002): 401-12.

Reed, Ron. "Streaming Technology Improves Achievement: Study Shows the Use of Standards-Based Video Content, Powered by new Internet Technology Application, Increases Student Achievement." *T.H.E. Journal* 30, no. 7 (February 2003): 14-8.

Stey, John A. and Linda J. Walton. "Producing Training Videos for End-User Instruction." *Medical Reference Services Quarterly* 15, no. 1 (Spring 1996): 89-95.

Templeman-Kluit, Nadaleen and Ethan Ehrenberg. "Library Instruction and Online Tutorials: Developing Best Practices for Streaming Desktop Video Capture." *Feliciter* 49, no. 2 (2003): 89-90.

Index

Numbers followed by n indicate notes.

"Academic Libraries and Distance
Education" (Gandhi), 21-22
Adobe Premiere, 198
Adolescents, Internet usage patterns of,
46
Advanced Distance Learning Network
(ADLN), 195,198
Advertising, on the World Wide Web,
164
*Agreement on Guidelines for
Classroom Copying in
Not-For-Profit Educational
Institutions with Respect to
Books and Periodicals*, 182
Alfred University, 137
Annual Conference on Distance
Teaching and Learning, 136
Anxiety
in librarians, 70
library-related, 117
Apache Web server, 151,152
Apple Public Source License, 150-151
Archie search engine, 163
Ariel®, 155
ASKAL (Ask-a-Librarian) open source
software, 154
Ask-a-Librarian reference services, 9,
11-12,52,116,136
Ask Jeeves, 52
AskNow Virtual Reference Project,
99-114
effects on distance learning
students, 109-113
versus e-mail reference service, 112
institutional autonomy of, 113
participating libraries, 104

staffing of, 104-105
staff training for, 104
Telecommunications Infrastructure
(TIF) of, 103
usage statistics for, 113
Virtual Reference Toolkit® use in,
104,112
Association of College and Research
Libraries (ACRL)
*Guidelines for Distance Learning
Library Services*, 7,20-21,
23-24,25,26-27,136
Information Literacy Competency
Standards, 58,163
Auburn University, 58
Audioconferencing, in reference
services, 22
limitations to, 23
Austin Community College, 13

Berkeley Systems Distribution, 150
Bibliographic verification, 35-36
Blackboard (course management
system), 23,135-145,195,199
library web site links to, 38
students' evaluations of, 141-143
students' expectations of, 139
underutilization of, 41
Black's Law Dictionary, 181-182
Boston Library Consortium, 26
Branch campus libraries, 6
Budgets, for library services for
distance learners, 28
Burich, Nancy, 83
Bush, George W., 184

Camtasia Studio (screen-capture
    program), 129,194-200
  cost of, 195,197
  editing process in, 198
  encoding process in, 198-199
  preproduction phase of, 196
  recording process in, 196-198
  scriptwriting phase of, 196
Canadian Library Association,
    *Guidelines for Library
    Support of Distance and
    Distributed Learning in
    Canada*, 21
CDs, library instructional videos on, 128
Central Michigan University
  chat reference services, 14-15
  Off-Campus Library Services
    (OCLS), 7,9,10-12,16
  videoconferencing-based reference
    services, 13
Central Missouri State University,
    Blackboard-based library
    services, 135-145
  students' evaluations of, 141-143
  students' expectations of, 139
CGI scripts, 161
Chat reference services, 9,13-15,22,
    29-30,52
  AskNow Virtual Reference Project,
    99-114
  effects on distance learning
    students, 109-113
  versus e-mail reference service,
    112
  institutional autonomy of, 113
  libraries participating in, 104
  staffing of, 104-105
  staff training for, 104
  Telecommunications
    Infrastructure (TIF) of, 103
  usage statistics, 113
  Virtual Reference Toolkit® use
    in, 104,112
  of Central Michigan University,
    14-15

chat reference transcript analysis of,
    58
chat request button for, 57,101
co-browsing in, 30,102
collaborative, 26,57,58-59,93
  advantages and disadvantages
    of, 58
  AskNow Virtual Reference
    Project, 99-114
  Beta Test phase of, 60-74
  chat reference transcript analysis
    of, 67
  in Colorado, 58-59
  comparison with face-to-face
    reference services, 70,71,73
  disconnect rate in, 68
  effectiveness of, 71,73,74
  libraries participating in, 60-61
  local implementation of, 65-67
  marketing of, 66-67,72
  in New Jersey, 59
  preliminary evaluation of, 67-74
  staffing of, 61-62,66,67,69
  staff training for, 62-65,70-71
  survey of librarians' attitudes
    toward, 68-74,77-79
  of Texas A&M University
    System Libraries, 99-114
  24/7 Reference, 57
  underutilization of, 53
  of University of Texas System
    Libraries, 59-79
  use by non-University of Texas
    students, 70,71-74
HawkHelp (University of Kansas),
    81-98
  assessment of, 90
  Blackboard course support by,
    90-91
  collaboration in, 93
  Convey Systems' OnDemand
    software use in, 87,88,90-92
  development of, 83-87
  KANAnswer and, 83,84-85,
    87-88

operational issues in, 87-88
software selection for, 86-87
staff of, 89
staff training for, 88-89
vision for, 85,90
history of, 13-15
implementation of, 56-57
joint venture. *See* Chat reference
services, collaborative
library Web page access to, 39
limitations to, 15
LSSI software for, 14
marketing of, 57
of Nova Southeastern Law Library,
57
planning for, 56-57
quality standards for, 58
RAKIM, 154
software for, 57
of St. Thomas University Law
Library, 57
underutilization of, 53
of University of Buffalo, 57
Citation style guides, 115
"Classroom flip" technique, 162,166
Co-browsing, in chat reference
services, 30,102
Coffman, Steve, 15-16,103
Collaboration
in chat reference services. *See* Chat
reference services,
collaborative
consortial, in library services for
distance learners
advantages of, 41
of the Greater Western Library
Alliance, 33-42
in digital reference services, 102-103
Greater Western Library Alliance,
32-42
for information technology access,
47-48
librarian-faculty, 53,143-144
students' expectations of, 139
for library Web page development,
48-49

College students, "Net generation" of,
45-46,47
Colorado, Ask Colorado collaborative
virtual reference project,
58-59,102-103
Communication, library-patron, 8-9
CompuServe, 13
Computers in Libraries, 194
Copyright, definition of, 181
Copyright Act of 1976, 181
Copyright law, affecting distance
learning-related library
services, 179-192
Copyright Act of 1976, 181
Digital Millennium Copyright Act
(DMCA), 182-184,187
effect on e-reserves, 189-190
Fair Use Doctrine, 181-182,
186-187,191n
Technology, Education and
Copyright Harmonization Act
(TEACH), 184-187,188
benefits of, 185
critique of, 186-187,188
requirements of, 185-186,190
Correspondence courses, 6
Course/control open source software,
155
Course guides, 115
Web-based, 126-127
Course management systems
Blackboard, 23,135-145,195,199
library web site links to, 38
students' evaluations of, 141-143
students' expectations of, 139
underutilization of, 41
library web site links to, 38
Macro-Level Library Courseware
Involvement (MaLLCI), 23
Micro-Level Library Courseware
Involvement (MiLLCI), 23
Prometheus, 137
reference services within, 30
Web-Course-in-a-Box, 137
WebCT, 23,53,136,137,166-167
library web site links to, 38
underutilization of, 41

Databases, online, 9
  full-text, 47
  searching of, 161-162
    assistance for, 115
    simplicity of access to, 48
Devlin, Frances A., 83,90
Digital libraries, definition of, 7-8
Digital Millennium Copyright Act
    (DMCA), 182-184,187
Digital Reference Services Bibliography
    (Sloan), 21,56,83-84
Distance learners
  attitudes toward information
    technology, 44,45-46
  U.S. Department of Education-
    sponsored survey of, 44-45
Distance learning
  growth of, 6,99-100
  history of, 6
  modes of, 180
DLI2 International Digital Libraries
    Project, 156-157
DOCLINE, 195
Document delivery management
    system, 155
Document delivery services, 29,35-36,40

EBSCOhost, 62-63
eCollege.com, 137
E-commerce, 164
Educational Quarterly, 195
Eisenberg-Berkowitz Information
    Problem Solvings Model, 58
E-mail reference services, 9-12,22,
    29-30,136
  Ask-a-Librarian services, 9,11-12,
    52,116,136
  ASKAL open software management
    system for, 154
  as asynchronous service, 102
  benefits of, 100
  disadvantages of, 82,100
  history of, 9-12
  of Marshall University, 124

prevalence of, 9-10
reference interviews in, 100,
    168-169,170
Embry-Riddle Aeronautical University,
    13
Emory University Libraries, 12-13,155
EPrints open source software, 156-157
ERIC, 84
Evaluation, of library services for
    distance learners, 26-27
Excel, 37
Exite, 49
Expanded Academic ASAP, 84
EZProxy, 48

Fair Use Doctrine, 181-182,186-187,
    191n
FAQs (frequently-asked questions),
    115
Feliciter, 195-196
Florida Distance Learning Reference and
    Referral Center (RRC), 10,14
Focus groups, 27
Funding, of library services for distance
    learners, 28

Global Reference Network, 16
GNU project, 150
GNU Public License, 150
Google search engine, 49,51
Gopher search engine, 163
GRATEFUL MED, 195
Greater Western Library Alliance,
    33-42,93
  analysis of library-related Web sites
    of, 36-41
    Blackboard links, 38
    chat or virtual reference
      services, 39
    document delivery services, 40
    electronic reserves, 39
    electronic resources, 39

interlibrary loan services, 40
subject guides or pathfinders, 38-39
WebCT links, 38
purpose of, 33
Guidelines and standards, for distance
learning-related reference
services, 19-32
of the Association of College and
Research Libraries, 20-21,
23-24,25,26-27
of the Canadian Library Association,
21,24,25,27-30
for delivery methods for services,
29-30
for equivalent services, 23-24
for evaluation of services, 26-27
for facilities and resources, 29
for finances, 28
of the Indian Library Association,
21,25-26,27
journal articles about, 21-23
of the Medical Library Association,
21,24,25,28
for mission statements, 26
for partnerships with other libraries,
25-26
for personalization of services, 24
for personnel, 28-29
for proactive librarianship, 25
for promotion and marketing, 25,
27-28
*Guidelines for Distance Learning
Library Services* (Association
of Research and College
Libraries), 7,20-21,23-24,25,
26-27,136
*Guidelines for Library Support of
Distance and Distributed
Learning in Canada*, 21

Hanson, Carol, 169
HawkHelp (chat reference service), 81-98
assessment of, 90
Blackboard course support by, 90-91
collaboration in, 93

Convey Systems' OnDemand
software use in, 87,88,90-92
development of, 83-87
KANAnswer and, 83,84-85,87-88
operational issues in, 87-88
software selection for, 86-87
staffing of, 89
staff training for, 88-89
vision for, 85-90
Help sites, for online users, 115-134
library users' attitudes toward,
115-116
library users' avoidance of, 116,124
of Marshall University, 118-133
chat reference component,
124,125
content development of, 123-124
course guide component, 126-127
design of, 118-119
design refinements of, 119-122
as FAQs (frequently-asked
questions) site, 118,122,125
impact on library Web site
development, 122-123
Information Delivery Service
(IDS) component of,
128-130,131
learning modules component,
127-128
relationship with virtual
reference services, 124-126
streaming video component,
130-131
student feedback about, 121-122
subject guide component,
122-123,126-127
tutorial component, 127-128,132
usage statistics, 132
Higher Education Funding Councils,
Joint Information Systems
Committee, 156-157
How-To-Do-It Manual for Librarians
series, 56
HTML pages, 155-156

*Implementing Digital Reference
    Services: Setting Standards
    and Making It Real* (Lankes
    et al.), 58
Indiana University, Academic
    Information Environment, 10
Indian Library Association, 21,25-26,27
Information delivery service (IDS),
    128-130
Information literacy instruction
    Internet Navigator (online information
        literacy instruction course),
        159-177
    ACRL Information Literacy
        Standards basis for, 163
    classroom flip technique in, 166
    history of, 163-165
    integration of reference services
        into, 167-174
    as a model, 165-167
    modules of, 165-166
    search engines for, 163,164
    students' evaluation of, 174-175
    syllabus for, 167
    pitfalls in, 161-162
    relationship with reference services,
        160-161
Information service management
    system, 154
Information technology
    distance learners' attitudes toward,
        44,45-46
    simplicity of access to, 43-54
Instant messaging, 46,101
Interlibrary loan services, 35-36,40
Internet, accuracy of information on,
    46,49
Internet Navigator (online information
    literacy instruction course),
    159-177
    ACRL Information Literacy
        Standards basis for, 163
    classroom flip technique in, 166
    history of, 163-165

integration of reference services
    into, 167-174
as a model, 165-167
modules of, 165-166
search engines for, 163,164
students' evaluation of, 174-175
syllabus for, 167
Internet Reference Services Quarterly,
    21

JavaScript, 155-156
JSTOR, 62-63

Kansas State Library, KANAnswer
    chat reference service of, 83,
    84-85,87-88
Katz, William, 58
Kentucky Virtual Library, 10
Kentucky Virtual University, 10
Kluwer, 62-63

LaTrobe University, School of
    Nursing, 14
Learning, online, components of, 161
Learning modules, for online "help"
    site use, 126-127
LibData open source software, 156
LibQUAL, 115
Librarianship, proactive, 25
"Librarians know best" syndrome,
    118,120
Libraries, students' use of, 46,47
*Library and Information Science
    Abstracts (LISA)*, 101-102
Library instruction. *See also*
    Information literacy
    instruction
    tutorials in
        audio use in, 86-87
        effectiveness of, 120-121
        face-to-face, 86-87

for online "help" site use, 126-127
Searchpath, 137
self-scoring and self-paced, 161
software for development of,
155-156
video use in, 86-87
Library services
for distance learners
simplicity of access to, 43-54
students' access to, 100
types of, 180
online, students' lack of awareness
about, 47
Library services for Distance Learning:
The Fourth Bibliography
(Slade), 83-84
Library tours, virtual, 115
Library users, desire to be independent,
116-117
Linux operating system, 151,152
LISA, 101-102
LOEX, 126

Macro-Level Library Courseware
Involvement (MaLLCI), 23
Macromedia Fireworks MX, 125
Maddox, Rebecca, 56
Maricopa Community College, 14
Marketing
of collaborative chat reference
services, 66-67,72
of library services for distance
learners, 25,27-28
Marshall University Libraries, online
library assistance site
(HELP), 118-133
chat reference component, 124,125
content development of, 123-124
course guide component, 126-127
design of, 118-119
design refinements of, 119-122
as FAQs (frequently-asked
questions) site, 118,122,125

impact on library Web site
development, 122-123
Information Delivery Service (IDS)
component of, 128-130,131
learning modules component,
127-128
relationship with virtual reference
services, 124-126
streaming video component of,
130-131
student feedback about, 121-122
subject guide component, 122-123,
126-127
tutorial component, 127-128,132
usage statistics for, 132
Medical Library Association, 21,24,
25,28
Miami University of Ohio, 154
Micro-Level Library Courseware
Involvement (MiLLCI), 23
Microsoft Windows Movie Maker, 130
Mission statements, 26
MIT (Massachusetts Institute of
Technology) open source
software license, 150
Modular Online Software for
Self-paced Tutorials
(MOSST) open source
software, 155-156
Monash University College, 9
MOSST (Modular Online Software for
Self-paced Tutorials) open
source software, 155-156
MySQL, 154,155,156-157

National Cancer Institute, 124
National Science Foundation, 156-157
"Net generation," of college students,
45-46,47
New Jersey, consortial chat reference
services in, 58-59
North Carolina State University, 14
Nova Southeastern Law Library, 57

OAI (Open Archives Initiation), 156
OCLC (Online Computer Library
Center), 56
*Off-Campus Library Services
Directory* (3rd ed.), 6,9-10
Ohio, OhioLINK collaborative virtual
reference project, 102-103
Ohio State University, 137,155
Online Computer Library Center
(OCLC), 56
Open Archives Initiation (OAI), 156
Open Citation Project, 156-157
Open learning universities, history of, 6
Open source software (OSS), 147-158
definition of, 149
"free," 150,151
guidelines for evaluation of, 157
licensing of, 149-151
principles of, 148-150
source codes for, 148-149
types of, 154-156
use in distance library services,
151-158
cross-platform simplicity of, 152
philosophical and pragmatic
dimensions of, 153-154
rationale for, 151-152
support costs of, 151-152
Oregon State University, 154
Outreach, to distance learners, 140-141

Pace University, 137
Palo Alto Community College,
110-111
Partnerships. *See also* Collaboration
among libraries, 25-26
Pathfinders, 126
Periodicals, electronic indexes to, 34
PERL programming language, 151,
155,156-157
Personalization, of library services for
distance learners, 24
Personnel, for library services for
distance learners, 28-29

Pew Internet and American Life
Project, 46,49,101
PHP programming language, 151,154,
155,156
PostgresQL, 154
PowerPoint, 104,128,129,130
Pratt, Stephen, 194,197,198, 200
Project Muse, 62-63
Prometheus, 137
Promotion, of library services for
distance learners, 25,27-28
ProQuest, 62-63
Prospero open source software, 155
Push-pull technology, 86

Q&A NJ, 26
Question Point, 16,62,63,126
QuickStart tutorial, 126

Radio-button quizzes, 161
RAKIM open source software, 154
RDM (Reference Desk Manager) open
source software, 154
Ready reference questions, 35-36
Reference books, students'
understanding of, 172
Reference Desk Manager (RDM) open
source software, 154
Reference interviews, 53
definition of, 168
in the electronic environment, 8,22-23
by e-mail, 100,168-169,170
Reference Librarian, The, 124
Reference librarians, role of, 35
Reference services, for distance
learners. *See also* Chat
reference services; E-mail
reference services
audioconferencing in, 22
limitations to, 23
digital/virtual
asynchronous, 102
collaborative approach in, 102-103

cost of, 102
definition of, 101-102
synchronous, 102
types of, 35-36
face-to-face, 8-9
guidelines and standards for, 19-32
of the Association of College
and Research Libraries,
20-21,23-24,25,26-27
of the Canadian Library
Association, 21,24,25,27-30
for delivery methods for
services, 29-30
for equivalent services, 23-24
for evaluation of services, 26-27
for facilities and resources, 29
for finances, 28
of the Indian Library
Association, 21,25-26,27
for innovation, 25
journal articles about, 21-23
of the Medical Library
Association, 21,24,25,28
for mission statements, 26
for partnerships with other
libraries, 25-26
for personalization of services, 24
for personnel, 28-29
for proactive librarianship, 25
for promotion and marketing, 25,
27-28
integrated into online library
instruction, 167-174
interactive, 52-53
Internet-based, historical overview
of, 5-17
on-site, 29
time-consuming nature of, 22-23
toll-free fax lines, 6,22
toll-free telephone lines, 6,22
users' avoidance of, 117
users' expectations of, 22
users' understanding of, 172
videoconferencing in, 22
limitations to, 23
Web-based, 43-54

Reference transactions, decrease in
number of, 143
Regent University, 137-138
Research
Internet-based, 46
librarian *versus* student attitudes
toward, 120-121
ResearchGuide open source software,
156
Reserves, electronic, 39
effect of copyright law on, 189-190
open source software management
system for, 155
Reserves Direct, 155
Resource sharing, 25-26
Rochester Institute of Technology, 137

St. Thomas University Law Library, 57
ScienceDirect, 62-63
Scout Portal Toolkit (SPT) open
source software, 156
Scout Project, 156
Screen-capture programs
Camtasia Studio, 194-200
cost of, 195,197
editing process in, 198
encoding process in, 198-199
preproduction phase of, 196
recording process in, 196-198
scriptwriting phase of, 196
Macromedia's RoboDem, 195
Search engines, 49,163,164
students' preference for, 34
Searching, online, 161-162
assistance for, 115
Searchpath, 137
Simon Fraser University, 155
Smart Sound Movie Maestro, 130
SnagIt software, 128
Software, closed source, 149
Southeastern Louisiana University, 14
Southern Oregon University, 195
SPT (Scout Portal Toolkit) open
source software, 156

Stallman, Richard, 150
"Statistics, Measures, and Quality
    Standards for Assessing
    Digital Reference Library
    Services" (McClure et al.), 58
Stephen F. Austin State University, 14,53
    Ralph W. Steen Library, 50-52
Stetson University, 137
Streaming video, 86-87,130-131,
    193-200
    benefits of, 194
    Camtasia Studio screen-capture
        program for, 194-200
    cost of, 195,197
    editing process in, 198
    encoding process in, 198-199
    preproduction phase of, 196
    recording process in, 196-198
    scriptwriting phase of, 196
    definition of, 194
    Macromedia's RoboDem
        screen-capture program for,
        195
    Windows Media Player for, 194
Subject guides, 115
    of Canadian universities, 126
    as library help site component,
        122-123,126-127
    software for development of, 156
    usability studies of, 126
SurveyMonkey.com, 68

Technology, Education and Copyright
    Harmonization Act
    (TEACH), 184-187,188
    benefits of, 185
    critique of, 186-187,188
    requirements of, 185-186,190
TechSmith, Camtasia Studio
    screen-capture program of,
    194-200
Telephone reference services, 29

Texas A&M University System
    AskNow Virtual Reference Project,
        99-114
    effects on distance learning
        students, 109-113
    versus e-mail reference service,
        112
    institutional autonomy of, 113
    libraries participating in, 104
    staffing of, 104-105
    staff training for, 104
    Telecommunications
        Infrastructure (TIF) for, 103
    usage statistics, 113
    Virtual Reference Toolkit® use
        in, 104,112
    Trans Texas Video Network
        (TTVN) of, 110
TexShare, 60
Trans Texas Video Network (TTVN),
    110
Tutor.com, 104,106,107,108,109,115
Tutorials, in library instruction
    audio use in, 86-87
    effectiveness of, 120-121
    face-to-face, 86-87
    for online "help" site use, 126-127
    Searchpath, 137
    self-scoring and self-paced, 161
    software for development of, 155-156
    video use in, 86-87
24/7 Reference software, 26

United States Department of Education, 56
Universities, open learning, history of, 6
University of Alaska, Fairbanks, 10
University of Arizona, 117
University of Buffalo, 57,117
University of California, Riverside, 137
University of Kansas Libraries,
        distance learning-related
        library services of, 81-98
    electronic reserves, 82
    e-mail reference services, 82

HawkHelp chat reference service,
    81-98
assessment of, 90
Blackboard course support by,
    90-91
collaboration in, 93
Convey Systems' OnDemand
    software use in, 87,88,90-92
development of, 83-87
KANAnswer and, 83,84-85,
    87-88
operational issues in, 87-88
software selection for, 86-87
staffing of, 89
staff training for, 88-89
vision for, 85,90
University of Maryland University
    College, 40
University of Michigan, 156
University of Minnesota, 156
University of Nebraska, Omaha,
    126,154
University of South Florida, 10
University of Tennessee, 86,195
University of Texas System Libraries,
    collaborative chat reference
    service, 59
Beta Test phase of, 60-74
chat reference transcript analysis of,
    67
comparison with face-to-face
    reference services, 70,71,73
disconnect rate in, 68
effectiveness of, 71,73,74
libraries participating in, 60-61
local implementation of, 65-67
LSTA Library Cooperation Grant
    for, 59-60
marketing of, 66-67,72
preliminary evaluation of, 67-74
staffing of, 61-62,66,67,69
staff training for, 62-65,70-71
survey of librarians' attitudes
    toward, 68-74,77-79

use by non-University of Texas
    students, 70,71-74
Virtual Reference Coordinator of,
    59-60,62,63,67
University of Utah, 164-165
University of Washington Libraries,
    50-51
University of Wisconsin, Eau Claire,
    193-194
University of Wisconsin, Parkside, 137
Utah Academic Library Consortium,
    Internet Navigator (online
    information literacy
    instruction course), 159-177
ACRL Information Literacy
    Standards basis for, 163
classroom flip technique in, 166
history of, 163-165
integration of reference services
    into, 167-174
as a model, 165-167
modules of, 165-166
search engines for, 163,164
students' self-evaluation of, 174-175
syllabus for, 167

VCR (video cassette recorders), 44
VHS format videos, 194-195
Videoconferencing, in reference
    services, 9,12-13,22
limitations to, 23
Video presentations. *See also*
    Streaming video
in library instruction, 128
Videos, 115
VHS format, 194-195
Virtual Reference Desk, 56
Virtual Reference Desk Conference
    Proceedings, 84,93
Virtual Reference Toolkit®, 104,112
Voice-over Internet Protocol (VoIP),
    15-16,86
VTEL equipment, 13

Washington State Library, 84
Wasik, Joann W., 56
Web-Course-in-a-Box, 137
WebCT, 23,53,136,137,166-167
    library web site links to, 38
    underutilization of, 41
Weber State University, 164,169
Web sites/pages, of libraries, 36-41
    copyright of, 189
    course-specific pages, 48-51
    design of, 48-52
        usability studies for, 50-51
    for distance learning courses, 29-30
    pushing of, 102
    role in user/library interaction, 115
    students' attitudes toward, 47
    survey of
        Blackboard links, 38
        chat or virtual reference
            services, 39

document delivery services, 40
electronic reserves, 39
electronic resources, 39
subject guides or pathfinders, 38-39
WebCT links, 38
Western Cooperative for Educational
    Telecommunications, 91
Wilson's Library Literature, 101-102
Windows Media Encoder, 198
Windows Media Viewer, 198
Worcester Polytechnic Institute
    Advanced Distance Learning
        Network (ADLN) 195,198
    Camtasia screen-capture program,
        194-200
WorldCat, 62-63
World Wide Web, market segments of,
    164

Yahoo, 49

BOOK ORDER FORM!

Order a copy of this book with this form or online at:
http://www.haworthpress.com/store/product.asp?sku=5616

Internet Reference Support for Distance Learners

_____ in softbound at $29.95 ISBN-13: 978-0-7890-2938-6. / ISBN-10: 0-7890-2938-3.
_____ in hardbound at $49.95 ISBN-13: 978-0-7890-2937-9. / ISBN-10: 0-7890-2937-5.

COST OF BOOKS _____

POSTAGE & HANDLING _____
US: $4.00 for first book & $1.50
for each additional book
Outside US: $5.00 for first book
& $2.00 for each additional book.

SUBTOTAL _____

In Canada: add 7% GST. _____

STATE TAX _____

CA, IL, IN, MN, NJ, NY, OH, PA & SD residents
please add appropriate local sales tax.

FINAL TOTAL _____

If paying in Canadian funds. convert
using the current exchange rate,
UNESCO coupons welcome.

❑ BILL ME LATER:
Bill-me option is good on US/Canada/
Mexico orders only; not good to jobbers,
wholesalers, or subscription agencies.

❑ Signature _____

❑ Payment Enclosed: $ _____

❑ PLEASE CHARGE TO MY CREDIT CARD:

❑ Visa ❑ MasterCard ❑ AmEx ❑ Discover
❑ Diner's Club ❑ Eurocard ❑ JCB

Account # _____

Exp Date _____

Signature _____
(Prices in US dollars and subject to change without notice.)

PLEASE PRINT ALL INFORMATION OR ATTACH YOUR BUSINESS CARD

Name

Address

City   State/Province   Zip/Postal Code

Country

Tel   Fax

E-Mail

May we use your e-mail address for confirmations and other types of information? ❑ Yes ❑ No We appreciate receiving
your e-mail address. Haworth would like to e-mail special discount offers to you, as a preferred customer.
We will never share, rent, or exchange your e-mail address. We regard such actions as an invasion of your privacy.

Order from your **local bookstore** or directly from
The Haworth Press, Inc. 10 Alice Street, Binghamton, New York 13904-1580 • USA
Call our toll-free number (1-800-429-6784) / Outside US/Canada: (607) 722-5857
Fax: 1-800-895-0582 / Outside US/Canada: (607) 771-0012
E-mail your order to us: orders@haworthpress.com

For orders outside US and Canada, you may wish to order through your local
sales representative, distributor, or bookseller.
For information, see http://haworthpress.com/distributors

(Discounts are available for individual orders in US and Canada only, not booksellers/distributors.)

Please photocopy this form for your personal use.
www.HaworthPress.com

BOF05